ONTARIO

REPORT
of
THE ROYAL COMMISSION
on
METROPOLITAN TORONTO

H. CARL GOLDENBERG, O.B.E., Q.C., LL.D.
Commissioner

June, 1965

FREDERIC H. FINNIS, M.B.E.
Secretary and Research Director

CURRICULUM DIVISION
APR 1 8 1967
LIBRARY

June 10, 1965.

To His Honour
    The Lieutenant Governor
        of the Province of Ontario.

May It Please Your Honour:

By a Commission issued under the authority of The Public Inquiries Act, Revised Statutes of Ontario, 1960, Chapter 323, and in accordance with the terms of Order-in-Council OC-1864/63, dated the 20th day of June 1963, Your Honour did appoint me Your Commissioner to inquire into and to report upon the structure and organization of the Municipality of Metropolitan Toronto and other matters related thereto.

I have completed the inquiry and beg to submit to Your Honour the following Report.

    Your obedient servant,

                                    H. CARL GOLDENBERG
                                        Commissioner.

CONTENTS

		PAGE
LETTER OF TRANSMITTAL		iii
THE ORDER-IN-COUNCIL		xi
THE ROYAL COMMISSION		xiii
FOREWORD		xv
I.	THE AREA	1
	1. The Area Municipalities	1
	2. The Fringe Municipalities	4
	3. The Conservation Area	7
II.	THE PEOPLE	10
	1. Population Growth	10
	2. Origins	12
	3. Age Distribution	14
	4. Occupations and Earnings	15
	5. The Fringe Municipalities	18
III.	FROM TOWNSITE TO METROPOLIS	20
	1. The Nineteenth Century	20
	2. From 1900 to 1930	21
	3. Developing Crisis: 1930-1953	21
	4. Seeking a Solution	24
IV.	THE STRUCTURE OF METRO	26
	1. The Cumming Report	26
	2. Recommendations of the Cumming Report	27
	3. The Municipality of Metropolitan Toronto Act	28
	i. Distribution of Powers	29
	ii. Metropolitan Council	31
	iii. Metropolitan School Board	32
	iv. Metropolitan Toronto Planning Board	33
	v. Toronto Transit Commission	34
	vi. Metropolitan Board of Commissioners of Police	35
	vii. Metropolitan Licensing Commission	35
	4. Related Boards and Commissions	36
	i. Metropolitan Separate School Board	36
	ii. Metropolitan Toronto and Region Conservation Authority	36
	iii. Toronto and York Roads Commission	37

		PAGE
V.	METROPOLITAN AND LOCAL SERVICES	38
	1. Water Supply	39
	i. Achievements of Metro	39
	ii. Rates	40
	iii. Conclusions	41
	2. Sewage Disposal	41
	i. Achievements of Metro	41
	ii. Local Sewer Renewal Needs	42
	iii. Conclusions	42
	3. Public Transportation	42
	i. Achievements	42
	ii. Finances	43
	iii. T.T.C. and Metro	45
	iv. Conclusions	46
	4. Roads	46
	i. Achievements of Metro	46
	ii. Provincial and Metro Expressways	47
	iii. Suburban Roads	48
	iv. Local Roads	48
	v. Conclusions	49
	5. Traffic Management	49
	i. Traffic Control	49
	ii. Parking	50
	iii. Conclusions	51
	6. Public Housing	51
	i. Housing Agencies	51
	ii. Limited Achievement	52
	iii. Conclusions	53
	7. Health and Welfare	54
	i. Care of the Aged	54
	ii. Chronically Ill and Convalescent Care	54
	iii. Hospital Grants	55
	iv. Emergency Ambulance Service	55
	v. Public Assistance	56
	vi. Public Health	57
	vii. Conclusions	58
	8. Waste Disposal	58
	9. Parks and Recreation	59
	10. Police	60

		PAGE
	11. Administration of Justice	61
	12. Licensing	62
	13. Fire Protection	63
	14. Public Libraries	65
	15. Air Pollution Control	67
	16. Conclusion	68
VI.	METROPOLITAN PLANNING	70
	1. The Legislation	70
	2. The "Unofficial Official Plan"	71
	3. Need for an Official Plan	71
	4. The Planning Area	74
	5. Conclusions	75
	i. The Metro Official Plan	75
	ii. Metro's Planning Powers	76
	iii. Local Planning Authorities	77
	iv. The Metropolitan Planning Board	77
	v. Extension of Metropolitan Planning Area	77
VII.	THE TAX BASE	78
	1. Assessed Valuation, 1954-1964	78
	2. Residential and Non-Residential Assessment	80
	3. Tax-Exempt Properties	84
	4. Conclusions	86
VIII.	MUNICIPAL CURRENT EXPENDITURES	87
	1. Gross Current Expenditures	87
	2. General Government	88
	3. Public Works	90
	4. Protection to Persons and Property	90
	5. Recreation and Community Services	90
	6. Public Welfare	92
	7. Health	93
	8. Sanitation and Waste Removal	95
	9. Conclusions	96
IX.	TAXATION AND OTHER REVENUES	97
	1. Tax Revenues	97
	2. Provincial Grants	97
	3. Metro and Local Tax Levies	100
	4. The Tax Burden	105
	5. Conclusions	107

		PAGE
X.	CAPITAL EXPENDITURES AND DEBT	108
	1. Capital Financing, 1954-1963	108
	2. Net Debt	111
	3. Debt Charges	114
	4. Conclusions	116
XI.	EDUCATION IN METRO: 1954-1964	118
	1. School Organization	118
	2. Growth of the Public School System	121
	i. Enrolment	121
	ii. Number of Schools	122
	iii. Teaching Staff	123
	3. Growth of the Separate School System	126
	4. Assessment and Finance	126
	i. Assessment Per Pupil	127
	ii. Maintenance Assistance Payments	129
	iii. Public School Operating Costs	132
	iv. Taxation	137
	v. Capital Costs	139
	5. Conclusions	143
XII.	EDUCATION: A NEW STRUCTURE	144
	1. Introduction	145
	2. School Districts	146
	3. The Metropolitan Toronto Board of Education	148
	4. District Education Councils	149
	5. Central and District Responsibilities	149
	6. Finance	152
	i. Current Expenditures	152
	ii. Capital Expenditures	153
	7. Administrative Arrangements	154
	8. Conclusions	154
	Appendix: Proposed School District Boundaries	155
XIII.	METRO'S BOUNDARIES AND THE FRINGE AREAS	157
	1. Urban Development	157
	2. Population in the Fringe	158
	3. Taxable Resources in the Fringe	162
	4. Metro and the Fringe	165
	5. Conclusions	169

XIV.	REORGANIZATION OF METROPOLITAN TORONTO	172
	1. Metro's Achievements and Continuing Problems	172
	2. Maintenance of the Status Quo	173
	3. Amalgamation	175
	4. Consolidation	179
	i. A Four-City System	181
	ii. Financial Implications	184
	iii. Provincial Road Grants	188
	iv. Partial Exemption of Dwellings	188
	5. Integration of Municipal Staffs	189
XV.	THE METROPOLITAN COUNCIL AND PROPOSED CITY COUNCILS	191
	1. The Metropolitan Council	192
	2. The Chairman of Metropolitan Council	194
	3. The City Councils	195
XVI.	CONCLUSION	199
XVII.	SUMMARY OF RECOMMENDATIONS	200
	APPENDICES:	
	A. List of Submissions Received at Public Hearings	209
	B. List of Tables	211
	C. List of Maps and Charts	213

THE ORDER-IN-COUNCIL

ONTARIO
EXECUTIVE COUNCIL OFFICE

OC-1864/63

Copy of an Order-in-Council approved by His Honour the Lieutenant Governor, dated the 20th day of June, A.D. 1963.

Upon the recommendation of the Honourable the Prime Minister, the Committee of Council advise that pursuant to the provisions of The Public Inquiries Act, R.S.O. 1960, Chapter 323, and effective from June 18th, 1963, a Commission be issued appointing

Mr. H. Carl Goldenberg, O.B.E., Q.C.,

of the City of Montreal, as Commissioner, designating him as The Royal Commission on Metropolitan Toronto,

(1) to inquire into and report upon

    (a) the structure and organization of the Municipality of Metropolitan Toronto and, more particularly, of the Metropolitan Council and the Metropolitan School Board, their functions and responsibilities and the relations with the area municipalities and the local school boards respectively and with municipalities and planning boards within the Metropolitan Toronto planning area,

    (b) the purposes and objectives of the establishment of the Metropolitan Corporation and the Metropolitan School Board, the extent of the accomplishment of such objectives and whether such objectives can be better achieved under a new or revised system of local government, having regard to the past and future development and needs,

    (c) the boundaries of the metropolitan area and of the area municipalities and their suitability in the light of the experience gained through the operations of the metropolitan government, with due regard to probable future urban growth within or beyond the present metropolitan limits and future service requirements,

    (d) any related matters affecting the government of the Toronto metropolitan region.

(2) after due study and consideration to make such recommendations with respect to the matters inquired into under the terms set out herein as the Commissioner sees fit to the Prime Minister and the Executive Council of Ontario.

The Committee further advise that pursuant to the said Public Inquiries Act the said Commissioner shall have the power of summoning any person and requiring him to give evidence on oath and to produce such documents and things as the Commissioner deems requisite for the full investigation of the matters into which he is appointed to examine;

And the Committee further advise that all Government departments, boards, agencies and committees shall assist, to the fullest extent, the said Commissioner who, in order to carry out his duties and functions, shall have the power and authority to engage such staff, secretarial and otherwise, and technical advisers as he deems proper.

Certified,

(Sgd.) J. J. YOUNG
Clerk, Executive Council.

THE ROYAL COMMISSION

(Sgd.) W. Earl Rowe

PROVINCE OF ONTARIO

ELIZABETH THE SECOND, by the Grace of God of the United Kingdom, Canada and Her other Realms and Territories Queen, Head of the Commonwealth, Defender of the Faith.

TO H. CARL GOLDENBERG, of the City of Montreal, in Our Province of Quebec, An Officer of Our Order of the British Empire and One of Our Counsel learned in the Law,

GREETING:

WHEREAS in and by Chapter 323 of The Revised Statutes of Ontario, 1960, entitled "The Public Inquiries Act", it is enacted that whenever Our Lieutenant Governor in Council deems it expedient to cause inquiry to be made concerning any matter connected with or affecting the good government of Ontario or the conduct of any part of the public business thereof or of the administration of justice therein and such inquiry is not regulated by any special law, he may, by Commission appoint one or more persons to conduct such inquiry and may confer the power of summoning any person and requiring him to give evidence on oath and to produce such documents and things as the commissioner or commissioners deem requisite for the full investigation of the matters into which he or they are appointed to examine;

AND WHEREAS Our Lieutenant Governor in Council of Our Province of Ontario deems it expedient to cause inquiry to be made concerning the matters hereinafter mentioned:

NOW KNOW YE that WE, having and reposing full trust and confidence in you the said H. Carl Goldenberg DO HEREBY APPOINT you to be Our Commissioner to inquire into and report upon

1. (a) the structure and organization of the Municipality of Metropolitan Toronto and, more particularly, of the Metropolitan Council and the Metropolitan School Board, their functions and responsibilities and their relations with the area municipalities and the local school boards respectively and with municipalities and planning boards within the Metropolitan Toronto planning area,

(b) the purposes and objectives of the establishment of the Metropolitan Corporation and the Metropolitan School Board, the extent of the accomplishment of such objectives and whether such objectives can be better achieved under a new or revised system of local government, having regard to the past and future development and needs,

(c) the boundaries of the metropolitan area and of the area municipalities and their suitability in the light of the experience gained through the operations of the metropolitan government, with due regard to probable future urban growth within or beyond the present metropolitan limits and future service requirements,

(d) any related matters affecting the government of the Toronto metropolitan region.

2. After due study and consideration to make such recommendations with respect to the matters inquired into under the terms set out herein as the Commissioner sees fit to the Prime Minister and the Executive Council of Ontario.

AND WE DO HEREBY CONFER on you Our said Commissioner the power to summon any person and require him to give evidence on oath and to produce such documents and things as you Our said Commissioner deem requisite for the full investigation of the matters into which you are appointed to examine.

AND WE DO HEREBY FURTHER CONFER upon you, Our said Commissioner, the power to require all our departments, boards, agencies and committees to assist you to the fullest extent, and in order to carry out your duties and functions, the power and authority to engage such staff, secretarial and otherwise, and technical advisers as you deem proper.

TO HAVE, HOLD AND ENJOY the said Office and authority of Commissioner for and during the pleasure of Our Lieutenant Governor in Council for Our Province of Ontario.

IN TESTIMONY WHEREOF We have caused these Our Letters to be made Patent, and the Great Seal of Our Province of Ontario to be hereunto affixed.

WITNESS: THE HONOURABLE WILLIAM EARL ROWE, A Member of Our Privy Council for Canada,

LIEUTENANT GOVERNOR OF OUR PROVINCE OF ONTARIO

at Our City of Toronto in Our said Province, this twentieth day of June in the year of Our Lord one thousand nine hundred and sixty-three and in the twelfth year of Our Reign.

BY COMMAND

(Sgd.) JOHN YAREMKO
Provincial Secretary

FOREWORD

During the course of the proceedings of this Commission, seventy-five briefs were submitted at public hearings which extended from April 21, 1964, to June 11, 1964. Additional briefs were filed but were not heard formally.

By touring the area a number of times and meeting informally with mayors, reeves, councillors and municipal officers, I obtained considerable information on the subject matter of my inquiry. I made several tours with present and former officials of Metro and the area municipalities in order to clarify a variety of matters which had been drawn to my attention. Memoranda and studies on particular aspects of the inquiry were prepared at my request. I am grateful for the helpful co-operation extended to me at all times by the departments of the Government of Ontario, the Metropolitan Corporation, the municipalities, the school boards, and interested organizations and individuals.

I am greatly indebted to the following committee which I asked to advise me on necessary changes in the educational structure: Dr. R. W. B. Jackson, Dr. George E. Flower and Dr. E. Brock Rideout, of the Ontario College of Education; Mr. W. J. McCordic, Executive Secretary of the Metropolitan School Board; Mr. David L. Tough, Superintendent of Secondary Schools, North York Board of Educaton; Mr. Douglas W. Gilmour, Solicitor, Toronto Board of Education; and Mr. J. Richard Davidson, School Trustee, Ward 9, Toronto.

For background information, I am particularly indebted to the Hon. Leslie M. Frost, Q.C., P.C., LL.D., former Prime Minister of Ontario; Mr. Frederick G. Gardiner, Q.C., LL.D., the first chairman of Metropolitan Council; Mr. Lorne R. Cumming, Q.C., LL.D., formerly chairman of the Ontario Municipal Board and later Deputy Minister of Municipal Affairs; and Mr. A. J. B. Gray, Metropolitan Assessment Commissioner. I owe thanks to Professor K. Grant Crawford, Director of the Institute of Local Government, Queen's University, who rendered service as a special consultant.

To Mr. Frederic H. Finnis, M.B.E., Secretary and Research Director of the Commission, Mr. Thomas J. Plunkett, technical consultant, Mr. Lionel Feldman, research associate, Mr. J. W. Peat, accounting consultant, and Ann MacGregor, research associate, I express my special appreciation for services rendered loyally and competently.

PLATE 1

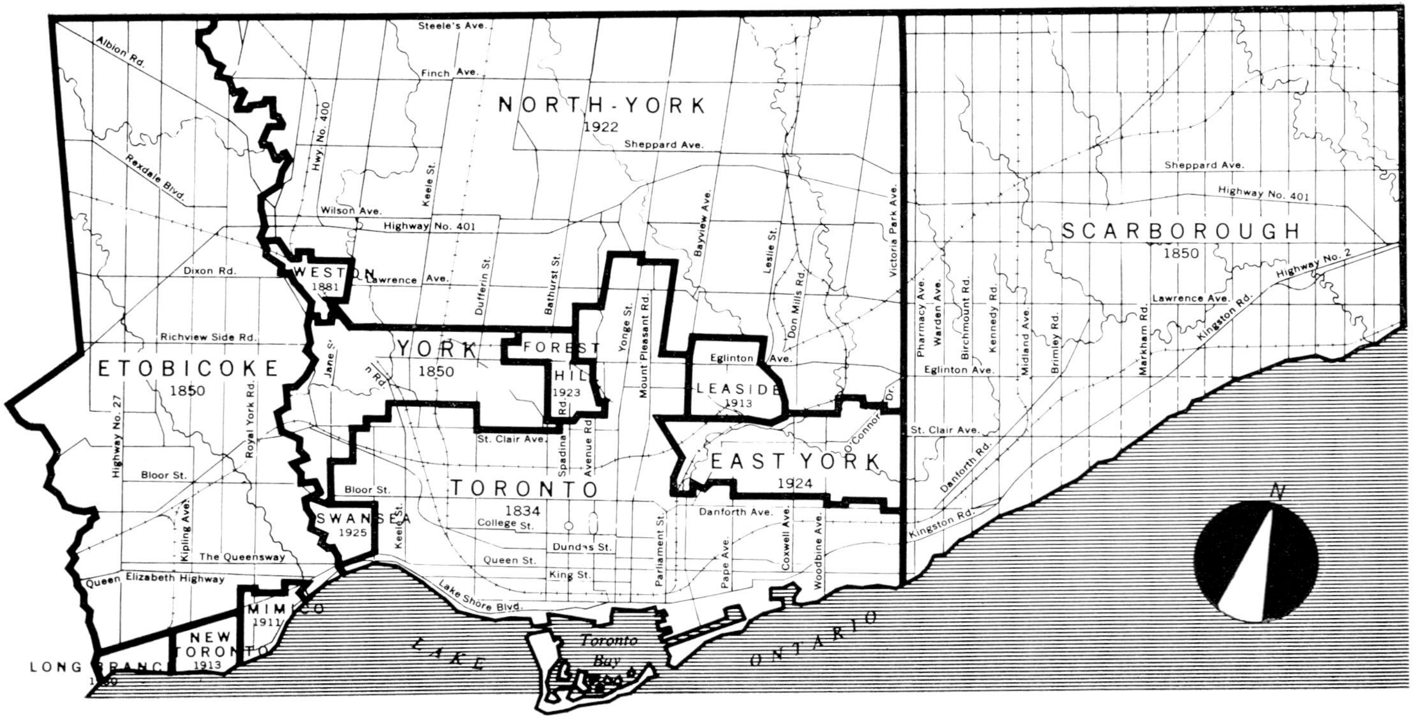

The Municipality of Metropolitan Toronto

CHAPTER I

THE AREA

Metropolitan Toronto, situated on the north shore of Lake Ontario in close proximity to one-third of the Canadian market and to the heavily populated industrial regions of the United States, contains more than one-quarter of the population of Ontario and eight per cent of the population of Canada. A great commercial, industrial and cultural centre, it has experienced a tremendous growth since 1953, when it became the first metropolitan region in North America to establish a federal system of metropolitan government.

1. THE AREA MUNICIPALITIES

The 241 square miles of the Municipality of Metropolitan Toronto include the City of Toronto and twelve suburban municipalities: the towns of Leaside, Mimico, New Toronto and Weston, the villages of Forest Hill, Long Branch and Swansea, and the townships of North York, Scarborough, Etobicoke, York and East York. These thirteen "area municipalities," as they are described in The Municipality of Metropolitan Toronto Act, 1953, which are the constituent units of what is commonly referred to as "Metro," vary widely in size and in population, as is shown in Table 1.

Table 1

METROPOLITAN TORONTO: AREA AND POPULATION

Municipality	Area		Population (1963)[1]	
	Square Miles	Per Cent of Metro	Total	Per Cent of Metro
Township of Scarborough	70.0	29.0	240,371	14.5
Township of North York	68.1	28.3	307,584	18.6
Township of Etobicoke	44.8	18.6	177,537	10.7
City of Toronto	35.1	14.6	630,339	38.1
Township of York	8.0	3.3	126,311	7.6
Township of East York	5.9	2.4	70,176	4.2
Town of Leaside	2.4	1.0	18,453	1.1
Village of Forest Hill	1.5	.6	21,126	1.3
Town of New Toronto	1.2	.5	11,785	.7
Village of Swansea	1.1	.5	9,371	.6
Town of Mimico	1.0	.4	18,150	1.1
Town of Weston	1.0	.4	9,983	.6
Village of Long Branch	.9	.4	11,129	.7
Metropolitan Toronto	241.0	100.0	1,652,315	100.0

[1]Source: Annual Report of Municipal Statistics, Province of Ontario, 1963.

The three outlying townships of Scarborough, North York and Etobicoke, with 44 per cent of the total population, occupy more than 75 per cent of the land area of Metro. The City of Toronto, with 38 per cent of the population, covers less than 15 per cent of the land area. The remaining 18 per cent of the population is distributed among nine municipalities, including five with an area of about one square mile apiece. The disparities in size are shown on Plate 2.

The area municipalities vary not only in size and population but also in the extent of their development. The Metropolitan Planning Commissioner estimates that Metro is now developed to about two-thirds of its designated urban capacity under the proposed Official Plan. The City, which is the central core of the area, and the inner ring of area municipalities are almost fully developed; their problem is now redevelopment and renewal. On the other hand, the three outlying townships, with their large land areas and more recent growth, are still in various stages of development. The proposed Metropolitan Official Plan (Table 5) shows that, in 1963, 47 per cent of the area of Scarborough, 33 per cent of North York and 32 per cent of Etobicoke was agricultural or vacant land.

The Metropolitan Area extends north from the shore of Lake Ontario for a distance of 12 miles to Steeles Avenue, and east from Etobicoke Creek for 24 miles to the Pickering Town Line. Its boundaries, shown on the map on Plate 3, are as follows:

1. On the south, the boundary is the lakeshore from the border of Pickering Township on the east to the west bank of Etobicoke Creek.

2. On the west, the boundary is the western boundary of Etobicoke. It follows Etobicoke Creek in a northwesterly direction to a point south of Malton Airport, the international air terminal for Metropolitan Toronto, situated almost entirely in the adjoining municipality of Toronto Township. After fringing the east side of the airport, the boundary continues north to a point where the boundaries of three adjoining townships, Vaughan in the north, Toronto Gore in the northwest and Toronto Township in the west, all coincide with the northwest point of Etobicoke.

3. On the north, commencing at this north-west point, the boundary is formed by the centre line of Steeles Avenue which runs almost due east to the eastern boundary. Steeles Avenue is also the southern boundary of two large rural townships, Vaughan and Markham, and the northern boundary of the three largest metropolitan area municipalities, the townships of Etobicoke, North York and Scarborough.

4. On the east, the boundary is the eastern boundary of Scarborough, which is the boundary between this township and Pickering Township.

In the centre of Metro is the City of Toronto, its southern boundary extending along the lakeshore to the borders of Scarborough on the east and Etobicoke on the west. These townships occupy, respectively, the whole eastern and western parts of Metropolitan Toronto, except for the three small lakeshore

PLATE 2

City of Toronto	35.1	14.6%
North York	68.1	28.3%
Scarborough	70.0	29.0%
Etobicoke	44.8	18.6%
York	8.0	3.3%
East York	5.9	2.4%
Forest Hill	1.5	0.6%
Leaside	2.4	1.0%
Mimico	1.0	0.4%
New Toronto	1.2	0.5%
Long Branch	0.9	0.4%
Weston	1.0	0.4%
Swansea	1.1	0.5%
Metropolitan Toronto	241.0	100%

METROPOLITAN TORONTO: AREA IN SQUARE MILES

municipalities of Mimico, North Toronto and Long Branch in the west formed from the southern part of Etobicoke Township during the period from 1911 to 1920. These six area municipalities—the City, Etobicoke, Scarborough and the three lakeshore municipalities—are the only ones with direct physical access to the lake.

The boundaries of Metropolitan Toronto are still rural to a large degree. The eastern boundary on the Metro side is entirely rural north of Highway 401 up to the northern boundary formed by Steeles Avenue. Through this north-east rural section runs the Rouge River Valley which is designated by the Metropolitan Planning Board as a recreational area for all time. Residential development north and south of Highway 401 in Pickering Township has not yet reached the metropolitan border, but such development in the extreme south-west pocket of the Township, formed by the Rouge River and the border, has been approaching the boundary. On the Metro side, opposite this pocket, a rather scattered residential development has already reached the border, with some small industrial development in the far south-east corner. The land in Pickering Township adjoining the latter development is also designated for industrial use.

On the western boundary, Etobicoke Creek, which forms the southern part, passes through parkland at its mouth on both sides of its banks. North of the parkland the creek runs through open recreational areas until some industrial development is reached at the Queen Elizabeth Way. From this point to Highway 5 (Dundas Street) the area is designated for industrial development, which is now very evident, but north of Dundas Street all the way to the northern boundary of Steeles Avenue, the boundary area is largely rural, except for Malton and residential development in the area of Bloor Street and Burnhamthorpe Road.

While development on the Pickering side of the eastern boundary has been light, development in Toronto Township, on the western boundary, is more intense and much more industrial and commercial in nature. This reflects the predominantly east-west flow of trade along Lake Ontario to the United States border, facilitated by highways, railways and waterways. The development in Toronto Township south of Highway 5 is a natural extension of growth from Metropolitan Toronto.

On the northern boundary there has been little residential or industrial development on either side of Steeles Avenue, except in the Bathurst-Yonge-Bayview area. However, the picture is changing with the location of the C.N.R. marshalling yards in Vaughan Township and the building of York University at Keele Street and Steeles Avenue in North York.

2. THE FRINGE MUNICIPALITIES

While large portions of its boundary areas are still rural, Metropolitan Toronto forms part of an urban belt that extends eastward to Oshawa and westward to Hamilton. A substantial ribbon of urban development also extends northward along Yonge Street beyond the boundaries of Metro to the far side of Richmond Hill. Proximity to Metro is exerting pressure for urban development in the municipalities and settlements on its fringe, whose residents commute daily to Toronto in large numbers.

The areas surrounding the borders of Metro comprise thirteen municipalities, which, together with the thirteen area municipalities of Metro, form the Metropolitan Toronto Planning Area. The Planning Area, shown on Plate 3, covers 720 square miles or three times the area of Metro, and includes parts of three counties. The area and population of the fringe municipalities, divided into northern, western and eastern groups, are shown in Table 2.

Table 2

FRINGE MUNICIPALITIES: AREA AND POPULATION

Municipality	Area (sq. miles)[1]	Population (1963)[2]
Northern Fringe		
Township of Vaughan	107	17,493
Village of Woodbridge	1	2,443
Town of Richmond Hill	2.5	18,696
Township of Markham	103	14,800
Village of Stouffville	2.5	3,457
Village of Markham	3	5,265
Township of Toronto Gore	24	1,154
Total	243.0	63,218
Eastern Fringe		
Township of Pickering	113	21,891
Village of Pickering	1	1,816
Town of Ajax	4.5	8,111
Total	118.5	31,818
Western Fringe		
Township of Toronto	115	70,859
Town of Streetsville	1.5	5,340
Town of Port Credit	1	7,147
Total	117.5	83,346

Sources: [1]Metropolitan Toronto Planning Board.
[2]Annual Report of Municipal Statistics, Province of Ontario, 1963.

In the east, Pickering Township, in Ontario County, includes the Town of Ajax and the Village of Pickering within its geographic boundaries. Bordering on Lake Ontario, its area of 113 square miles holds a small population of less than 22,000 people, clustered mainly in its south-west section. Very largely rural, it is traversed by Highways 2 and 401, as well as by the C.N.R. main line and the C.N.R. by-pass to the new marshalling yards in Vaughan Township. Ajax, with a population of little more than 8,000, has an unusually large industrial development for a town situated so close to the industrial complex of Metropolitan Toronto.

PLATE 3

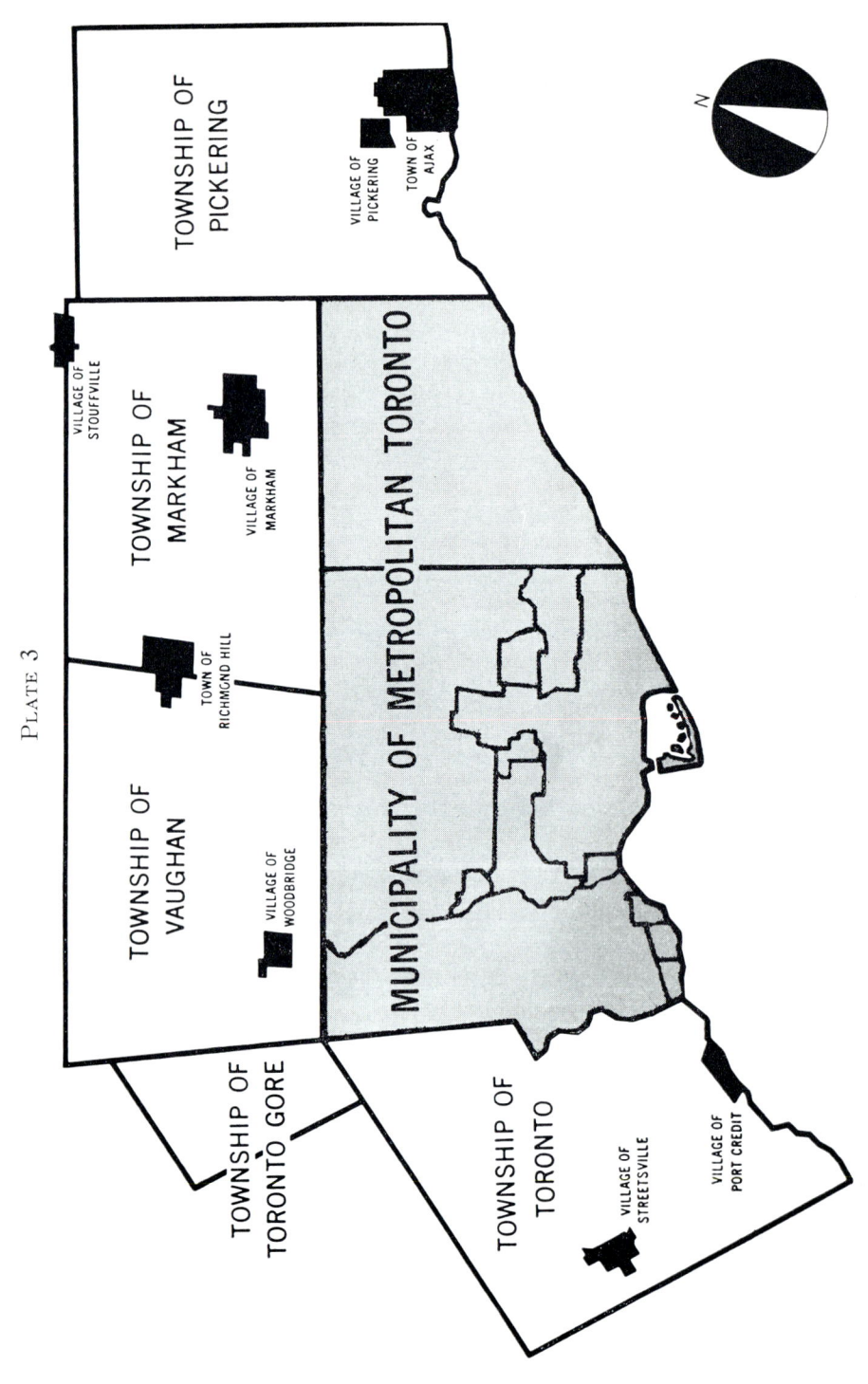

METROPOLITAN TORONTO PLANNING AREA

In the west, Toronto Township, in Peel County, includes the towns of Port Credit and Streetsville within its geographic boundaries. It has an area of 115 square miles, slightly larger than that of Pickering, but its population of over 70,000 is more than three times the population of Pickering. Bordering on Lake Ontario, Toronto Township is particularly well served by railways and highways. Traversed by both C.N.R. and C.P.R. lines, by Highway 2 in the south, the Queen Elizabeth Way and Highway 5 in its south-central part, and by Highway 401 in its northern section, the Township, still largely rural, is experiencing a growing urban development in the area south of Highway 5. Port Credit, extending about two miles along the lakeshore, is now the site of new docking facilities for lake cargo vessels.

North-west of Metro, in Peel County, is the small rural township of Toronto Gore, with a population of 1,100 in an area of about 24 square miles.

Extending across Metro's northern boundary are the rural townships of Vaughan and Markham, in York County, each with an area of more than 100 square miles. Vaughan, with a population of 17,500, includes the Village of Woodbridge within its geographic boundaries. Markham's population is less than 15,000 and its geographic boundaries include the villages of Markham and Stouffville. Situated on the ribbon development along Yonge Street, some five miles north of Steeles Avenue, is the Town of Richmond Hill, with a population of more than 18,500.

These six dormitory municipalities on Metro's northern border are particularly dependent on Metro for their development. The municipalities on its eastern and western fringes border on Lake Ontario and are geographically in a position to provide their own water and sewage services for purposes of development; the northern municipalities are not in this favourable position since they can have access to Lake Ontario only through Metropolitan Toronto. Accordingly, as stated in the brief submitted to the Commission by the County of York: "The economic, social and physical development of the southern part of the county is inextricably bound to Metropolitan Toronto; the wider area is also affected but to a decreasing intensity."

3. THE CONSERVATION AREA

The tremendous growth in urbanization in the past decade has made it necessary to provide protection of the many water courses flowing through the metropolitan region in order to preserve the quality and quantity of the water and to control pollution of the river systems. The Metropolitan Toronto and Region Conservation Authority was created in 1957 to carry out a programme of flood control and water conservation and land, forest and wild life conservation.

The Authority has jurisdiction over an area of approximately 1,000 square miles, including the watersheds of the Humber, Don and Rouge Rivers and the Etobicoke, Mimico, Highland, Petticoat, Duffin and Carruther's Creeks. The area, as shown in Plate 4, extends from Long Branch, at the mouth of the

Etobicoke Creek, northwest into Dufferin County at the headwaters of the Humber, eastward into Uxbridge Township, and south to Ajax at the mouth of Carruther's Creek. Its boundary on the north is the watershed between Lake Simcoe and Lake Ontario and, on the west, the watershed between the Etobicoke Creek and the Credit River.

The conservation area covers all of Metropolitan Toronto and all of the Metropolitan Planning Area except, on the west, Streetsville, Port Credit and the western section of Toronto Township, which are in the Credit River watershed, and, on the east, a narrow strip on the eastern boundary of Pickering Township. Extending north and north-west beyond the Planning Area, it also covers all or part of eleven additional municipalities, including the Town of Brampton.

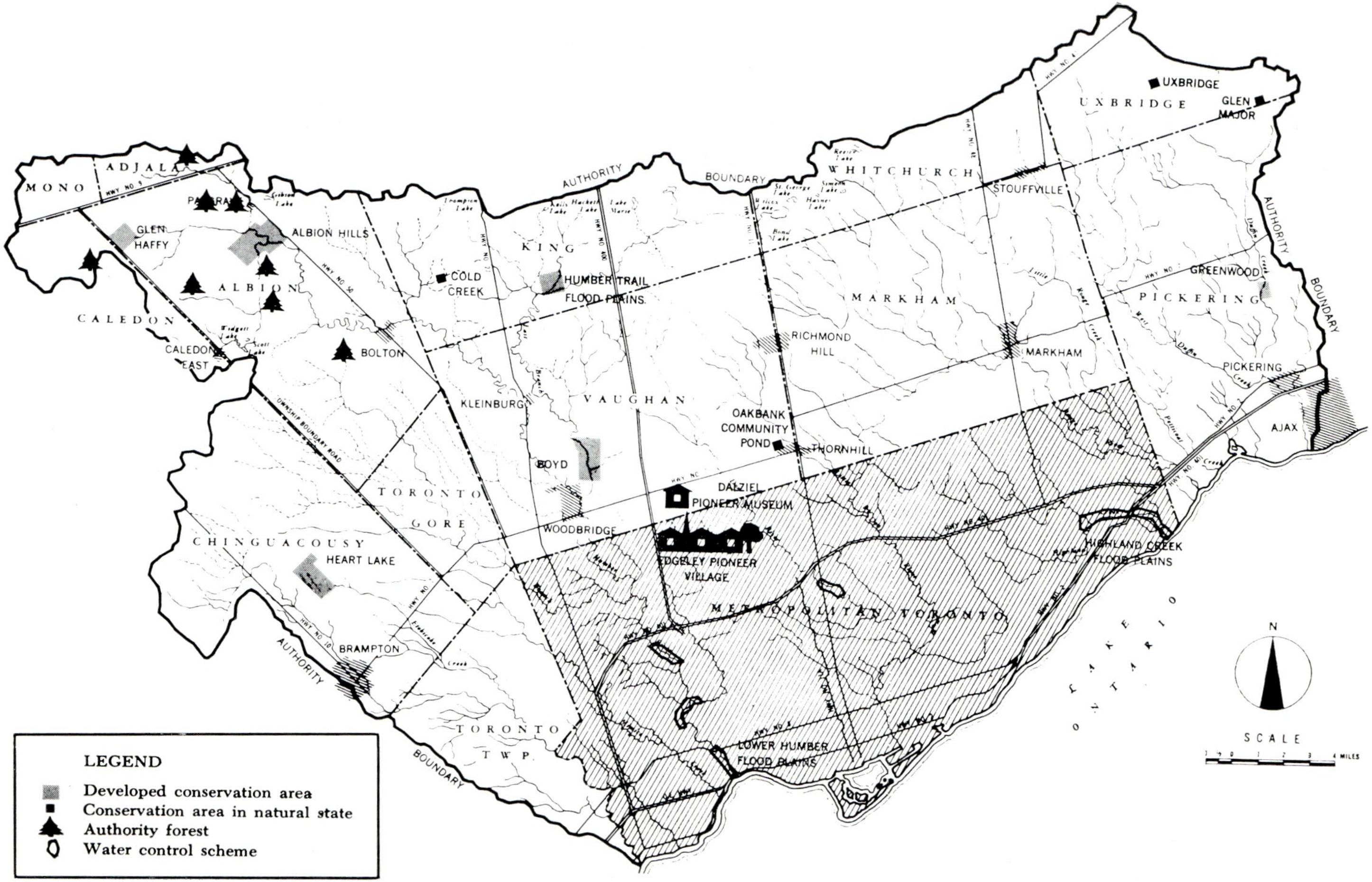

PLATE 4

METROPOLITAN TORONTO AND REGION CONSERVATION AUTHORITY

CHAPTER II
THE PEOPLE

More than one-quarter of the people in Ontario live in Metropolitan Toronto. With a population of more than 1,750,000, Metro includes within its boundaries the municipalities which rank first, second, fifth, sixth and eighth in the Province. The order, based on 1963 population figures, is as follows:

Toronto	630,339
North York	307,584
Ottawa	276,769
Hamilton	271,300
Scarborough	240,371
Etobicoke	177,537
London	171,116
York	126,311
Windsor	112,049

1. POPULATION GROWTH

At the end of the Second World War, the area which is now the Municipality of Metropolitan Toronto had a population of 942,762; in 1963 the figure was 1,652,315, an increase of more than 76 per cent. The average annual increase between 1945 and 1953 was about 29,000 or eight per cent of the total for Canada; in the first ten years of Metro the average was 48,000 annually or approximately twelve per cent of the total for Canada. Immigration accounted for a substantial part of the increase between the census years 1951 and 1961.

The rise of more than 40 per cent in Metro's population since 1953, as Table 3 shows, is reflected only in the suburbs. These doubled their population, the figure rising from 507,000 in 1953 to 1,022,000 in 1963. Almost 62 per cent of the people lived in the twelve suburbs in 1963, as compared with 43 per cent ten years before. The proportion of the population of the area living in the three outlying townships, where most of the increase took place, rose from 22 per cent in 1953 to 44 per cent in 1963. In the same period, the proportion in the City declined from 57 per cent to 38 per cent and in the inner ring of suburbs from 21 per cent to 18 per cent. In terms of population, the gap between the larger and the smaller suburbs has materially widened.

More than 41 per cent of the average annual growth in the area in this period took place in North York. With an average increase of 19,700 persons per annum, its population grew by almost 180 per cent to 307,500, which is more than 18.5 per cent of Metro's total. For 1964 the Metropolitan Assessment Department shows a population of 341,000 for North York. In the ten-year period, 1953-1963, Scarborough, with an average annual increase of more than 16,000, tripled its population, which rose to more than 240,000. Etobicoke, with a population of 177,500 in 1963, showed an increase of more than 150 per cent over 1953, its average increase having exceeded 10,700 annually.

Table 3

METROPOLITAN TORONTO: POPULATION, 1953 AND 1963

Municipality	1953 Population	1953 Per Cent of Metro	1963 Population	1963 Per Cent of Metro	Average Annual Increase or Decrease	Per Cent Change 1953 to 1963
Toronto	665,502	56.7	630,339	38.1	−3,516	−5.3
North York	110,311	9.4	307,584	18.6	19,727	178.8
Scarborough	78,803	6.7	240,371	14.5	16,157	205.0
Etobicoke	70,209	6.0	177,537	10.7	10,733	152.9
York	100,463	8.6	126,311	7.6	2,585	25.7
East York	65,736	5.6	70,176	4.2	444	6.7
Forest Hill	17,719	1.5	21,126	1.3	341	19.2
Leaside	15,910	1.3	18,453	1.1	254	16.0
Mimico	12,301	1.0	18,150	1.1	585	47.5
New Toronto	9,744	.8	11,785	.7	204	20.9
Long Branch	9,140	.8	11,129	.7	199	21.8
Weston	8,374	.7	9,983	.6	161	19.2
Swansea	8,344	.7	9,371	.6	102	12.3
Metro	1,172,556		1,652,315		47,976	40.9

Source: Annual Reports of Municipal Statistics, Province of Ontario, 1953 and 1963.

The three outer townships accounted for 46,615 of the average annual population growth in Metro of approximately 48,000 between 1953 and 1963, and their combined population now exceeds that of the City of Toronto. In 1953 the population of the City was 665,000, as compared with 260,000 for the three suburbs; by 1963 the population of these suburbs had risen to 725,000, while that of the City had declined to 630,000. The inner ring of area municipalities showed a more modest rate of growth. Mimico's population increased by more than 47 per cent, while the increase in the others ranged from less than 7 per cent in East York to more than 25 per cent in York.

Population density in Metro as a whole rose from 7.6 persons per acre in 1953 to 10.7 in 1963, as shown in Table 4. Only two municipalities experienced a decrease: the City of Toronto, from 29.8 to 28 persons per acre, and Leaside, because of an addition of 320 acres through boundary adjustments, from 13 persons per acre in 1953 to 12 in 1963.

With about 28 persons per acre, the City and Mimico show the highest density, followed by York Township with 24.7 persons per acre. In the remaining inner suburbs density now ranges from 12 in Leaside to 22 persons per acre in Forest Hill. The three large outer suburbs, while still below the average for Metro, have considerably increased their densities since 1953: from 2.5 to 7 persons per acre in North York; from 2.4 to 6.2 persons per acre in Etobicoke; and from 1.7 to 5.4 persons per acre in Scarborough.

The pattern of distribution of the population increase in the Toronto metropolitan area has been the same as in almost all metropolitan centres in North America. As a general rule, the growth has taken place outside the central city. The 1960 United States Census showed that between 1950 and 1960, eight of the ten largest core-cities in metropolitan areas experienced an absolute population decline. Thus, in this decade, New York City showed a loss of 1.5 per cent while its suburbs increased their population by 75 per cent.

Table 4

METROPOLITAN TORONTO: POPULATION
Densities Per Acre, 1953 and 1963

Municipality	1953			1963		
	Population[1]	Land Acreage[2]	Population Density Per Acre	Population[1]	Land Acreage[2]	Population Density Per Acre
Toronto	665,502	22,336	29.8	630,339	22,528	28.0
North York	110,311	43,712	2.5	307,584	43,584	7.0
Scarborough	78,803	44,800	1.7	240,371	44,800	5.4
Etobicoke	70,209	28,672	2.4	177,537	28,672	6.2
York	100,463	5,120	19.6	126,311	5,120	24.7
East York	65,736	3,968	16.6	70,176	3,776	18.6
Forest Hill	17,719	960	18.4	21,126	960	22.0
Leaside	15,910	1,216	13.1	18,453	1,536	12.0
Mimico	12,301	640	19.2	18,150	640	28.3
New Toronto	9,744	768	12.7	11,785	768	15.3
Long Branch	9,140	576	15.9	11,129	576	19.3
Weston	8,374	640	13.1	9,983	640	15.6
Swansea	8,344	704	11.8	9,371	704	13.3
Metro	1,172,556	154,112	7.6	1,652,315	154,304	10.7

Sources: [1]Annual Reports of Municipal Statistics, Province of Ontario, 1953 and 1963.
[2]Assessment Department, Metropolitan Toronto.

2. ORIGINS

The 1961 Census of Canada showed that about two-thirds of the population of Metropolitan Toronto was born in Canada. Immigration since 1946, principally from the British Isles and Western Europe, has provided almost one-quarter of the present population.

The majority of post-war immigrants have settled in the central city. In 1961 immigrants who had entered Canada since 1946 constituted 29 per cent of the population of the City of Toronto. They were 31 per cent of the population of York Township, and in the rest of the inner ring the range was from 10 per cent in Leaside to 23 per cent in Mimico. In the outer ring, the figures were 14 per cent for Etobicoke, about 15 per cent for Scarborough and some 19 per cent for North York.

Table 5 indicates the diversity of origins of the population of Metro. The 1961 Census showed 59 per cent to be of British origin in the area as a whole. In the City less than 52 per cent was of British origin; in York Township, less than 50 per cent; in Forest Hill, 35 per cent; and in the rest of the inner ring the

Table 5

METROPOLITAN TORONTO: POPULATION

Origins

Municipality	Population	Born in Canada %	Immigrated 1946-61 %	Br. Isles %	French %	German %	Italian %	Netherlands %	Polish %	Russian %	Scandinavian %	Ukrainian %	Other European %	Asiatic %	Other %
Toronto	672,407	58.1	29.1	51.7	4.1	4.6	11.6	1.0	4.0	.6	.7	3.9	12.9	1.8	3.0
North York	269,959	70.7	19.4	57.6	2.6	4.2	5.8	2.2	3.9	1.8	1.0	1.3	16.7	.7	2.1
Scarborough	217,286	76.6	15.5	74.7	3.4	4.7	2.2	2.2	1.1	.2	.9	1.3	4.5	.8	3.9
Etobicoke	156,035	77.1	13.9	70.9	2.7	4.2	4.7	2.0	2.8	.3	1.0	2.8	4.8	.7	3.0
York	129,645	55.4	31.2	49.7	2.4	4.1	18.2	1.2	4.1	1.0	.6	2.9	12.9	.7	2.1
East York	72,409	66.3	17.0	71.7	3.1	3.5	4.4	1.3	.9	.2	.9	1.1	7.9	1.2	3.6
Forest Hill	20,489	67.0	13.8	35.2	1.2	2.7	1.9	.7	11.9	10.0	.3	.6	33.3	.8	1.2
Leaside	18,579	75.5	10.4	84.2	1.9	3.0	1.3	1.3	.7	.2	.9	.6	3.8	1.1	.8
Mimico	18,212	66.6	22.8	66.6	4.3	5.4	5.7	2.0	2.9	.2	1.0	3.1	5.4	.7	2.5
New Toronto	13,384	69.2	16.4	65.8	5.9	3.2	2.8	1.3	5.3	.8	1.0	4.1	7.2	.5	2.2
Long Branch	11,039	71.5	17.3	74.3	5.4	3.3	1.6	1.4	3.2	.1	1.2	3.5	4.0	.4	1.4
Weston	9,715	72.7	15.9	76.4	2.7	3.7	2.0	3.6	1.7	.1	.9	1.5	3.6	.2	3.6
Swansea	9,628	62.9	20.8	63.8	2.1	5.2	1.1	1.1	6.0	.5	.8	6.6	10.3	.6	1.7
Metro	1,618,787	65.4	23.0	59.2	3.4	4.3	8.3	1.5	3.4	.8	.8	2.6	11.3	1.2	2.8

Source: 1961 Census of Canada.

proportion ranged from 64 per cent in Swansea to 84 per cent in Leaside. In the outer municipalities the figures were approximately 58 per cent in North York, almost 75 per cent in Scarborough and 71 per cent in Etobicoke.

Italians form the second largest group, constituting more than 8 per cent of the total population, a little less than 12 per cent of the population of the City of Toronto, and more than 18 per cent of the population of York Township.

People of various other European origins form 30 per cent of the total population, more than 4 per cent being of German origin, over 3 per cent of French origin, more than 3 per cent of Polish origin and more than 2 per cent of Ukrainian origin. In each case the largest number lives in the City.

3. AGE DISTRIBUTION

There are striking differences between the age distribution of the population in Toronto and the inner suburbs and that of the three outer suburbs. Table 6, based on the 1961 Census, shows that, while children under 15 years constituted 28 per cent of the population of the area as a whole, the figure was considerably higher in the three outer suburbs and lower in the inner ring, except Long Branch. The proportion was 37 per cent in Scarborough and more than 33 per cent in both North York and Etobicoke. In contrast, the figure for Toronto was 23.5 per cent and, except for Long Branch with 30 per cent, the range in the inner suburbs was from 17.2 per cent in Swansea to 25.7 per cent in York.

Table 6

METROPOLITAN TORONTO: POPULATION

Age Distribution

	Under 15 years	Per Cent of Total Population	70 Years and Over	Per Cent of Total Population
Toronto	158,007	23.5	48,663	7.2
North York	89,829	33.3	8,020	3.0
Scarborough	80,382	37.0	5,585	2.6
Etobicoke	51,582	33.1	5,145	3.3
York	33,369	25.7	6,354	4.9
East York	16,519	22.8	4,356	6.0
Forest Hill	3,805	18.6	1,234	6.0
Leaside	3,479	18.7	1,069	5.7
Mimico	4,390	24.1	726	4.0
New Toronto	3,306	24.7	741	5.5
Long Branch	3,307	30.0	423	3.8
Weston	2,396	24.7	581	6.0
Swansea	1,655	17.2	815	8.5
Metro	452,026	27.9	83,712	5.2

Source: 1961 Census of Canada.

In respect of older people, 70 years of age and over, the picture is different. These represented about 5 per cent of the population of the area as a whole. In Toronto the proportion was more than 7 per cent and in the inner suburbs it ranged from almost 4 per cent in Long Branch to 8.5 per cent in Swansea. In the three outer suburbs, the figure was 2.6 per cent in Scarborough, 3 per cent in North York and 3.3 per cent in Etobicoke.

Such differences in age distribution between the more central sections and the outlying suburbs are a characteristic of metropolitan areas. It is young people with families who tend to move to the developing suburbs. Older people prefer the more established residential neighbourhood where mobility does not depend upon the ownership and operation of a motor car. The resultant differences in age composition are significant in terms of actual and prospective school costs in the outer suburbs, with their high proportion of young people, and in terms of costs for the care of elderly persons in the inner areas, where they tend to concentrate.

4. OCCUPATIONS AND EARNINGS

With the City of Toronto, which is the capital of Ontario and a great commercial, industrial and financial centre, as its core, and with industrial and commercial development in the suburbs, the Metropolitan Area provides a wide diversity of employment in its 5,000 factories, its commercial and financial establishments, its service industries, in government, and in educational and other institutions.

The 1961 Census reported a Metro labour force of some 715,000. Table 7 shows the number employed by occupational classification. Table 8 analyzes the labour force by area municipalities. The following comparisons are noted.

Table 7

METROPOLITAN TORONTO: POPULATION

Occupations

	Males	Females	Total
Managerial	63,763	6,068	69,831
Professional and Technical	51,518	27,265	78,783
Clerical	52,436	99,285	151,721
Sales	36,706	17,672	54,378
Service and Recreation	40,971	44,151	85,122
Transport and Communication	33,758	5,036	38,794
Primary	4,455	149	4,604
Craftsmen, Production Process and Related Workers	150,781	35,650	186,431
Labourers	26,042	3,430	29,472
Total	460,430	238,706	699,136

Source: 1961 Census of Canada.

Table 8

METROPOLITAN TORONTO: POPULATION

Per Cent of Labour Force Employed by Occupational Classification

Municipality	Labour Force	Managerial	Professional and Technical	Clerical	Sales	Service and Recreation	Transport and Communication	Primary	Craftsmen, Production Process and Related Workers	Labourers
		%	%	%	%	%	%	%	%	%
Toronto	320,161	6.2	9.8	20.6	5.9	15.8	5.5	.7	26.9	5.5
North York	107,425	16.4	14.7	20.0	9.9	8.8	3.9	.7	21.2	2.4
Scarborough	84,828	10.8	10.6	22.3	9.7	8.1	6.0	.7	26.4	2.6
Etobicoke	61,431	16.5	13.7	20.4	9.9	6.6	5.0	.6	23.2	2.5
York	60,200	6.6	7.4	21.4	6.3	10.5	6.1	.6	33.5	5.6
East York	34,580	7.6	9.3	26.3	7.8	10.1	6.3	.4	27.5	3.2
Forest Hill	9,107	30.1	20.8	16.2	9.9	12.8	1.9	.3	5.8	.7
Leaside	8,989	17.7	20.6	27.6	11.6	5.7	3.2	.1	10.7	.9
Mimico	9,198	7.9	9.1	25.5	7.5	8.7	7.1	.3	28.5	3.6
New Toronto	5,480	4.7	5.8	19.9	5.4	11.6	7.4	.6	38.0	4.5
Long Branch	4,780	6.0	7.1	22.4	5.7	9.7	7.5	.3	36.3	3.4
Weston	4,413	8.3	13.0	22.8	7.4	9.8	5.7	.6	27.5	2.8
Swansea	4,822	10.0	14.6	28.1	7.9	9.7	3.9	.4	22.2	1.9
Metro	715,414	9.8	11.0	21.2	7.6	11.9	5.5	.6	26.1	4.1

Source: 1961 Census of Canada.

Production workers constitute the largest group, 26 per cent, of Metro's labour force. Toronto and the inner ring show higher proportions: New Toronto, 38 per cent; Long Branch, 36.3 per cent; York, 33.5 per cent; Mimico, 28.5 per cent; East York and Weston, 27.5 per cent each; and Toronto, approximately 27 per cent. At the other extreme are Forest Hill with approximately 6 per cent and Leaside with 10.7 per cent. In the three outer suburbs the range is from 21 per cent to 26.4 per cent.

Clerical workers form the second largest group and represent 21 per cent of the area labour force. The highest percentages are shown by Swansea, 28 per cent; Leaside, 27.6 per cent; East York, 26.3 per cent; and Mimico, 25.5 per cent. Forest Hill, with 16.2 per cent, shows the lowest figure. In the three outer suburbs the range is narrow, from 20 to 22.3 per cent.

In the service and recreation group, the Metro figure of approximately 12 per cent is exceeded only by Toronto, with almost 16 per cent, and Forest Hill, with approximately 13 per cent. Leaside, with 5.7 per cent, and Etobicoke, with 6.6 per cent, are at the other extreme.

Professional and technical workers constitute 11 per cent of the Metro labour force. In Forest Hill and Leaside they represent almost 21 per cent, in North York and Swansea about 15 per cent, almost 14 per cent in Etobicoke and 13 per cent in Weston. In the remaining municipalities the range is from less than 6 per cent in New Toronto to more than 10 per cent in Scarborough. Toronto shows a figure of less than 10 per cent.

The managerial group represents less than 10 per cent of the total labour force. This percentage is exceeded by Forest Hill with 30 per cent, Leaside with 17.7 per cent, North York and Etobicoke with 16.5 per cent each, and Scarborough with almost 11 per cent. Swansea shows 10 per cent and the range in the remaining units is from less than 5 per cent in New Toronto to a little more than 8 per cent in Weston. The figure for Toronto is 6 per cent.

Labourers represent 4 per cent of the Metro labour force. The figure for Toronto is 5.5 per cent and in the inner ring ranges from less than one per cent in Leaside and Forest Hill to 5.5 per cent in York. In the three outer suburbs the proportion is 2.5 per cent.

With differences in occupational patterns, average wage and salary incomes by municipality also show variations. The 1961 Census reports these as follows:

AVERAGE WAGE AND SALARY INCOME (MALES)
(1961 Census of Canada)

Leaside	$5,817	Mimico	$4,231
Forest Hill	5,791	East York	4,145
Etobicoke	5,516	Long Branch	4,082
North York	5,084	New Toronto	3,884
Scarborough	4,786	York	3,706
Swansea	4,634	Toronto	3,583
Weston	4,355		

The bulk of the wages and salaries earned in the area is, of course, derived from employment in Toronto. On the basis of the Census figures, the City shows the lowest male average wage and salary income. But the comparison is deceiving. It is a comparison between municipalities with populations ranging from about 10,000 in Swansea and in Weston to more than 630,000 in Toronto, whose population also includes the lowest income groups in the area. It therefore becomes necessary to look beyond the overall averages.

The Census presents its data by "census tracts" which "are designed to be relatively uniform in area and population" and "fairly homogeneous with respect to economic status and living conditions". Swansea, Weston and Long Branch, for example, each constitutes a single census tract, for which the average figure is as shown above. Leaside is divided into three and Forest Hill into four census tracts; the highest figures for these municipalities, which show the highest overall average for the area, are $6,401 and $7,240, respectively. Toronto is divided into 135 tracts, with average wage and salary incomes ranging from a low of $2,289 to a high of $9,093. In this light, the comparison as such between the overall average for Toronto and the corresponding figure for other area municipalities loses much of its significance.

5. THE FRINGE MUNICIPALITIES

In the decade from 1953 to 1963, when Metro's population rose by some 40 per cent, the population of the 13 fringe municipalities, which are included in the Metropolitan Planning Area, increased by almost 96 per cent. The details are shown in Table 9.

The fringe population rose from 91,000 in 1953 to 178,000 in 1963. It is distributed geographically as follows: 83,000 or 46.5 per cent in the west; 63,000 or 35 per cent in the north; and 32,000 or 18 per cent in the east. Toronto Township alone contains 40 per cent of the total, and, with a population of 71,000, ranked sixth among the 26 municipalities in the Planning Area in 1963. It doubled its population in the ten-year period.

The growth in the fringe reflects pressure for urban development in predominantly rural areas in close proximity to Metro. The western section experienced the largest percentage increase, 102.5 per cent, followed by the north with 92.5 per cent, and the east with 86 per cent. The Town of Richmond Hill, built around the northern extension of Yonge Street, showed an increase of more than 460 per cent. The larger part of the work force of the fringe, except Ajax, is employed in Metropolitan Toronto.

While the fringe population rose by 96 per cent between 1953 and 1963, as compared with an increase of 40 per cent in Metro, the increase in the whole of the fringe averaged only about 8,700 persons annually, as compared with an average annual increase of 48,000 in Metro. With the extension of the provincial and metropolitan expressway systems, increased pressures for development, particularly in the northern fringe, may be forecast. In the interests of orderly growth and to curtail "urban sprawl", the proposed Metropolitan Official Plan delineates an urban development area within which urban land uses will be confined.

Table 9

FRINGE MUNICIPALITIES: POPULATION, 1953 and 1963

Municipality	1953	1963	Per Cent of Total 1963	Per Cent Change 1953 to 1963
Northern Fringe				
Township of Vaughan	11,636	17,493	9.8	50.3
Village of Woodbridge	1,909	2,443	1.4	28.0
Town of Richmond Hill	3,310	18,606	10.4	462.1
Township of Markham	11,406	14,800	8.3	29.8
Village of Stouffville	1,893	3,457	1.9	82.6
Village of Markham	1,913	5,265	3.0	175.2
Township of Toronto Gore	777	1,154	.6	48.5
Total	32,844	63,218	35.4	92.5
Eastern Fringe				
Township of Pickering	11,045	21,891	12.3	98.2
Village of Pickering	944	1,816	1.0	92.4
Town of Ajax	5,124	8,111	4.5	58.3
Total	17,113	31,818	17.8	85.9
Western Fringe				
Township of Toronto	35,199	70,859	39.7	101.3
Town of Streetsville	1,409	5,340	3.0	279.0
Town of Port Credit	4,556	7,147	4.0	56.9
Total	41,164	83,346	46.7	102.5
Fringe Municipalities—Total	91,121	178,382	100.0	95.8

Source: Annual Reports of Municipal Statistics, Province of Ontario, 1953 and 1963.

CHAPTER III

FROM TOWNSITE TO METROPOLIS

1. THE NINETEENTH CENTURY

In 1793 John Graves Simcoe, the first Lieutenant-Governor of Upper Canada, selected Toronto as the capital of the recently created province and changed its name to York. Its choice as a townsite was largely dictated by expected military requirements but its harbour also pointed to commercial possibilities. In the same year the southern part of the province was divided into nineteen administrative counties, one of which embraced the embyro townsite of York and was named the County of York. Later in the year, part of the southern portion of York County, covering the larger part of the area now included in Metropolitan Toronto, was partitioned off as a township and was also named York.

For a few years the new Town of York grew slowly. By 1800 the population, including soldiers, was only 300. But it increased markedly with the wave of immigrants to Upper Canada after the termination of the War of 1812 and the Napoleonic Wars. Many of the newcomers settled in the Town, and by 1834 York could boast of over 9,000 inhabitants. In that year it was incorporated under its original Huron name as the City of Toronto, with an area of 7,400 acres. At the time of incorporation the city boundaries extended to Parliament Street on the east, Front Street on the south, a short way past Bathurst Street on the west, and on the north almost to Dundas Street. Yonge Street was already steering urban development northward.

In 1836 the Township of York held its first council elections and in 1850, together with the Townships of Etobicoke and Scarborough, became an incorporated municipality under the Baldwin Act of 1849 which laid the foundation of the system of local government in Ontario.

Transportation was the key to the development of the region. It was in the railway age of the 1850's, with its rapid industrial growth, that the Toronto area may be said to have become a metropolitan community. In 1855 the Northern Railway connected the City with Georgian Bay and made Toronto a great lumber port. In 1856 the Grand Trunk linked Montreal, Toronto and Hamilton and by 1860 operated all the way from Rivière du Loup in Quebec to Sarnia in the southwest part of Ontario. At the same time Toronto became the eastern terminus of the Great Western, originally built from Hamilton to Windsor. Dominating communications to the region and far beyond, Toronto effectively organized the economic life of a wide surrounding area.

By this time the City's population had reached about 45,000 and in the surrounding Township of York small towns and villages were springing up. The last of these to be incorporated in this period was the Town of Weston, established as a village in 1881. The City soon proceeded to expand by absorbing newly built-up areas. The annexation of Yorkville Village in 1883 was the first of a series of annexations which only terminated when North Toronto was annexed in 1912. These annexations, which increased the City's area by about 15,500 acres, were, in a sense, a by-product of the electric street car. The new method of public transportation made possible a great expansion of urban development throughout the surrounding area during the period from 1885 to 1914, sometimes referred to as the "street car era".

2. FROM 1900 TO 1930

At the turn of the century there were some 25,000 people in the suburbs of the City, which itself had a population of about 200,000. Immigrants were starting to build beyond the Humber River in the west and, as a result, Mimico and New Toronto were incorporated as villages out of the southern part of Etobicoke Township in 1911 and 1913, respectively. Both were raised to the status of towns a little later, Mimico in 1917 and New Toronto in 1920. In 1913 Leaside was incorporated as a town of 42 persons.

After the First World War population growth was again very rapid. The City soon reached the 500,000 mark but was not interested in increasing its area further while a considerable amount of land within its own boundaries still remained undeveloped. Annexations were therefore confined to minor territorial adjustments, the largest being the annexation of 93.8 acres north of Danforth Avenue and east of Woodbine in 1920. In 1928 a committee of City department heads recommended a policy of no further annexations "until such time as undoubted compensating advantages existed". This was adopted as policy by a succession of city councils. Further expansion of the built-up area was therefore to take place within newly created municipalities carved out of York Township.

The period between the end of the First World War and the beginning of the depression of the 1930's saw five new municipalities incorporated in the area. In 1922 the northern part of the Township of York was incorporated as the Township of North York. There followed the incorporation of the Township of East York in 1923; the Village of Forest Hill in 1924; the Village of Swansea in 1925; and, finally, the Village of Long Branch in 1930.

Accordingly, by 1930, the metropolitan area was composed of a central city with a population of 621,590 and twelve suburban municipalities with a combined population of about 162,400.

3. DEVELOPING CRISIS: 1930-1953

From 1930 to 1945 the economic depression and the Second World War forced the postponement of essential expenditures on municipal services. But the need for these services did not diminish; it merely went unfulfilled, building up a backlog to plague the later years. The depression so adversely affected municipal finances that by 1935 all the municipalities in the area, except Toronto, Forest Hill and Swansea, were in default and under the supervision of the Department of Municipal Affairs.

During this period the population continued to increase, although at a comparatively slow rate. Table 10 shows that from 1930 until the commencement of the war, the annual increase averaged only 9,300. The figure rose to 12,500 during the war but this was to be less than half the post-war rate of growth. For the first eight years after the war, from 1945 to 1953, the population increased annually by an average of 28,700 persons.

Table 10

CITY AND SUBURBS: POPULATION GROWTH, 1930-1953

Year	City of Toronto	Suburbs	Total	Average Annual Increase	Per Cent of Population in Suburbs
1930	621,596	162,362	783,958	—	20.7
1939	649,123	218,597	867,720	9,307	25.2
1945	681,802	260,960	942,762	12,507	27.7
1953	665,502	507,054	1,172,556	28,725	43.2

Sources: Civic Advisory Council of Toronto, 1st Report, Section 2, of the Committee on Metropolitan Problem 1950; The Cumming Report, 1953; Annual Report of Municipal Statistics, Province of Ontario, 1953.

By 1953 the population of the twelve suburban municipalities had risen to 507,000 and that of the City to 665,000. Thus, during the 23 year period, from 1930 to 1953, the suburbs increased their population by more than 200 per cent while the City showed only a modest seven per cent increase. In fact, the City's population began to decline after the war. The post-war development of the Toronto metropolitan area was to be similar to that of most metropolitan areas in North America. It was marked by the very rapid mushrooming growth of the suburbs: North York, for example, grew from a rural township of some 26,000 people in 1945 to become the fifth largest municipality in Canada, with a population of more than 340,000 in 1964.

Caught in the post-war "population explosion" and the mounting backlog of services, the area, fragmented into 13 municipal units, was faced with economic, financial and social crises and the problem of political organization. The rapidly expanding suburbs urgently required increased services of all kinds, and, more particularly, water, sewage disposal, roads, and, above all, schools. Most serious were the problems of water supply and sewerage facilities. All the water must come from Lake Ontario, and all sewage must drain into it, but only six of the thirteen municipalities have direct physical access to the lake. The lack of proper sewage facilities became a menace to public health and serious water shortages forced occasional curtailment of the use of water in the suburbs. Arterial road development was grossly inadequate to handle the rapidly increasing volume of traffic. Public transportation and the existing highway network were poorly integrated. The need for new school facilities was staggering. Other services had to be expanded to meet the requirements of a phenomenal post-war growth.

The outlying suburbs, where growth was so fast and so great, and some in the inner ring, were not in a position to finance the enormous expansion of services required by their people. Since they were essentially dormitory municipalities, the ratio of industrial to residential assessment was low. Except for the City and the towns of New Toronto and Leaside, residential property formed by far the greater proportion of the total assessment. The lack of commercial and industrial assessment created a serious imbalance in the economic structure of the mushrooming suburbs. Taxes rose steeply and this led to intermunicipal competition for industry. Industries requiring room for expansion were encouraged to move to the suburbs and new industry was attracted to the suburbs by offers of land at low prices.

With each municipality seeking capital funds on its own credit, borrowing by the growing suburbs became more and more difficult as interest rates rose. The large sums required for capital purposes could only be obtained in the open market in competition with established and stable communities. By the early 1950's it became increasingly evident that, unless the whole of the financial resources of the area could be drawn upon, the outlying townships would cease to expand for want of essential physical services which they could not provide individually.

The problems of the suburbs were such that they tended to overshadow the social and economic problems developing in the City. It faced a large backlog of public works. Its residential population was declining as many of its younger people, the newly prosperous and the more affluent immigrants settled in the suburbs. The older residents remained in the City, and it attracted large numbers of immigrants who came to Canada in the post-war years. Residential areas which had greatly deteriorated continued to be used, partly because of suburban policies discouraging the construction of cheaper homes within the reach of families of low or moderate incomes. The City had to provide expanded welfare services. With the growing number of suburban commuters and the steady rise in the ratio of motor vehicles to population, it was also faced with the need for extensive street improvements to relieve traffic congestion. On the horizon were vast problems of renewal and redevelopment.

With area-wide and local problems, it was apparent by about 1950 that a radical solution was essential to ensure further growth of the region on an orderly basis. The existing intermunicipal agreements for the provision of certain services did not meet basic needs.

4. SEEKING A SOLUTION

Although for about 25 years the City had been officially opposed to any move to annex surrounding municipalities, it was apparent to some that the seeds of future problems were being sown by the policy of "no further annexations". Even before the adoption of this policy, a bill had been introduced in the Ontario Legislature in 1925 seeking to establish a metropolitan area of Toronto. The bill died on the floor of the House.

In the 'thirties and 'forties, three reports recommended a reorganization of the area. In 1935, A. F. W. Plumptre, of the Department of Political Economy of the University of Toronto, urged unification of the urban sections, in a report to the Minister of Municipal Affairs. In 1949 there were two reports. In the first, the Toronto and York Planning Board recommended the unification of the City with the other seven municipalities lying between the Humber River and the Township of Scarborough. The second, by the Civic Advisory Council of Toronto which, at the request of the Mayor of Toronto, had set up a committee to study metropolitan problems, offered alternative proposals, one of which was the creation of a metropolitan form of government.

In 1947 the Town of Mimico applied to the Ontario Municipal Board for an order to create an area for the joint administration of such major municipal services as education, fire and police protection, administration of justice, health and welfare, planning, sewage disposal and public utilities, including transportation and main highways. No definite boundaries were set out in this application, except that the inner suburbs were to be included in their entirety together with "the urban sections" of Etobicoke, North York and Scarborough. A number of preliminary hearings were held and the Ontario Municipal Board finally ordered public hearings to open in January 1950.

Before the hearings could take place, there were new developments. On January 16, 1950, the Hon. Leslie M. Frost, Prime Minister of Ontario, called together the heads of the thirteen municipalities which now constitute the area municipalities of Metropolitan Toronto and suggested that they form themselves into a Toronto Area Committee to consider four specific questions which be submitted to them. The committee's reply a few weeks later indicated that there was little hope of the municipalities settling their problems amicably among themselves.

Meanwhile, on January 18, 1950, Long Branch filed an application with the Municipal Board for the amalgamation of New Toronto, Mimico, Long Branch and Etobicoke. The situation was further complicated when, on February 2, 1950, the City of Toronto, reversing its long-standing policy of no further annexations, applied for an order amalgamating the City with all the surrounding municipalities, except the more rural parts of Scarborough and Etobicoke.

Faced with three different applications covering parts of the same area, the Ontario Municipal Board gave the City's application priority over that of

Mimico and indefinitely postponed hearing the application from Long Branch. As it turned out, the last named application was never heard. The City's application, however, was held to be beyond the Board's jurisdiction because only parts of Scarborough and Etobicoke were included for purposes of the proposed amalgamation. This was remedied on May 15, 1950, when the City of Toronto applied for total amalgamation with the twelve surrounding municipalities.

The public hearings of the Mimico and the revised Toronto applications were held concurrently and commenced on June 19, 1950. They termed one year later. On January 20, 1953, the Ontario Municipal Board, under the chairmanship of Mr. Lorne R. Cumming, Q.C., issued the historic report, known as the Cumming Report, which culminated in the creation of the Municipality of Metropolitan Toronto.

CHAPTER IV

THE STRUCTURE OF METRO

After almost a year of public hearings and a further eighteen months of deliberations, the Ontario Municipal Board, in its Decisions and Recommendations of January 20, 1953, commonly referred to as the Cumming Report, rejected the application of Toronto for amalgamation and of Mimico for the creation of an area for the joint administration of certain area-wide services. In their place, it proposed its own solution which was to be substantially enacted in The Municipality of Metropolitan Toronto Act.

1. THE CUMMING REPORT

The Board rejected the Mimico plan because it held that the Board of Management, which would be set up for the "administration and management of existing facilities", would have "no power to plan extensions or improvements of existing services or to build new schools, public works and other projects which might be needed throughout the area. It would therefore be quite powerless to provide the most urgent requirements of the metropolitan area during the present period of rapid expansion."

With respect to the Toronto application, the Board found "many obvious advantages" in total amalgamation. The formation of one municipal government would "expedite the planning, construction or acquisition of adequate coordinated water supply and sewage disposal systems, urgently needed arterial highways, major parks and recreation areas, an extended public transportation system, and other physical needs of the area". Amalgamation would also "provide a drastic solution of all problems attributable to the existing inequitable and illogical distribution of taxable resources". It would concentrate borrowing powers in a single authority, with debentures secured by the combined assets and tax-paying powers of the whole area. Capital expenditures could be planned and undertaken on an area-wide priority basis according to need, and conflicting local plans of development could be harmonized.

The Board found, however, that these manifest advantages were outweighed by serious objections. First, it concluded that amalgamation "would result in immediate and prolonged administrative confusion of the most serious kind". Secondly, it foresaw "a substantial increase in taxation due to the practical necessity of bringing all suburban wage and salary scales and working conditions up to city levels". In addition, demands for improved services in the suburbs equal to those in other areas would prove "difficult if not impossible to resist". The evidence showed that "per capita costs in general tend to increase with the size of the municipality".

A third objection was "the proposed concentration of all municipal duties and responsibilities in a single all-powerful council which would be expected to deal wisely and adequately with both local and metropolitan problems". The Board was impressed by evidence on the actual operations of the local councils which showed the amount of "time expended in detailed consideration of a great variety of local problems and the nature and volume of business transacted in numerous and lengthy meetings of the councils and their various committees". It felt that it would be unrealistic to expect a single council to undertake the burdens and responsibilities of all the area governments, and "at the same time to give sufficient consideration to the many difficult problems confronting the metropolitan area as a whole and to provide the kind of leadership it requires".

Finally, the Board concluded that, however great the need for local government reform, "the complete dissolution of the existing municipal institutions and the creation of a form of government which appears to be bitterly opposed by eleven of the thirteen municipalities concerned" could not be justified.

2. RECOMMENDATIONS OF THE CUMMING REPORT

In disposing of the Toronto and Mimico applications, the Municipal Board had discharged its statutory responsibilities. Having found, however, "that the applicants have clearly proved the need of some major reform of the existing form of local government," it proceeded to "assume the responsibility of presenting its own proposals for the organization of a suitable form of metropolitan government in the Toronto area". The Honourable Leslie Frost, Prime Minister of Ontario, later told the Legislative Assembly that he had intimated to Mr. Cumming that "any views the Municipal Board had on the solution of the problem would be welcome".

The Board's solution was the application of the principle of federation to local government in the area. It pointed out that "the principle of municipal federation in counties has always been an important feature of the organization of municipal institutions in Ontario", and that its proposals embodied a "number of fundamentals of the county type of federation which have survived the test of long experience".

The Board recommended the creation of a new joint central authority to be called "The Metropolitan Council", with exclusive responsibility for the "functions and services considered vitally necessary to the continued growth and development of the entire area as an urban community", and the retention of local governments for local purposes, which "is not only desirable but necessary". Under the Board's proposals, each of the thirteen area municipalities was to continue its separate existence without boundary changes and was to retain full responsibility for local services not assigned to the new authority. The specific division of powers recommended by the Board was substantially enacted by The Municipality of Metropolitan Toronto Act. The Board foresaw "the gradual and orderly transfer to the central authority of certain additional powers" over a period of time but recommended that such transfer "should await the gradual development of public opinion after the new system has been placed in operation".

With respect to the composition of the Metropolitan Council, the Cumming Report recommended equal representation for the City, on the one hand, and the suburbs, as a group, on the other, "notwithstanding the theoretical advantages of representation by population". It proposed a nine-member council, four from the City and four from the twelve suburbs, with a chairman to be appointed by the Lieutenant Governor in Council. The City's four members would be appointed by resolution of the City Council, while the four suburban members would be elected by the twelve suburbs divided into four groups for this purpose, the municipal councils within each group choosing their representative in joint session. Under this proposal there would be a "Western Division" composed of the western suburbs; a "North-Western Division" composed of York and Forest Hill; a "Northern Division" composed of Leaside and North York; and an "Eastern Division" composed of Scarborough and East York.

The board was of the opinion that the responsibilities of the new Council would require the full time of every member. It was also of the opinion that members should not be considered delegates or representatives of local councils. Accordingly, it recommended that a member, officer or employee of any local council or board elected or appointed to the Metropolitan Council should be deemed to have resigned automatically from his position in the local municipality.

While the Cumming Report proposed a Metropolitan Council for area-wide municipal services, it did not propose the creation of a Metropolitan School Board. Local boards of education would be continued, retaining almost all their powers and responsibilities, but the Metropolitan Council would provide a major source of revenue and exercise "an overall coordinating and financing authority". By financing capital expenditures and maintenance and administration costs up to certain standards through uniform metropolitan taxation, as recommended, the Council would exercise a centralized control "limited to matters which are considered essential to the success of the basic scheme". This scheme was to make available the combined resources of the entire area to support education.

3. THE MUNICIPALITY OF METROPOLITAN TORONTO ACT

The Government of Ontario acted quickly on the Report. Bill 80—"An Act to provide for the Federation of the Municipalities in the Toronto Metropolitan Area for Certain Financial and Other Purposes"—was introduced in the Legislature with a minimum of delay. On April 2, 1953, only six weeks from the date of the Report, "The Municipality of Metropolitan Toronto Act" received Royal Assent. Thirteen days later the first Metropolitan Council was sworn in. In the nine and a half months which followed, it prepared the plans for the change-over to the new system, and on January 1, 1954, the new metropolitan government commenced operations.

i. *Distribution of Powers*

The Municipality of Metropolitan Toronto Act, 1953, referred to in this report as "the Metro Act", provided for a division of powers between the Metropolitan Corporation and the area municipalities along the lines recommended by the Cumming Report. In general, matters of area-wide concern were assigned to the Metropolitan Council or to quasi-independent metropolitan boards, while those of local concern remained the responsibility of the area municipalities. Two major changes in the division of powers were made in 1956, effective January 1, 1957, when the Act was amended to provide for unification of the police forces under a Metropolitan Board of Commissioners of Police and to transfer responsibility for licensing to a Metropolitan Toronto Licensing Commission. Civil defence and control of air pollution have also become metropolitan responsibilities. Accordingly, the distribution of powers is now as follows:

POWERS OF THE METROPOLITAN CORPORATION

Assessment and Taxation—Assessment of real property, both metropolitan and local, throughout the area. On the basis of this assessment, the Metropolitan Corporation levies on the area municipalities for its requirements according to the proportion which the assessment of each bears to the assessment of the whole area.

Debenture Borrowing—Borrowing of money, subject to the approval of the Ontario Municipal Board, for the Metropolitan Corporation, the Toronto Transit Commission, any area municipality, and any board of public school trustees in the area, by the issuing of debentures on the credit of the Metropolitan Corporation.

Water Supply—Construction and maintenance of all works for the production, treatment and storage of water and all trunk mains; the wholesale distribution of water to the area municipalities, with power to fix wholesale rates and to set standards for local distribution systems in the area municipalities.

Sewage Disposal—Construction and maintenance of trunk sewer mains and sewage treatment works to provide a metropolitan sewage disposal system, and to set standards for local works connected to a metropolitan work.

Roads—Establishment of a metropolitan road system and designation of highways as metropolitan roads, with power to prescribe speed limits thereon and to control traffic over and to limit access to such roads.

Transportation—Construction, maintenance and operation by the Toronto Transit Commission of all forms of public transportation within the metropolitan area, except steam railways and taxis.

Education—Co-ordination of educational facilities in the area by the Metropolitan School Board, which also makes maintenance assistance payments to each local board in respect of every pupil.

Parks—Establishment of metropolitan parks and recreation areas and assumption, with the approval of the Ontario Municipal Board, of existing parks.

Health and Welfare—Provision of homes for the aged, hospitalization and burial of indigents, maintenance of neglected children, and post-sanitorium care of tuberculosis patients.

Administration of Justice, etc.—Provision and maintenance of a court house and a jail, and conveyance of prisoners; juvenile and family court; magistrates' courts; provision of Registry office and Land Titles Office accommodation.

Police—Police services throughout the metropolitan area under the Metropolitan Board of Commissioners of Police.

Licensing—Licensing of trades and businesses by the Metropolitan Toronto Licensing Commission.

Housing and Redevelopment—All powers of a municipality in the fields of housing and redevelopment.

Planning—Preparation of an official plan for the Metropolitan Planning Area by the Metropolitan Planning Board.

Air Pollution Control.

Civil Defence.

POWERS OF THE AREA MUNICIPALITIES

Fire Protection.

Water Supply—Construction and maintenance of local distribution systems and retail sale of water to consumers.

Sewage Disposal—Local sewage collection and construction and maintenance of local sewage collection systems.

Garbage Collection and Disposal.

Roads—Construction and maintenance of local streets and sidewalks, including sidewalks on metropolitan roads.

Planning, etc.—Planning by local planning boards in conformity with the Metropolitan Official Plan when it becomes effective; zoning.

Education—Operation of schools by the local board of education, the area municipality being responsible for costs above the metropolitan grants.

Recreation and Community Services—Local parks; recreation programmes; community centres and arenas; public libraries.

Traffic Control, etc.—Traffic regulations on local streets; street lighting; municipal parking lots.

Housing—All powers of a municipality in the fields of housing and redevelopment.

Health and Welfare—Public health services; general welfare assistance and social work services; maintenance of non-wards.

Hydro-Electric Power—Local distribution.

Licensing and Inspection—Preparation and enforcement of building by-laws; marriage licenses; dog licensing.

Taxation—Levying and collection of taxes for local purposes, including the metropolitan levy.

Under this distribution of powers the Metropolitan Corporation and the area municipalities each have certain exclusive functions and share responsibility for others. The shared functions, such as water supply, sewage disposal and roads, fall under metropolitan jurisdiction in their area-wide aspects and under local jurisdiction in their local aspects. In the fields of housing and redevelopment, Metro and the area municipalities have equal powers.

ii. *Metropolitan Council*

The Municipality of Metropolitan Toronto Act enacted the basic scheme and most of the recommendations of the Cumming Report with two major exceptions, the first affecting the composition of the Metropolitan Council and the second affecting education. The legislation accepted the principle of federation and separated the twelve suburban municipalities from the County of York for municipal purposes. Toronto, as a city, was already separate.

The Report had recommended a council of nine full-time members holding no local office, of whom four would be appointed by the Toronto City Council, four would represent the suburbs with one elected from each of four groups of suburbs, and the ninth would be the chairman to be appointed by the Lieutenant Governor in Council. The term of office was to be "not less than three years". The Report pointed out that, as the council was to be a taxing body, its members should be elected, but it saw serious objections to the direct election of the members of the first council.

The Act accepted the principle of equal representation of the City and the suburbs as a group, but in other respects departed from the recommendations. It provides that the powers of the Metropolitan Corporation are to be exercised by a Metropolitan Council composed of the following: from Toronto, the Mayor, the two of the four controllers who received the highest number of votes at the preceding municipal election, and the alderman from each of the nine wards who received the highest number of votes in the ward; from the suburbs, the heads of the council in each municipality. Each suburb is given one representative and one vote, regardless of population. The Council is thus composed of twenty-four members and the chairman, if he is not chosen from the Council membership. The term of office coincides with the term of local office, which was originally one year but, by an amendment to the Act effective in 1956, is now two years.

The chairman is the head of the Council and its chief executive officer. The first chairman was appointed by the Lieutenant Governor in Council but the Act provided that thereafter the Council was to elect one of its own members "or any other person" as chairman, originally for one year but now for two years. A chairman who has not been elected from among the members of the Council, votes only in the event "of an equality of votes"; if he has been elected from the Council, he has a second or casting vote in such a situation. The first chairman, Mr. Frederick G. Gardiner, Q.C., appointed by the Lieutenant Governor in Council in 1953 to hold office until the end of 1954, was re-elected by the Council at each election until his retirement in 1961, when he was succeeded by Mr. William R. Allen, Q.C.

Part VII of the Municipal Act requires all cities with a population of not less than 100,000 to have a board of control. The Cumming Report did not recommend such a board for Metro because the Metropolitan Council was not to be a municipal government in the ordinary sense of the term. The Council was given authority, however, to set up standing and other committees and, as early as May 1953, provided by by-law for the appointment of an executive committee composed of the chairman and four other members. In 1958 the Act was amended to give statutory authority for the establishment of an executive committee composed of the chairman and four or six other members of the Council, one-half from Toronto and one-half from the area municipalities. It also empowered the Council to authorize the committee to exercise any and all powers of a board of control under the Municipal Act, and such powers were duly conferred on the committee by by-law. Accordingly, the executive committee, now consisting of the chairman of Council, who is also chairman of the committee, and six members, prepares the annual budget, awards all contracts, nominates all heads and deputy heads of departments, and initiates policy proposals; it may only be overruled on the award of contracts and on nominations of officials by a two-thirds vote of the Council.

The Council has also established the following standing committees: welfare and housing, works, transportation, and parks and recreation. Each has seven members, including the chairman.

iii. *Metropolitan School Board*

With respect to education, the Cumming Report said that "the fundamental problem is to find an equitable method of financing capital and maintenance costs", and recommended that a portion of these costs be financed on a metropolitan basis. The powers were to be exercised by the Metropolitan Council which was not to assume "the functions of a metropolitan board of education": the local school boards were to retain almost all their powers. The Metro Act, however, created a Metropolitan School Board of 22 members constituted along the lines of the Metropolitan Council.

The Board is composed of the chairman of the Toronto Board of Education, the member from each of the nine City wards who received the largest number of votes in the ward, the ten chairmen of the suburban school boards,[1] and two representatives appointed by the Metropolitan Separate School Board,[2] one of whom must be from the City and the other from the suburbs. The chairman of the Metropolitan Board, like the chairman of the Metropolitan Council, is selected from among the twenty-two members or from outside.

---

[1] The three lakeshore municipalities of Long Branch, New Toronto and Mimico have a combined school board; hence there are only ten suburban boards instead of twelve.

[2] This Board operates Roman Catholic schools pursuant to provincial legislation. Its representatives on the Metropolitan School Board do not participate in proceedings exclusively affecting the public elementary schools.

The Act confers upon the Board the responsibility of co-ordinating the area's requirements for school accommodation and school sites. Each local school board must submit its proposals in this regard, with their estimated cost, for review by the Board, which may revise them before submitting a composite proposal to the Metropolitan Council.

The Metropolitan Corporation assumed all school debenture liabilities of the area municipalities outstanding on January 1, 1954. Debt created subsequently for the erection of new schools and the acquisition of lands for school sites was apportioned between the Metropolitan Corporation and the area municipalities, the former assuming the portion of school debt which is recognized by the Province of Ontario for legislative grant purposes. This policy was recently changed; the Metropolitan Corporation now assumes all debt incurred from January 1, 1964, for the municipal share of standard school construction costs under a ceiling cost formula, the area municipalities continuing to be responsible for all costs in excess of the ceiling.

The general legislative grants for school purposes, with a few exceptions, are paid to the Metropolitan Board, which makes maintenance assistance payments to each local school board in respect of each resident pupil in amounts which it determines annually for each category. The amount per pupil in each category must be uniform for each board within the area. The Act also confers on the Metropolitan Board the power to define the boundaries of attendance areas, to determine the charges to be made for non-resident pupils, including their transportation, and to fix the cost of special classes.

To meet its expenditures and obligations, the Board submits its estimates annually to the Metropolitan Council, which, in turn, levies the required amount on the area municipalities. This levy, however, finances only a part of total school costs. The Act specifically preserves all the powers, duties and responsibilities of each local board of education which are not inconsistent with its provisions. Accordingly, each area board prepares and adopts its own current estimates to finance the additional expenditures for its own pupils and submits such estimates for levy by the local council.

iv. *Metropolitan Toronto Planning Board*

The Metropolitan Corporation is the designated municipality for the Metropolitan Toronto Planning Area under The Planning Act. This Act applies to it, subject to Part XIV of The Municipality of Metropolitan Toronto Act which excludes powers with respect to redevelopment, subdivision control, zoning and building by-laws, but authorizes agreements with area municipalities or others relating to conditions of approval of subdivision plans.

The Act provides that the Planning Board is to be constituted as under The Planning Act, except that the membership is at all times to include two persons recommended by the Metropolitan School Board.

As originally established in 1953, the Board consisted of fourteen members: nine appointed by the Metropolitan Council from outside its membership; three

Council representatives—the Chairman of Metropolitan Council, the Mayor of Toronto and a suburban member of the Planning and Parks Committee (since renamed the Parks and Recreation Committee); and two representatives of the Metropolitan School Board. In 1957 the Board's composition was altered to include all of the foregoing (except the suburban member of the Planning and Parks Committee) and, in addition, four representatives from the fringe areas, the four chairmen of the standing committees of Council, a suburban councillor, and the chairman of the Toronto Transit Commission. The addition, in 1959, of a representative from the Separate School Board brought the Board to its present strength of 24 members.

For the purpose of representation on the Board, the thirteen fringe municipalities which are included in the Metropolitan Planning Area are divided into four districts, with one representative from each, as follows:

West District—Toronto Township, Streetsville, Port Credit.
North-West District—Toronto Gore Township, Vaughan Township, Woodbridge.
North-East District—Richmond Hill, Markham Township, Markham Village, Stouffville.
East District—Ajax, Pickering Township, Pickering Village.

As a planning board governed by the provisions of The Planning Act, the Board has the duty to prepare an official plan for the area and recommend it to the Council for adoption. After adoption by the Council, the plan must be submitted to the Minister of Municipal Affairs for his approval. Upon such approval the plan becomes official.

v. *Toronto Transit Commission*

The Municipality of Metropolitan Toronto Act created the Toronto Transit Commission as successor to the Toronto Transportation Commission and conferred upon it full powers with respect to "the construction, maintenance, operation, extension, alteration, repair, control and management" of all forms of local public passenger transportation in the Metropolitan Area, except steam railways and taxis. The assets of the Toronto Transportation Commission, including the capital stock of Gray Coach Lines Limited held by it, and of the area municipalities in respect of public passenger transportation were vested in the new Commission without compensation to the former Commission or to any municipality, subject to assumption by the new Commission of all liabilities in respect of the property transferred.

Under the Act, the original commissioners were to be the three members of the former Toronto Transportation Commission and two members appointed by the Metropolitan Council, who were to be ratepayers and residents of an area municipality other than the City of Toronto. Except in the case of the first members, the term of office was to be five years and commissioners were to retire in rotation. The term was reduced to three years on a staggered basis in 1963, when the Metropolitan Council was also authorized to reduce the membership from five to three. The Commission still consists of five members who must be appointed on the affirmative vote of at least two-thirds of the members of the Council present and voting.

The salary of the commissioners is fixed by the Council, to which an annual financial statement and general report on operations must be submitted. The Commission may not acquire land to be paid for by borrowing without the approval of Council, and the debentures for all sums necessary to finance the Commission's undertakings are issued by Metro, the Council retaining "its authority with reference to providing the money required for such works" (sec. 116(e)).

While setting up these relationships between the Metropolitan Council and the Transit Commission, sec. 115(c) of the Act specifies that the Commission's "powers, rights, authorities and privileges shall not be exercised by any area municipality or its council or by the Metropolitan Corporation or the Metropolitan Council". It was originally intended that the Commission should be financially self-sustaining: sec. 116(1)(c) authorized it to fix tolls and fares so that its revenue "shall be sufficient to make all transportation facilities under its control and management self-sustaining, after providing for such maintenance, renewals, depreciation, debt charges and reserves as it may think proper". In 1962 the Act was amended to authorize the Metropolitan Corporation to contribute to the capital costs of the Commission with the approval of the Municipal Board (sec. 116a), and in 1963 to authorize contributions to operating costs (sec. 116a(2)).

vi. *Metropolitan Board of Commissioners of Police*

Under the original distribution of powers, and until January 1, 1957, the police services remained a responsibility of the area municipalities. On that date all police services were unified under a Metropolitan Board of Commissioners of Police. The Board is composed of five members: the chairman of the Metropolitan Council; a member of the Council appointed by it, who, by custom, has always been the Mayor of Toronto; and three members designated by the Lieutenant Governor in Council, of whom one is a judge of the County Court of the County of York and two are magistrates.

vii. *Metropolitan Licensing Commission*

A second change in the distribution of powers became effective on January 1, 1957, when licensing became a metropolitan function. The Metropolitan Licensing Commission was created with certain statutory powers, including, inter alia, the licensing and regulation of teamsters, cab owners and drivers, auctioneers, bill posters, driving schools and instructors, electrical workers, and plumbers. Its powers may be extended by by-law of the Metropolitan Council, under the provisions of any Act, to cover "the licensing, revoking of a license, regulating, governing, prohibiting or limiting of any trade, calling, business or occupation or the person carrying on or engaged in it . . ." (sec. 211(2)). A number of by-laws extending the Commission's powers have been passed.

The Commission was originally composed of the chairman of the Metropolitan Council or his delegate, and two magistrates designated by the Lieutenant Governor in Council. In 1963 the Act was amended to provide that the Commission shall be composed of the chairman of the Metropolitan Council or his delegate, and two members appointed by the Metropolitan Council who are not members of the council of an area municipality. The Commission elects its own chairman.

4. RELATED BOARDS AND COMMISSIONS

The Metro Act makes reference to boards and commissions created under other legislation on which Metro is represented or which are represented on Metro bodies. They include the Metropolitan Separate School Board, the Metropolitan Toronto and Region Conservation Authority and the Toronto and York Roads Commission.

i. *Metropolitan Separate School Board*

The Metropolitan Separate School Board was created by a special Act, assented to on April 22, 1953, which set up a metropolitan area for separate school purposes. The area covers all the area municipalities, except Mimico and the Union Section in the south part of Etobicoke bordering on Mimico, which have retained their own separate school boards. There are no other local separate school boards.

The Metropolitan Board has complete administrative and financial control over schools under its jurisdiction. In this respect a pattern had been set by its predecessor, the Toronto and Suburban Separate School Board, created in 1941 with administrative and financial authority over separate schools in the City and the greater part of the suburbs. The assessment for separate school purposes, since the inception of Metro, is made by the Metropolitan Assessment Commissioner and the tax rate for separate elementary schools is uniform throughout the area under the Board's jurisdiction.

Members of the Board are elected by separate school supporters biennially by wards, with one member for each ward. The original Board consisted of fifteen members, of whom nine represented Toronto and six the suburbs. In 1956, an additional suburban ward was created, raising total membership to sixteen. Two more suburban wards were created in 1964.

The Board is represented by two members on the Metropolitan School Board who do not participate in proceedings affecting public elementary schools since The Separate Schools Act provides for education up to Grade 10. The Board is also represented by one member on the Metropolitan Toronto Planning Board.

ii. *Metropolitan Toronto and Region Conservation Authority*

The Conservation Authorities Act, 1946, permitted a group of municipalities in a watershed or a group of watersheds to form a conservation authority for the purpose of carrying out a programme to conserve the natural resources of the area within its jurisdiction. At the inception of Metro four such authorities, the Etobicoke-Mimico, the Humber, the Don and the Rouge-Duffin-Highland-Petticoat Creek, had been formed. Recognition of the need for a regional approach and for a more substantial financial base, as well as the impetus provided by the disastrous flood following Hurricane Hazel in October 1954, led in 1957 to the amalgamation of the four authorities and the formation of the Metropolitan Toronto and Region Conservation Authority. The area under its jurisdiction has been described in Chapter I.

The Authority is administered by 55 appointed members: 3 members, including the chairman, are appointed by the Province of Ontario, 26 by Metro, and 26 by member municipalities outside Metropolitan Toronto. The work of the Authority is financed by levies on the member municipalities and by federal and provincial grants. The annual municipal levy is based on population. Accordingly, the Municipality of Metropolitan Toronto contributes 92 per cent of the municipal share.

iii. *Toronto and York Roads Commission*

Prior to the formation of Metro, the City of Toronto and the County of York shared in the costs of construction and maintenance of suburban roads in the County, each paying 25 per cent and the Province 50 per cent. The Toronto and York Roads Commission was established in 1916, with two representatives each from the City and the County and one from the Province.

The Cumming Report, taking cognizance of the financial implications to the County if the southern municipalities were separated from it, pointed to "the need for a special adjustment between the metropolitan area and the remaining county arising from the fact that the northern municipalities with less than fifteen per cent of the County equalized assessment would have to assume the County's portion of the cost of maintenance of nearly sixty per cent of the mileage of the existing county and suburban roads". Accordingly, implementing recommendations of the Report, the Metro Act provided that the Toronto and York Roads Commission be continued (sec. 104), and that all roads forming part of the county road system on December 31, 1953, other than those vested in a local municipality or assumed by Metro under the Act, continue to form part of the county road system as "suburban roads". Part VIII of The Highway Improvement Act, providing for the division of costs of suburban roads, was made to apply to the Metropolitan Corporation (sec. 101).

Metro thus became responsible for 25 per cent of the approved costs of suburban roads in the County, the expenditures on which are planned by the Toronto and York Roads Commission in co-operation with Metro's Roads Department and Planning Board. The composition of the Commission was also changed to provide for two representatives from the County, two from Metro, and a fifth selected by these four or, failing this, by the Lieutenant Governor in Council.

CHAPTER V

METROPOLITAN AND LOCAL SERVICES

On December 31, 1963, the Municipality of Metropolitan Toronto completed its first decade. In this period of rapid growth and development, water and sewage problems of crises proportions were overcome; transportation facilities for both city and suburban residents were immensely improved by expressway and rapid transit construction; and urgently needed new school accommodation was provided for the greatly expanded school population of the outer suburbs. Metro established and maintained a high credit rating which made possible the financing of vast projects. There were impressive accomplishments in other directions. There are also areas where expectations have not been fulfilled.

Metro's achievements in its first ten years must in large part be credited to the vision and driving force of Mr. Frederick G. Gardiner, Q.C., first chairman of the Metropolitan Council, who, with the co-operation of representatives of the area municipalities and of a staff of very able civic officials, took charge of the Metropolitan Corporation at its birth and led it through its first eight years, until his retirement in 1961. The area's rapid development has continued under his successor, Mr. William R. Allen, Q.C.

In its first decade, Metro concentrated its efforts on physical service needs. This was properly its first priority; it was largely to satisfy these needs on an area-wide basis that Metro was created. Accordingly, with projected expenditures of $585 million, its 1955 ten-year capital budget allocated 76 per cent for roads, sewers and water supply, 21 per cent for education, and 3 per cent for housing, welfare and recreation. The achievements in the provision of basic services have now made possible some changes in emphasis. The 1964 ten-year capital budget of more than a billion dollars is distributed as follows: 36 per cent for roads, sewers and water supply, about 30 per cent for public transit, 28 per cent for education, and 6 per cent for the social services.

In considering the accomplishments in the matter of physical services, it is well to recall that they were largely made possible by the credit rating of the City of Toronto and the transfer of physical plant by the City to Metro. Toronto, in turn, has benefited materially from the improvements and additions to the plant by Metro which were necessary for orderly development in a period of remarkable growth.

The following sections examine the development of Metro's services and the performance by area municipalities of local services which are of metropolitan interest. The recommendations are based on the continuance of a metropolitan form of government.

1. WATER SUPPLY

Periodic water shortages and offensive and dangerous conditions with respect to sewage disposal and treatment were two of the principal problems faced by the area after the Second World War. Under the Metro Act, the Metropolitan Corporation assumed "all works for the production, treatment and storage of water vested in each area municipality or any local board thereof and all trunk distribution mains connected therewith . . ." (sec. 39). It became the wholesale distributor of water to the area municipalities, which, in turn, distribute it locally to domestic and industrial consumers.

i. *Achievements of Metro*

Prior to 1954 the City of Toronto and the Town of New Toronto had the only adequate waterworks systems in the area. These were assumed by Metro, which then proceeded to expand and extend waterworks facilities to meet development requirements. In the ten years which followed, the capacity of pumping stations was increased from 618 million to 989 million gallons per day; the treatment capacity increased from 245 million to 345 million gallons per day; the storage capacity rose from 93 million gallons to 162 million gallons, with an additional 25 million gallons in reserve storage at the purification plants and pumping stations; and the 94 miles of trunk distribution mains grew to 202 miles.

A major step was the doubling, between 1957 and 1959, of the capacity of the R. C. Harris Plant, which previously belonged to Toronto, from 100 million to 200 million gallons per day. The Scarborough and New Toronto treatment plants were also enlarged and the Island water filtration plant was rebuilt. Storage capacity was increased by the construction of the new Lawrence, Eglinton and Richview reservoirs. The John Street Pumping Station, formerly part of the Toronto plant, was completely rehabilitated.

Annual water consumption rose from 51 billion gallons in 1954 to more than 70 billion gallons in 1963. Watering restrictions, which had been common in many sections of the area during the summer months, ceased in 1959 and the supply both for domestic and industrial purposes has been unrestricted since then. On October 28, 1963, following a referendum, a water fluoridation system went into operation.

Over the ten-year period, Metro's capital expenditures on its waterworks exceeded $64 million, representing almost 90 per cent of capital expenditures on waterworks in the area. Continuing development now necessitates a further growth of the metropolitan waterworks system. Construction began in 1963 of a new westerly purification plant—The Ross L. Clark Water Purification Plant—with an initial capacity of 100 million gallons per day and provision for future expansion to 300 million gallons per day. A new easterly purification plant is also projected, as well as new trunk mains on the periphery of the area, the enlargement of existing reservoirs, and construction of two new reservoirs in Markham and Vaughan townships, respectively. Further capital expenditures of approximately $38.5 million are anticipated in the next five or six years.

ii. *Rates*

While Metro was successfully fulfilling one of its major objectives in solving the problem of water supply, its policy on water rates created considerable tension. The Metro Act authorizes the Metropolitan Council to fix the rates for water supplied to area municipalities and to charge different rates to different municipalities, provided that the rates will be sufficient to make the system self-sustaining. The Toronto and New Toronto waterworks, assumed by Metro, had been a source of profit to these municipalities which had sold water to the suburbs at higher rates than those charged to their own residents. Their plants having been taken over without compensation, the City and New Toronto felt entitled to preferential rates under Metro.

At the outset Metro introduced a system of varying rates. As "producing" municipalities, the City and New Toronto paid 8.72 cents and 6 cents per 1,000 gallons, respectively, while the other area municipalities paid from 13 cents to 24 cents. In 1954 the Metropolitan Works Department proposed a uniform rate of 10.8 cents per 1,000 gallons for 1955. Instead, Council adopted a compromise plan proposed by the City and established a graduated scale of 15 cents per 1,000 gallons up to three billion gallons and 9.09 cents per 1,000 gallons beyond this quantity, except for New Toronto where the rate was to be 9.09 cents for all consumption. As the largest consumer, averaging about 38 billion gallons per year, Toronto's rate under this system, effective July 1, 1955, was about 9.13 cents per thousand gallons. In the suburbs the average rates decreased slightly.

There were rate increases in 1957 and 1958, when the rate became 20.15 cents per 1,000 gallons up to three billion gallons and 14.24 cents on purchases in excess of this quantity. New Toronto's rate increased to 14.24 cents per 1,000 gallons but was still the lowest of the suburban rates.

A further increase was necessary in 1959. The Metropolitan Works Department again proposed a uniform rate which Toronto had hitherto always successfully opposed. This time Council approved the change and fixed a uniform rate of 16.87 cents per 1,000 gallons, effective January 1, 1959. The rate will be increased to 19.90 cents on July 1, 1965.

In its brief to the Commission, the City of Toronto submits that: "Through the creation of Metro, the City of Toronto has been divested of its waterworks plant, has lost its substantial annual surplus on waterworks operations and has been forced to almost double its charges to consumers". This statement does not take account of what was in effect a saving to the City's residents during the five-year period, 1954-1958, when they enjoyed preferentially lower rates. The saving should be offset against the takeover of the City's plant by Metro without compensation but with liability for any outstanding debt. The submission also makes no allowance for the capital costs of renewal and enlargement of its plant which the City would in due course have had to bear, but which, instead, were assumed by Metro. Finally, the statement suggests that charges to consumers would not have risen if the City had retained its plant. This suggestion can scarcely be maintained in the light of the rise in costs and prices since 1954.

iii. *Conclusions*

In respect of water supply, Metro has achieved one of its principal objectives: it has solved the problem of adequate supplies of pure water throughout the area and is continuing to extend its waterworks facilities on a planned basis.

2. SEWAGE DISPOSAL

With only six of the thirteen area municipalities having direct access to Lake Ontario, the availability of a fresh water supply was dependent upon water pollution control by the extension of sewage facilities to the other municipalities. In 1954 there were nineteen sewage treatment plants in the Metro area, most of them seriously overloaded and not related to any general system of sewage disposal. Large areas of suburban housing were served only by septic tanks installed in clay soils which prevented their efficient operation. Seepage, uncontrolled storm water run-off and disposal of partially treated sewage into natural drainage channels turned streams and rivers, particularly the Don and the Humber into open sewers.

Under the Metro Act, the Metropolitan Corporation became responsible for all permanent sewage treatment plants and trunk sewers and trunk sewer systems for the collection and disposal of sewage. It assumed this plant from the area municipalities, which retained the local mains. Metro was empowered to levy sewage service rates on the whole or a designated part of an area municipality; to contract with any municipality outside Metro's boundaries to receive and dispose of sewage and land drainage; and to regulate, govern and establish standards for the design, construction and maintenance of local works connected or to be connected to a metropolitan work or water course.

i. *Achievements of Metro*

Under the overall plan adopted by Metro, all sewage was to be fed into large trunk mains leading to a number of major disposal plants along Lake Ontario, where it would be treated before discharge into the lake.

Metro completely remodelled the main sewage treatment plant at Ashbridge's Bay, which it assumed from the City, enlarged its capacity from 84 million to 120 million gallons per day, and installed secondary treatment facilities. The minor plants assumed were also remodelled; others were renovated; and 13 overloaded upstream plants were eliminated. Additional treatment capacity of 62 million gallons per day was provided by construction of the new Humber plant, enlargement of the Highland Creek plant, and construction of the new Lakeview plant, which is operated jointly by Metro and Toronto Township and in the construction of which Metro participated with the Township and the Ontario Water Resources Commission. These plants are served by some 170 miles of trunk sewers. Certain areas of Markham and Vaughan have been connected to the Metro system, on a fee basis, to prevent pollution of upstream waters, and several major storm interceptor sewers have been built.

Capital expenditures on Metro's sewage system to the end of 1963 amounted to $87 million. To complete works in progress, the Metropolitan Finance Commissioner estimates further capital expenditures of $40 million for trunk sewers and sewage treatment plants, including enlargement of the main plant at Ashbridge's Bay.

ii. *Local Sewer Renewal Needs*

Notwithstanding Metro's major achievements in respect of sewage disposal, the area faces a continuing problem in the need for a sewer renewal and enlargement programme in much of Toronto and the rest of the core area. The Metropolitan Corporation assumed responsibility for trunk sanitary sewers and the enlargement of the sanitary trunks has been of particular benefit to the outer suburbs, where sanitary and storm sewers are separate. But in much of Metro's core area the systems are combined and a heavy rainfall overloads the trunks and causes undesirable discharge of contaminants to the lake.

The inadequacy of the combined sewer systems, built to serve a city of single family dwellings and small commercial buildings, may restrain development and re-development. A renewal programme, involving either the separation of storm and sanitary sewers or the installation of greatly enlarged trunk sewers to carry combined sewage, is necessary. The area as a whole would benefit from such improvements which would ensure a higher quality of raw water in its supply system and less pollution of the lake water.

iii. *Conclusions*

Metro has to a large degree achieved its objective of solving the area-wide sewage problems which existed in 1954. It thereby made possible the rapid development of the outer suburbs. In the City of Toronto, York, East York and other parts of the core area, however, the sewer systems are now inadequate in relation to development and re-development needs. Since redevelopment of the core is a matter of area-wide concern, the area as a whole should share in financing the municipal costs of the necessary trunk sewer renewal programmes.

3.   PUBLIC TRANSPORTATION

The Toronto Transit Commission ("T.T.C."), as outlined in Chapter IV, was created by the Metro Act as successor to the Toronto Transportation Commission, with exclusive power to provide public passenger transportation in the Metropolitan Area, other than steam railways and taxis.

i. *Achievements*

The Transit Commission's first task was the reorganization of the system and the extension of services to the suburban areas. Its achievements have been impressive. In ten years it increased the number of surface routes from 53 to 80 and the one-way route mileage from 244 to 428. The annual mileage of bus services operated in the suburbs has doubled, increasing from 5 million miles in 1955 to 10 million in 1963. The Commission now operates 583 miles of streetcar and subway track and bus routes, and, in 1963, carried 271 million passengers. Five fare zones have been reduced to two: an inner zone extending to about five miles from the core area and a second zone consisting of the rest of the Metropolitan Area.

In 1954 the Yonge Street Subway, Canada's first subway, consisting of 4.56 miles of rapid transit lines extending from Union Station to Eglinton Avenue, constructed and independently financed by the former Commission, was completed at a cost of some $64 million. In 1958, following intensive study by T.T.C., Metropolitan Council and the Metropolitan Planning Board, agreement was reached on the construction and financing of the Bloor-Danforth-University extension of 9.85 miles. The University Avenue section (two miles), connecting with the Yonge Street Subway at Union Station and extending to Bloor Street, was opened in February 1963. The Bloor-Danforth Subway, extending eight miles from Keele Street to Woodbine Avenue, is now under construction and the target date for completion has been advanced from 1968 to 1965. In 1963, Council approved eastern and western extensions to this line—to Warden Avenue and St. Clair Avenue in Scarborough (about three miles) and to Bloor Street and Montgomery Road in Etobicoke (about three miles)—with completion scheduled in 1967 or 1968. In September 1964, the Executive Committee of Metro Council recommended that the western terminus be moved from Montgomery Road to Islington Avenue.

By 1968 the subway system will consist of about 21 miles of rapid transit lines. Further extensions of the Bloor-Danforth Subway and a northerly extension of the Yonge Street Subway are under study, and the ten-year capital budget makes provision for a Spadina Expressway route.

ii. *Finances*

The great expansion in transit services and facilities has materially affected the financial position of the Transit Commission and its relationship to the Metropolitan Council. The system it assumed in 1954 had always operated at a profit, improving and extending its facilities and equipment without any assistance from municipal taxation. T.T.C., too, was required by the Act to fix rates so that it would be financially self-sustaining, although the Cumming Report had suggested "that the underlying liability of the metropolitan area for the provision of possible future deficits in this publicly owned system should be given formal recognition in any legislation . . ." In this, the Report foresaw what was soon to happen.

In June 1955, T.T.C. reported to the Metropolitan Council on its financial position. The costs of servicing a much larger area, increases in operating costs, and heavy interest charges on the Yonge Street Subway had produced a net operating deficit of $1.9 million in 1954, which was met from a fare stabilization fund. For 1955 the Commission estimated a deficit of $3.1 million, which, after exhausting the balance in this fund, would leave a net deficit of $2.5 million. Under authority of an amendment to the Metro Act, Council made a grant of $2.3 million to T.T.C. in 1956 to cover its losses. On July 1, 1956, the Commission increased the basic adult fare from 10 cents to $12\frac{1}{2}$ cents.

T.T.C. showed surpluses in 1956, 1957 and 1958, a small deficit in 1959, surpluses in 1960 and 1961, and a deficit of $823,000 in 1962. On May 1, 1960, the fare was raised to 15 cents, modified on May 1, 1961, to $14\frac{2}{7}$ cents on the basis of 7 tickets for $1.00. On May 1, 1963, there was a further fare increase to $16\frac{2}{3}$ cents, that is, 6 tickets for $1.00. On May 3, 1963, Council, authorized by an amendment to the Act, approved payment of a subsidy of $2.5 million to the Commission on account of its 1963 debenture interest charges, conditional upon revocation of the last fare increase. On May 20, 1963, the Commission reverted to the $14\frac{2}{7}$ cents fare. Notwithstanding the subsidy, it showed a deficit of almost $500,000 for 1963. On January 1, 1964, the basic adult fare was increased to $16\frac{2}{3}$ cents.

A major factor contributing to operating losses in this period was the continued decline in the number of fare-paying passengers—an experience which T.T.C. shared with other carriers in North America. The decline in the Toronto area between 1953 and 1963 was about 38 per cent, as compared with an average decline of 48 per cent in other Canadian cities and about 57 per cent in the United States. During 1963 the trend was reversed, the number of passengers carried increasing by almost 2.3 million over 1962. The first increase in many years coincided with the reduction in the number of fare zones from five to two, which meant substantially reduced fares for many suburban riders. Despite an increase in fares from seven to six tickets for one dollar at the beginning of 1964, the number of passengers carried has continued to rise, the first eight months of 1964 showing an increase of 2.5 million passengers over the corresponding period of 1963. T.T.C. now shows an operating surplus, which, however, has only been made possible by relief from debt charges resulting from the assumption of subway debt by the Metropolitan Corporation.

On the basis of agreements reached, and under authority of amendments to the legislation, capital expenditures on subway construction are shared by the Metropolitan Corporation and the Transit Commission. A basis for sharing the costs was originally agreed on in 1958, at which time Council also decided that a two mill area-wide levy, which had been imposed initially in 1957 for general municipal purposes, should be applied in each of the years 1959 to 1968, inclusive, solely to reduction of the Metropolitan Corporation's share of financing subway construction. The proceeds of this levy to the end of 1964 were approximately $47.5 million.

The agreement for sharing the costs of subway construction was revised in 1963: the Metropolitan Corporation assumed responsibility for all right-of-way costs and the Transit Commission for all operating equipment costs of the Bloor-Danforth-University line and its eastern and western extensions into Scarborough and Etobicoke. To relieve T.T.C. of heavy annual debt charges, Metro, as authorized by the Ontario Municipal Board in January 1964, also assumed responsibility, on the same basis, for approximately $49 million of unmatured debenture debt of the Yonge Street Subway.

The estimated cost of the Bloor-Danforth-University Subway is $277.7 million. The T.T.C. share of this amount, to be financed by Metropolitan Toronto debentures, is $82.2 million. Metro's share is $195.5 million, which, according to estimates, will be financed as follows: $86.7 million by the two mill levy; $9.3 million by sales of surplus lands; $21.4 million by subsidies from the Provincial Government under Part XIII-A of The Highway Improvement Act, enacted in 1963 to authorize the Minister of Highways to pay an amount not exceeding $33\frac{1}{3}$ per cent of the expenditure on right-of-way construction on the Bloor-Danforth line after April 1, 1964; and $78 million by the issuance of Metropolitan Toronto debentures. In 1961 the Provincial Government undertook direct purchase of $60 million of Metro debentures issued for the project. Metro has also received permission to borrow approximately $29.5 million under the Federal-Provincial-Municipal Works Assistance Program, which will reduce interest costs and which provides that 25 per cent of the moneys advanced will be forgiven to the extent that the works are completed by April 1, 1966.

iii. *T.T.C. and Metro*

In 1962 the Metro Act was amended to authorize the Metropolitan Corporation to contribute to the capital costs of the Transit Commission with the approval of the Ontario Municipal Board (sec. 116a), and the requirement that T.T.C. operate on a self-sustaining basis was made subject to the new provision (sec. 116(1)c). In 1963 the Act was further amended to authorize the Corporation to "contribute to the cost of operating the transportation system operated by the Commission" (sec. 116a(2)).

The inability of T.T.C. to finance the costs of the increasing and diversified transportation needs of the area on a self-sustaining basis has affected its relationship to the Metropolitan Council. With tax revenues paying more than 40 per cent of the development costs of the transit system over a ten-year period, the Council necessarily acquired a voice in decisions on transportation policies and projects and fares, which was not envisaged by the legislation. In law, T.T.C. continues to operate as a quasi-independent commission solely responsible for public transportation. In fact, Council has determined the fare structure from time to time and, more recently, the course of development of rapid transit facilities. A number of briefs to this Commission have therefore submitted that the changed circumstances call for more direct control of T.T.C. by the Metropolitan Corporation. It was recommended, inter alia, that T.T.C. be made directly responsible to a committee of Council or that it be abolished and replaced by a new Metro department.

In considering the suggested changes, it is well to note the powers conferred on Council with respect to the Transit Commission by the Metro Act. Council appoints the commissioners of T.T.C. and fixes their salaries. It may reduce their number from five to three. It retains its authority with reference to providing the money for T.T.C. undertakings and alone can issue the necessary debentures. In exercising the more recent authority conferred on it to contribute to the capital and operating costs of T.T.C., Council has been in an effective position to influence policies on fares and the planning of subway routes. It cannot, therefore, be said that Council is without control over the Transit Commission.

Considering that transportation is a basic component in the overall planning and development of the area, I am of the opinion that a more formal coordination between Metro and T.T.C. is desirable. I do not find, however, that such coordination requires the abolition of T.T.C. and the transfer of its functions to a Metro department. The nature of the service provided by the Transit Commission and its record of efficient administration are reasons for leaving the provision of public transportation in its hands.

iv. *Conclusions*

The Transit Commission, with the financial participation of the Metropolitan Corporation, has achieved major objectives in providing a high standard of mass transit services in the area.

There should be a more formal coordination between Metro and T.T.C. To this end, the chairman of Metropolitan Council should ex officio be a full member of the Toronto Transit Commission. There should also be a more formal coordination in overall transportation planning between the staffs of the Transit Commission, the Metro Planning Board and other agencies concerned, in order to ensure that proper consideration is given to all forms of transportation required to meet the present and prospective needs of Metro and the surrounding area.

4. ROADS

The Metro Act (sec. 76) provides that, subject to the approval of the Lieutenant Governor in Council, "the Metropolitan Council shall by by-law establish a metropolitan road system in the Metropolitan Area by assuming roads in any area municipality . . . and the by-law shall designate the roads to be assumed as metropolitan roads and intended to form the metropolitan road system". The Metropolitan Corporation is also empowered to establish and lay out new roads as part of the metropolitan road system.

i. *Achievements of Metro*

Under the authority of the Act, Metro assumed a basic network of 275 miles of arterial roads and streets in 1954. Since then it has increased the total to 355 miles by assuming an additional 47 miles of existing roads and constructing

18 miles of new arterial roads and 15 miles of new expressways. Improvements of the arterial system have included the widening of 60 miles of roads, the resurfacing of 118 miles and the improvement of 171 intersections by channelization to accommodate traffic movements.

To 110 major structures on the road system in 1953, Metro has added 101 new bridges, including 20 railway grade separations and major interchange construction at Royal York Road and Dundas Street; the Six Points in Islington; and the intersection of Bayview and Lawrence Avenues.

The development of Metro's expressway network has proceeded with construction of the western section of the Frederick G. Gardiner Expressway and the Don Valley Parkway, now extending to Lawrence Avenue in the north. These were linked in November 1964 and provide a six-lane highway from the Queen Elizabeth Way to Lawrence Avenue. Construction of the Spadina Expressway began in 1963. Of Metro's total expenditures of $200 million on roads, $135 million has been spent on the expressway system and the related extensions of Bayview Avenue and Lawrence Avenue.

Prior to 1954 the area municipalities had endeavoured to keep pace with the tremendous increase in the number of motor vehicles in the area but they could not cope with some of the major problems. For thiry years plans had been made to connect the adjacent municipalities of Scarborough, North York and Leaside across the two branches of the Don River but no method of financing the project could be devised. The Metropolitan Corporation connected the municipalities by constructing the Eglinton Avenue Extension, which now carries 33,000 vehicles per day. Another example of Metro's achievements are the seventeen lanes now crossing the Humber River at its mouth, as compared with the single four-lane bridge which formerly connected the Queen Elizabeth Way and Highway 2, on the west side of the Humber, to the Lakeshore Boulevard and Queen Street on the east side.

In his annual report for 1963, the Metropolitan Finance Commissioner estimated further capital expenditures of more than $145 million to complete works in progress, including the Frederick G. Gardiner Expressway, the Don Valley Parkway, the Spadina Expressway (including provision for future rapid transit facilities), and other major road improvements. Approximately 50 per cent of these expenditures will be recovered by way of Provincial Government subsidy.

ii. *Provincial and Metro Expressways*

The Gardiner Expressway and the Don Valley Parkway, which, when connected in November 1964, linked the Humber in the west and the Don in the east, supplement an extensive system of provincial expressways: Highway 401, traversing the northern part of Metro in an east-west direction, which is now being widened over a distance of 17 miles to a minimum of 12 lanes; Highway 27 in the west, running north through Etobicoke; and the Queen Elizabeth Way in the south. Two authorities, the Metropolitan Corporation and the provincial Department of Highways, are therefore responsible for essential components of the Metro expressway network. Expressway construction by these two authorities should be coordinated in terms of both overall transportation requirements and local development objectives.

iii. *Suburban Roads*

It has been shown in Chapter IV that Metro is responsible for 25 per cent of the approved costs of maintenance and construction of suburban roads in York County. In its first ten years Metro's share of these costs amounted to $3.75 million.

In his brief to the Commission, Mr. William R. Allen, Q.C., Chairman of the Metropolitan Council, submitted that Metro is comparable to a county organization and should not be responsible for road costs beyond its boundaries. The County of York, in its brief, pointed out that the current arrangement gives effect in the Toronto area to the statutory requirement for the sharing of suburban road costs throughout Ontario, and requested that it should be maintained. I do not find that the existing arrangement should be changed.

iv. *Local Roads*

Roads and streets which have not been assumed by the Metropolitan Corporation remain the responsibility of the area municipalities. In this connection, the Metropolitan Planning Commissioner, in his brief to the Commission, said that: "The establishment of proper collector road systems, designed to provide satisfactory internal communications within neighbourhoods and reasonable connections between adjoining neighbourhoods or communities, without requiring the excessive use of arterial roads, is essentially a local responsibility, discharged primarily in the course of subdivision design. While some of the municipalities are paying increasing attention to this vital requirement, in others this requirement has been neglected or undergone considerable distortion. As a result, some sections of Metropolitan Toronto have been developed with quite inadequate road systems, which has had a detrimental effect on the ability of the Metropolitan road system to perform its basic function." This view was supported by the brief of the Central Ontario Chapter of the Town Planning Institute of Canada. On the basis of the evidence submitted, I suggest that Metro should assume appropriate major local arterial roads.

The Planning Commissioner also pointed to the problem of control of access to arterial roads, which is largely in the hands of the area municipalities: "Here again, in some municipalities adequate attention is paid to the Metropolitan interests, through consultation prior to the granting of development approval and subsequently on the design and location of access points. In some other municipalities, there is almost no consultation, except in extraordinary circumstances. As a result a number of difficult situations have been created at specific locations on the Metropolitan road system which might have been avoided with a proper coordination of access control." In my opinion, the law should require approval by the Metropolitan authority of the design of access to metropolitan roads.

v. *Conclusions*

Metro's expressways and arterial road network constitute one of the major accomplishments of metropolitan government in the area.

The design of access to metropolitan roads should require the approval of Metro authorities, and Metro should assume appropriate major local arterial roads.

Since Metro and the Province are each responsible for essential components of the metropolitan expressway system, construction should be coordinated to meet the overall requirements of both transportation and local development.

To make transit operations possible on the roads on Metro's boundaries, where the dividing line is the middle of the road the Metropolitan Corporation should be authorized to assume such roads as metropolitan roads.

5. TRAFFIC MANAGEMENT

The construction of new roads or the widening of existing roads does not solve the traffic problems of an area like that of Metro without effective traffic management "to keep the traffic moving".[1] In this regard, Metro faces a problem of divided authority under which the Metropolitan Corporation is responsible for traffic control on metropolitan roads and the thirteen area municipalities are responsible for regulating traffic on local roads. Nevertheless, considerable progress towards uniform procedures and controls has been made.

i. *Traffic Control*

A Metropolitan Traffic Engineering Department was established in 1954 to prepare traffic by-laws and regulations for metropolitan roads and to assist the Roads Department in the design of road intersections and the Planning Board in transportation research. It was also to be responsible for measures to speed the flow of traffic and to promote safety on roads. The fragmentation of traffic control authority in the area required close co-operation with the thirteen area municipalities and thirteen police forces.

Unification of the police services in 1957 automatically placed the enforcement of traffic by-laws under a single authority. In 1959 all the area municipalities adopted uniform traffic control by-laws based on a Metro by-law adopted in 1958. In the latter year agreement was also reached for the installation of a system of pedestrian crosswalks by Metro at appropriate intersections in the area.

In 1962 an amendment to the Act empowered Metro to assume operation of all signal-light traffic control systems in the area, to control the systems by electronic computers, and to regulate traffic on highways within 100 feet of any

---
[1]Report of the Royal Commission on Local Government in Greater London, 1957-60, p. 108.

such system. Accordingly, all traffic signals in the area, whether on metropolitan or local roads, have been assumed by the Metropolitan Corporation, which has done pioneering experimental work in the electronic control of traffic. It is expected that by the end of 1965 traffic signals over the whole area will be controlled by an electronic computer-control system, which has been established at a cost of more than $3 million. An improvement of 20 to 25 per cent in traffic flow is anticipated.

Subject to the foregoing, the regulation of traffic on local streets and roads continues to be the responsibility of the area municipalities. Traffic engineering practices vary; for example, there is no uniform policy governing truck traffic, and no rational system of one-way streets. When the centrally controlled traffic signal system is in operation, the fragmented control of traffic on local streets will be even more out of date. It is clear that the traffic engineering services of the area should be unified under a single authority.

ii. *Parking*

The Metro Act (sec. 272) grants to the Metropolitan Corporation the powers of a municipality to establish parking lots and facilities and to set up a Parking Authority, and authorizes the Corporation to enter into an agreement with the Parking Authority of Toronto for the operation of Metro parking lots. Metro has to date not exercised these powers.

Parking is generally a problem in all large urban communities; in the Metro area, the problem is accentuated by one of the highest motor vehicle ratios to population on the continent coupled with the fact that the central area was developed before the age of the automobile. Off-street parking facilities, which are, in effect, an extension of the public street system, are essential to ensure the most efficient use of the streets. In 1952 the City of Toronto established a Parking Authority which operates off-street parking facilities on a self-sustaining basis. In North York, York and Etobicoke the authorities are financially dependent upon the local councils.

In view of the relationship of parking to the overall transportation system of the area, Metro has at various times considered the establishment of a metropolitan authority which would either assume the assets or operate through the agency of the Toronto Parking Authority. New problems of area-wide concern are now to the fore in the planning of parking facilities both to complement rapid transit and commuter train services and to encourage commercial developments along the route of the east-west subway. These are matters of metropolitan concern affecting traffic control policy, the financial operations of the transit system, and the amount of traffic entering the central part of the area.

The City of Toronto, in its brief to the Commission, submitted that an area-wide parking authority "would assist the proper coordination of all communications interests—arterial roads, mass transit, commuter rail service and traffic control". I am of the opinion that such an authority should be established.

iii. *Conclusions*

The traffic engineering services of the Metropolitan area should be unified under Metro.

Metro should establish an area-wide Parking Authority with responsibility for policy on the provision of parking facilities in the Metropolitan Area in conformity with metropolitan requirements and planning, and with power to operate such facilities directly or to enter into a contractual arrangement for their operation by the Toronto Parking Authority.

6. PUBLIC HOUSING

Section 217 of the Metro Act confers upon the Metropolitan Corporation all the powers of a municipality under The Housing Development Act or any other Act with respect to housing or building development, housing projects and redevelopment areas, without limiting or interfering with the powers of the area municipalities in these matters. Section 218 authorizes Metro to enter into agreements with an area municipality for sharing or contributing to its costs in the exercise of any of its powers in the matter of housing.

i. *Housing Agencies*

With the Federal Government contributing the largest share of the financing, under the National Housing Act and through Central Mortgage and Housing Corporation, five separate and distinct agencies have been operating in the public housing field in the Metro area, as follows:

(a) Metropolitan Toronto Housing Authority, a special authority created by the Provincial Government in 1955, administers low rental family housing projects which are subsidized jointly, under section 36 of the National Housing Act, by Central Mortgage and Housing Corporation and the Government of Ontario.

(b) Metropolitan Toronto Housing Company Limited, a non-profit company wholly owned by the Metropolitan Corporation, was incorporated to qualify under the "limited dividend" mortgage loan provisions of section 16 of the National Housing Act. It builds housing for elderly people and the projects are managed by the Metropolitan Department of Welfare and Housing.

(c) Housing Authority of Toronto, a housing agency of the City of Toronto created in 1947 to manage city housing projects, concerned itself originally with low rental or subsidized housing but now directs its efforts mainly to moderate rental family housing projects.

(d) City of Toronto Limited Dividend Housing Corporation Limited, created by the City of Toronto in 1956 to qualify for limited dividend mortgage loans under section 16 of the National Housing Act, builds and administers moderate rental housing on sites supplied by the City.

(e) York Township Housing Company Limited, owned by York Township, builds and administers housing for elderly persons.

ii. *Limited Achievement*

When Metro came into being on January 1, 1954, the only subsidized family housing units available were in Regent Park North, a project of the Housing Authority of Toronto, commenced in 1947 and completed with 1,397 dwelling units in 1959. Apart from Regent Park South, with 732 units, all other subsidized public housing constructed in the Metro area under section 36 of the National Housing Act was requested by the Metropolitan Council. As at September 1, 1964, the stock of low rental housing in Metro was 3,707 units, and the construction of 6,300 additional units is planned for the period 1964-1973. Under the Ontario Rent Certificate Plan, which provides for renting existing houses and apartments from private owners, the Metropolitan Toronto Housing Authority, as agent for the Province, has assembled 245 units.

All moderate rental "limited dividend" housing units, built under section 16 of the National Housing Act, were constructed by the City of Toronto Limited Dividend Housing Corporation Limited. The total stock, as at September 1, 1964, was 1,268 units, including 902 units in the Moss Park project.

Prior to Metro, low rental housing for elderly persons was provided in one project of 128 units by the York Township Housing Corporation, which has retained administration of the project. Since 1954, the Metropolitan Corporation, acting through its "limited dividend" Metropolitan Toronto Housing Company Limited, has constructed 1,866 units in separate projects in the City, Etobicoke, North York, Scarborough, York and East York, raising the total to almost 2,000 units. These make available bachelor and one-bedroom suites for citizens of Metro of limited income, who are over 60 years of age and have had ten years' continuous residence in Metro immediately prior to their application. Rents range from $35.75 to $50.00 monthly for bachelor suites and from $42.25 to $60.00 monthly for one-bedroom apartments.

Metro's major accomplishment in public housing has been in the provision of low rental units for elderly persons. Its record in this field is very good. The same cannot be said of the provision of subsidized low rental family housing. The existing stock of 3,700 units meets only a fraction of the need; the revised draft Metro Official Plan estimates requirements at 30,000 to 40,000 units by 1980, while a recent study estimates the current effective demand at 15,000 units.[1] But Metro's experience in public housing is by no means unique. In the whole of Canada only 12,500 units have been provided in the past fifteen years, of which more than 60 per cent are in Ontario. It is apparent that public housing has not yet attained wide political acceptance in Canada.

---
[1] *Good Housing for Canadians: A Study by the Ontario Association of Housing Authorities*, 1964, p. 91.

The lack of progress in public housing in the Toronto area should not be attributed solely to the metropolitan government. The situation has been substantially beyond its control. The multiplicity of authorities concerned in housing involves agreements between four governments and complicated administrative techniques. It has been estimated that more than eighty planning and engineering steps are necessary between the initiation of a project and the occupancy of public housing dwellings and that the normal time lapse is of the order of five years. A project must be initiated by a municipality or receive its approval if it is to be located within its boundaries. But the area municipalities with available land have been reluctant to accept public housing because of fear of its effects on municipal and school costs and on the values of existing residential properties and, generally, because of the opposition of local residents to public housing in their neighbourhood. By its opposition, a municipality can delay a project almost indefinitely. Examples of such delays were cited in evidence before the Commission.

The limited achievement in the Metro area must also be attributed to absence of a coordinated public housing programme. There has been no central housing authority responsible for planning, designing, constructing and administering public housing projects and allocating the units in accordance with the overall needs of the area, regardless of existing municipal boundaries. It is doubtful, however, whether an agency with such authority was feasible in the early years of metropolitan government. The law says that Metro's housing powers are not to limit or interfere with the corresponding powers of the area municipalities; an agency such as described would at the outset have caused major political controversy. In any event, the first priority of the Metropolitan Corporation was to provide the basic physical services upon which the development of the area depended. Even with its powers widened, Metro would not have been in a position to embark on a large-scale housing programme until its major water and sewage programmes had been substantially completed. These services had to be extended to the suburbs where most of the vacant sites available for housing are located. With the completion of its major projects, Metro, in 1962, endorsed the amalgamation of existing housing agencies and the formation of a metropolitan agency responsible for all aspects of public housing in the area. But negotiations to achieve this end were unsuccessful.

iii. *Conclusions*

The need for a central housing agency in Metro is established by the evidence. Public housing programmes will not be accelerated unless the multiplicity of authorities and the procedural complexities are reduced to a necessary minimum. This may now be achieved through the Ontario Housing Corporation, created by provincial legislation in 1964 with all the powers of a housing authority under The Housing Development Act and with responsibility for all aspects of housing in Ontario.

Amendments to the National Housing Act enacted in 1964 authorize the Federal Government to loan 90 per cent of the capital costs of public housing projects created and owned by provinces, municipalities or public housing agencies, and to pay 50 per cent of the annual operating losses. Under the policy adopted by the Ontario Housing Corporation, Ontario municipalities will no longer be required to contribute to capital costs. Their financial participation is to be limited to payment of 7.5 per cent of any operating losses incurred in housing other than for elderly people and, in the latter case, to waiving all realty taxes in excess of $25 per suite per annum.

The Ontario Housing Corporation, qualified for loans under the National Housing Act, should now act as a single agency on behalf of the federal and provincial governments in dealing with the Metropolitan Corporation in respect of all further low rental housing developments in the Metro area, with Metro assuming the remaining municipal financial responsibility therefor.

7. HEALTH AND WELFARE

Under Part IX of the Metro Act, the mandatory responsibilities of the Metropolitan Corporation for health and welfare services are limited to such matters as payment of the cost of post sanatorium care for consumptives, provision of homes for the aged, payments to Children's Aid Societies for the support of neglected children, and, since January 1, 1964, repayment to the area municipalities of the municipal share of the cost of mandatory services under the General Welfare Assistance Act. Metro has optional powers to make grants for the erection and maintenance of public hospitals and to construct and maintain public hospitals. The major public health and welfare services remain the responsibility of the area municipalities, with financial assistance from the Province.

i. *Care of the Aged*

It has been said in this report that Metro's record in the provision of low rental housing for elderly persons has been very good. Its record in providing institutional care for the aged, under its welfare responsibilities, has been equally good. Prior to 1954, 762 beds were available, all of which were in Lambert Lodge, which was transferred to Metro in that year. As at September 1, 1964, there were 2,262 beds in five separate locations, including Lambert Lodge, which now has only 710 beds due to remodelling for the Geriatric Centre.

ii. *Chronically Ill and Convalescent Care*

The Metro Act transferred Riverdale Isolation Hospital from the City of Toronto to the Metropolitan Corporation. In March 1964, The Riverdale Hospital Act vested the management, maintenance and operation of the hospital in a Board of Governors, to whom the real property was leased by Metro and to whom all the personal property of the hospital was transferred. The board is not a local board of the Metropolitan Corporation.

Riverdale Hospital now cares for chronically ill and convalescent patients. While it was a responsibility of Metro, its capacity was increased from 105 to more than 900 beds, thereby providing relief to the active treatment hospitals in the area. The City of Toronto continues to provide a similar service at Runnymede Hospital with 130 beds.

iii. *Hospital Grants*

Metro made grants in aid of hospital construction amounting to some $8 million from 1954 to 1963. In March 1958, the federal and provincial governments having increased their capital grants, Council voted to cease Metro grants. Accordingly, reflecting diminishing instalments on commitments, the grant declined from $1.2 million in 1958 to $200,000 in 1963. Rising construction costs and a severe shortage of hospital beds soon led to pressure for a resumption of Metro's original policy. In November 1963, Council voted to resume grants on the basis of 50 per cent of the regular provincial grant, and an amount of $500,000 was included in the 1964 operating budget for this purpose. I find that, in making grants in aid of hospital construction, the Metropolitan Corporation is discharging a proper responsibility.

Reports of a major survey of hospital needs in Metro show a current shortage of 2,360 active treatment beds, an anticipated shortage of 6,172 beds between 1963 and 1980, and a severe shortage of hospital beds for the care of children. In its brief to the Commission, the Social Planning Council of Metropolitan Toronto submitted that the problem of providing adequate hospital facilities in the area "is much more than a matter of financing. It is a problem of planning which must be tackled on the metropolitan level at least". On March 17, 1965, the Minister of Health officially endorsed a recommendation of a survey committee for the establishment of a Metropolitan Toronto region hospital coordinating council which "would maintain an up-to-date analysis of the needs and facilities for health services in the area and would make the necessary recommendations to meet any deficiencies that might occur". The appointment of such a council will be a forward step in planning for health needs.

iv. *Emergency Ambulance Service*

The City of Toronto provides the only publicly-owned emergency ambulance service in the metropolitan area, with eight well-equipped modern ambulances. Operating under the City's Department of Health, there are five ambulance stations strategically located. The ambulances are linked by two-way radios and a central dispatcher who has radio and telephone connections with the police and fire departments. Each ambulance has two attendants and both are trained as drivers and as first aid attendants. The ambulances provide transportation to the nearest general hospital for any type of emergency case from any location in the City. By agreement, the City ambulances also transport mentally ill patients for the Municipality of Metropolitan Toronto. Etobicoke provides an ambulance service under a contract arrangement, and in three municipalities each fire department has an ambulance.

It was submitted to the Commission that an emergency ambulance service should be available on a metropolitan basis. I agree. Ambulance service in a metropolitan area should have no regard to local boundaries. In the words of the Royal Commission on Greater London (1960), which recommended that the Greater London Council should be responsible for the service, "the area needed for this service is very much larger than that needed for the other personal health services". I also find that the service should be publicly owned and operated; it is of too vital concern to the citizens to be left in the hands of private ambulance operators.

Metro should take steps to provide a metropolitan public emergency ambulance service. A central despatch system for all ambulances serving emergency calls in Metropolitan Toronto is immediately necessary. It has been suggested that the emergency service should be operated by the police department or by the area fire departments. I suggest a contractual arrangement between the Metropolitan Corporation and the City of Toronto under which the service would be operated by the City for the whole area.

v. *Public Assistance*

The welfare services assigned to Metro are administered by the Metropolitan Welfare and Housing Department. Under provincial legislation, each of the area municipalities administers general welfare assistance, supplementary services and such optional services as it may choose. Nine services, including general welfare payments, nursing home care, and rehabilitation, are mandatory where the need is present, and the Province pays 80 per cent of the allowances paid to the recipients, subject to certain ceilings. The Province also shares in the costs of other services which may be provided.

With a relatively larger proportion of elderly persons and with the concentration of low-income families within its boundaries, the City is called upon to provide a greater variety of welfare services than the other municipalities. It bears the preponderant share of welfare costs, although it was afforded relief in 1964 when the Metropolitan Corporation assumed the municipal share (20 per cent) of the payments under The General Welfare Assistance Act. The other municipalities submit that their more limited services are adequate for the requirements of their people.

The Social Planning Council of Metropolitan Toronto submitted in its brief to the Commission that, with certain services being optional and with different interpretations given to the general welfare assistance legislation, there are inequalities in the provision of welfare services among the thirteen area municipalities. There are services which are provided in some municipalities and not in others and, in some instances, allowances under mandatory welfare assistance vary appreciably as the recipient moves out of one municipality into another. The Council also submitted that most of the services for which there is legislative provision are needed in the suburbs as well as in the older core of the area. It urged "that these services should be equally available to individuals and families with the same needs, no matter where they live in Metropolitan Toronto".

With Metro's thirteen municipalities varying so greatly in size, in the composition of their population and in resources, the needs for welfare services vary and there are variations in the standards of service provided. In 1963 the City of Toronto reported 340 full time welfare employees; in the suburbs the number was 37, distributed as follows: nine in North York, seven each in Scarborough, Etobicoke and York, four in East York, one each in Mimico, New Toronto and Long Branch, and none in Swansea, Weston, Forest Hill and Leaside.

While it is generally agreed that the personal services directly affecting the individual citizen require a local unit of administration, it is also agreed that such unit must be adequate for the purpose. Small autonomous units with limited resources, like some of the area municipalities, cannot provide the range of services which should be available under modern health and welfare programmes, and the services which they do make available are not always administered by trained personnel. This is not satisfactory. A consolidation of some of the municipalities, by enlarging the areas of service and spreading the costs, would lead to more equality in standards and in the range of welfare services provided in the Metro area.

vi. *Public Health*

Public health is the responsibility of the local boards of health in the area municipalities. Leaside and East York constitute an inter-municipal health unit. The basic services include nursing services, immunization, school dental services, medical care of infants and mothers, sanitary inspection and housing inspection. As in the case of the welfare services, the health services of the area vary in range and in quality, the City of Toronto necessarily providing the widest range. Per capita gross expenditures on health services in 1963 amounted to $5.74 in Toronto and, in the suburbs, ranged from 41 cents in Long Branch to $2.50 in York. For the reasons already set out in respect of welfare, a consolidation of some of the area municipalities would result in a more equitable distribution of health services in Metro.

In its brief to the Commission, Etobicoke Township recommended the appointment of a Metropolitan Health Officer who would be responsible for certain inspection services. Specific reference was made, among others, to the medical aspects of milk inspection, because of Metro-wide distribution of milk. I find that, if some inspection services should be performed for the whole area by a single agency, this does not necessarily require the establishment of a new metropolitan department. With fewer area municipalities, an inspection service could be assigned under contract to the City's Health Department, each municipality to pay its share of the cost. I suggest that a Metropolitan Board of Health Officers, consisting of the medical health officers of the area municipalities, should be formed to advise on such matters, to coordinate the health policies of the municipalities and, generally, to promote co-operation in maintaining high standards of health services throughout the area. The board could also set up standards in relation to service, equipment and staff training for the proposed metropolitan emergency ambulance service.

vii. *Conclusions*

In resuming grants in aid of hospital construction, the Metropolitan Corporation is discharging a proper responsibility.

The Metropolitan Corporation should take steps to provide a metropolitan public emergency ambulance service. Consideration should be given to a contractual arrangement with Toronto under which the City would operate the service.

A Metropolitan Board of Health Officers, consisting of the area health officers, should be formed to coordinate the public health policies of the local municipalities and to advise on health and sanitary inspection matters.

A consolidation of municipalities would lead to more equality in standards and in the range of health and welfare services provided in the Metro area. The aim should be to make these services equally available to individuals and families with the same needs, no matter where they live in Metropolitan Toronto.

8. WASTE DISPOSAL

Section 257 of the Metro Act authorizes the Metropolitan Corporation to acquire land and to erect buildings and machinery for the purposes of dumping and disposing of garbage, refuse and industrial waste, but only with the approval of the area municipality in which the land is situated.

While Metro has not acquired any sites, it has operated a total of twelve sites under agreement with the area municipalities concerned. By the end of 1964, however, only one metropolitan disposal site was still in operation and this was being rapidly filled up. As locally operated sites in almost every municipality are quickly being filled, there is now an urgent need to locate new sites to provide disposal and incineration facilities on an area-wide basis.

A system of disposal of industrial waste and some domestic refuse by the dumping of satisfactory fills in low-lying areas has been in operation for some years through the co-operation of the Metropolitan Parks Department and the Metropolitan Toronto and Region Conservation Authority. This has made possible the development of many low-lying marshy sites as park sites and green areas; it assisted, for example, in the creation of Marie Curtis Park in Long Branch. These land improvement operations are to be commended.

In its brief to the Commission, the Conservation Authority urged the need for a long-term programme for industrial and municipal waste disposal, on which a joint study with the Metropolitan Parks Department has been undertaken. The Authority also submitted that Metro alone should assume responsibility for all waste disposal in the Metropolitan Area. I agree with this recommendation.

9. PARKS AND RECREATION

Under section 223 of the Metro Act, the Metropolitan Council is empowered to acquire land for establishing public parks and recreation areas in the Metropolitan Area or in any adjoining local municipality in the counties of Ontario or Peel or in any local municipality in the County of York. With approval of the Municipal Board, Council may, under section 225, assume any existing park or recreation area in any area municipality without compensation but subject to assumption of responsibility for any outstanding debt. By agreement with the Conservation Authority, Council may manage and control lands vested in the Authority.

Lands acquired by Metro for park purposes are intended to be developed as regional parks serving large communities. Local parks providing recreation on a neighbourhood basis remain the responsibility of the area municipalities. In 1953 the only major regional parks in the area were High Park in the west end of Toronto and the Toronto Islands. Ownership of High Park, which has been attractively developed, has remained with the City of Toronto. The Toronto Islands were conveyed to Metro on January 1, 1956, and have since been extensively developed. The Metropolitan Corporation now operates approximately 4,400 acres of park lands, including horticultural gardens, two golf courses and the Riverdale Zoo. Capital expenditures of the Metropolitan Parks Department in the first ten years of Metro exceeded $12.5 million.

The metropolitan parks programme in large part hinges on the programme of the Conservation Authority. Under agreement with the Authority, Metro develops and maintains, for park and recreational purposes, flood plain lands and conservation lands acquired by the Authority. Five major parks are now under development in the Highland Creek, Black Creek, Don River, Rouge River and Humber River Valleys.

The acreage of metropolitan parklands by municipality is as follows:

	acres
Toronto	612.0
North York	1,239.4
Scarborough	1,088.4
Etobicoke	526.5
York	176.7
East York	340.4
Leaside	150.6
Long Branch	51.0
Weston	17.2
Swansea	60.1
Vaughan Township	71.2

The Metropolitan Parks Department is responsible for a considerable area of waterfront parkland in the east, including the Scarborough Bluffs. On the western lakeshore of Metro, between the Humber River and Etobicoke Creek, only Marie Curtis Park, in Long Branch, has been established. No steps have been taken to preserve the waterfront on the western fringe of the Metropolitan

Planning Area. As it would benefit the area as a whole, responsibility for the development of the waterfront for park and recreational purposes should be exercised by the Metropolitan Corporation.

10. POLICE

When Metro was formed each of the thirteen area municipalities retained its own police department. These varied in size, recruiting methods and standards, training, equipment, salaries and working conditions, and, accordingly, in the standards of service provided. There was no single communications network to link all the municipalities as each was concerned primarily with law enforcement within its own boundaries. There were difficulties in traffic control and the enforcement of licensing regulations. The ratio of policemen to population ranged from one officer for every 450 residents in Toronto to one for every 1,200 in Scarborough.

On January 1, 1957, under an amendment to the Metro Act, the police departments were unified under the Metropolitan Board of Commissioners of Police. The area is now divided for police purposes into five districts to serve the west-central, western, east-central, eastern, and northern sections, without regard to municipal boundaries. The whole area is now served by a central police communications system, supplemented by a complete mobile communications unit for use in an emergency. Specialized equipment has been furnished in all districts and new police stations have been built replacing the smaller and obsolete stations.

A Metropolitan Toronto Police College has been in operation since January 1959, and recruiting methods and training are now standardized. The uniform force has increased from 1,985 in 1956 to 2,402 in 1963 and a police cadet system has been instituted. Costs of the police service have risen from $12.7 million in 1957 to $19.8 million in 1963, salaries alone accounting for an increase of $6 million.

A number of briefs to the Commission complained that the police force is too centralized, with the result that some municipalities are receiving less protection than when they had their own force. It was submitted that local by-laws are not effectively enforced and, accordingly, that the responsibility for such enforcement should be restored to each municipality, the Metro police to remain responsible for communications and criminal investigation.

I find that the creation of the Metropolitan Police Force has considerably improved the service for the entire area. To divide the police function between the Metro force and a number of local forces would be a retrograde step. In 1964 the Board of Commissioners of Police created a Parking Control Unit of civilian personnel appointed as by-law enforcement officers to enforce parking regulations. This unit now consists of 45 officers and releases uniform police for the performance of their major functions. I am of the opinion that if this system, operating under the Police Commission, is extended to the enforcement of other by-laws, the requirements of the area municipalities would be met. The enforcement of local by-laws would also be greatly facilitated if the present variety in area by-laws were reduced by a consolidation of some of the area municipalities.

While I do not recommend the division of the police function between Metro and the area municipalities, I suggest that more effort should be made to improve relationships between the police force and the municipalities. There is value in identification of the policeman with the citizens of the locality which he serves. I commend to the Police Commission the following suggestions submitted by the Township of Scarborough:

> Our concern is that the Police Force is too centralized and there is too little association directly with the local municipalities. If there were a larger measure of authority at the local level there would be a greater participation by the Police in community functions to the end that their association with local residents would be on a more personalized level. We would suggest the following to help the situation:
>
> (a) The Police Commission be more closely associated with the local municipality.
> (b) District Chiefs of Police have more local authority.
> (c) Limit the transfer of personnel so that they can become more familiar with the local problems.

11. ADMINISTRATION OF JUSTICE

Under the Metro Act, the Metropolitan Corporation assumed the responsibility for maintaining the County Court House and the County Jail, the Juvenile and Family Court, the Magistrates Courts for the metropolitan area, the office of the Chief Coroner and the registry offices of the City and of the County of York.

A new Metropolitan Toronto Juvenile and Family Court building was constructed on Jarvis Street in Toronto in 1957, and a new County Court House is under construction on University Avenue. Magistrates Courts are now provided on an area-wide basis, with courts established in Toronto, New Toronto, York, Etobicoke, North York and Scarborough.

It was submitted to the Commission that the services of the Juvenile and Family Court should be expanded and that they should be decentralized by the establishment of court facilities in the outer suburbs, where children and adolescents form a large proportion of the population. However, Metro, which is responsible for payment of salaries and all other costs, has contended that it is bearing an undue burden and that the costs should be assumed by the Province. Expenditures on this service rose from some $250,000 in 1954 to more than $700,000 in 1963.

Considering, inter alia, the importance of the services provided and that the number of children appearing before the Court has increased from approximately 2,700 in 1953 to more than 10,000 in 1964, I find that there is an urgent need for additional services, facilities and staff. In my opinion the need for a properly staffed and serviced Metropolitan Juvenile and Family Court system, with court facilities in the large outer suburbs, is sufficiently immediate to warrant the necessary increase in Metro's budget for this purpose, pending a review of the sharing of costs of the administration of justice between the Province and the Metropolitan Corporation.

12. LICENSING

The licensing of businesses and trades was the responsibility of the area municipalities until January 1, 1957, when it was assumed by the Metropolitan Licensing Commission under an amendment to the Metro Act (sections 209-216). The Commission, exercising the powers of boards of commissioners of police under The Municipal Act, is empowered to license, to revoke licenses and to fix the fees to be paid for a license. It now licenses some eighty activities in the area.

Metropolitan licensing has made possible common minimum standards, uniform fees and regulations, and, in the case of taxicabs, area-wide licenses in place of the local licenses which, prior to 1957, had restricted drivers to operating within the boundaries of the municipality in which they were licensed.

The Commission has established seven districts, with two offices in Toronto and an office in Scarborough, North York, Etobicoke, York and New Toronto. Licenses affecting metropolitan-wide activities, such as taxicabs and tradesmen, are issued from the head office, while those affecting activities tied to a specific location, such as restaurants, are issued from the area offices. The Commission has also set up Boards of Examiners for plumbers, electricians and heating installers.

In briefs submitted by Scarborough, Etobicoke and Forest Hill, it was urged that the licensing function should be divided between the metropolitan government, which should retain responsibility for licensing metropolitan-wide activities, and the area governments, which should be responsible for licensing local businesses tied to a specific location. The Scarborough brief states that:

> The Commission is trying to administer many local licensing matters with a centralized organization and sub-offices. Reports required from Township Departments such as Fire, Building and Health are coordinated by the local municipality and reported to the Central Licensing Office. Often the application is made to the area office and the administrative problems of handling such a simple matter of a local license becomes complicated and frustrating to applicants when so many bodies are handling the application with the resultant delays. It is difficult to correct the delays because of the administrative monster that is necessary to coordinate these procedures. Local licenses could be far more effectively handled on the local level.
>
> The Municipal Act gives a licensing body the discretion to grant or refuse a license and we consider this an essential element of its function. A

particular type of business is sometimes very unsuitable to a particular location. With the centralized administration of the Metro Licensing Commission it is difficult, if not impossible, for it to act in such a discretionary way since it cannot be expected to be fully acquainted with a particular local situation. Within the federation concept, licenses of a Metro-wide nature should be handled by Metro and those of a local nature by the local Council.

The Licensing Commission, as has been shown, already recognizes a distinction between licensees whose activities are tied to a specific location and those whose operations are mobile and metropolitan-wide in nature. For the former it has found it necessary to establish a number of area offices. I find that, with a consolidation of some of the municipalities, the remaining units should assume responsibility for the licensing of local businesses which are tied to a specific location, as distinct from metropolitan-wide businesses and activities. This would be a proper function for the area municipalities, subject, where required, to minimum standards set by the Metropolitan Licensing Commission. The transfer of this responsibility to the local municipalities will enable the Commission to concentrate on the licensing of taxicabs and other businesses of area-wide concern.

To avoid duplicating the Commission's machinery for the issuing of licenses, consideration should be given to an arrangement between the area municipalities and the Commission under which, the municipality having made the decision, the license would be issued on its behalf and at its request by the Commission, with the fee paid to the local municipality.

While the Metropolitan Council appoints two of the three members of the Licensing Commission, fixes the salaries of the Commission, and has power to confer licensing powers on it in certain fields and to revoke such powers, the authority of the Commission itself is very wide. It may license and revoke licenses and alone fixes the fees for licenses. The law provides for an appeal to the Courts in the case of refusal or revocation of a license, but the Commission's authority in the matter of fees is final. To conform with our principles of government, the law should be amended to require approval by the Metropolitan Council of license fees adopted by the Commission.

13. FIRE PROTECTION

Fire protection in the Metropolitan Area is the responsibility of the area municipalities, and, in their briefs to the Commission, almost all municipalities submitted that this responsibility should remain with them. The City of Toronto alone presented a case for unification of the thirteen fire fighting services.

With municipal units so different in size and resources, fire protection standards in the area necessarily vary. The City, with its high population density and its pattern of residential, commercial and industrial development, provides a high standard of service, with a permanent skilled fire fighting force and modern fire fighting equipment. In the past ten years the suburbs have expanded their services considerably. Gross current expenditures per capita on fire protection in 1963 totalled $13.02 in Leaside, $12.31 in New Toronto and $11.12 in Forest Hill, as compared with $12.79 in Toronto. The figure for Swansea, with a volunteer force, was $2.54 and in the remaining suburbs the range was from $4.39 in Long Branch to $6.85 in East York.

Fire protection is the largest local service in terms of personnel. The increases in the number of fire department employees in the area between 1954 and 1963 are shown in the following table:

FIRE DEPARTMENTS: NUMBER OF EMPLOYEES

	1954	1963		1954	1963
Toronto	893	1,235	Leaside	16	48
North York	71	285	Mimico	7	13
Scarborough	77	224	New Toronto	13	22
Etobicoke	37	178	Long Branch	1	7
York	72	150	Weston	3	12
East York	39	79	Swansea	—	—
Forest Hill	31	35			
			Area Total	1,260	2,288

These increases in personnel reflect both improved services and a reduction in the work week. The improvement in services included establishment of new stations, expansion of existing facilities and provision of new services. It also included the partial replacement of volunteers by permanent employees. In Swansea, however, the force is still exclusively voluntary; in Long Branch it is composed of seven permanent and seventeen volunteer firemen; and as at October 30, 1964, there were twenty volunteers in the Etobicoke force, twelve in Weston, ten in New Toronto and one in Mimico. It will be noted that, apart from Etobicoke, the suburbs served by volunteers are in the inner ring.

While wholly or partly volunteer fire departments may be adequate for less developed areas, volunteer fire fighters cannot meet the standards which must be maintained by departments responsible for fire protection in a large urban metropolis. Municipalities which have to rely on volunteers and which, in some cases, are not able to afford certain expensive types of modern fire fighting equipment, are uneconomic units for the provision of adequate fire protection services in a metropolitan area.

The improvement in standards which should be effected in some parts of Metropolitan Toronto does not necessarily call for a level of service which is uniform throughout the area. The level of service should be commensurate with the requirements of the area served, having regard to such factors as population density and the stage of development reached and to its geographic location within the larger area. If the municipalities are economic units for the provision of the required standards of service, unification of the fire fighting services of the Metropolitan Area becomes unnecessary. I am of the opinion that under the consolidation of municipal units recommended in this report, fire protection can properly remain the responsibility of the area municipalities, with an effective mutual aid agreement under which each could request assistance from one or all of the others when necessary.

Where centralization is necessary, as in the case of a central communications system, the system could be operated under contract by the City of Toronto, with the costs shared among the municipalities on an agreed basis. The training of personnel might also be centralized in the City on a similar basis.

The fire chiefs should continue to constitute an area committee to advise on the foregoing matters and on other matters of mutual concern affecting the fire fighting services of the area.

14. PUBLIC LIBRARIES

The establishment of public libraries in Metro is the responsibility of the area municipalities. There are thirteen public library boards in the area operating under the provisions of The Public Libraries Act. Their operations are financed mainly by a local public library rate, which must be set to yield not more than 50 cents per capita of population, unless a majority of council decides otherwise. The boards also receive legislative grants from the Province.

Library service standards vary from municipality to municipality. The Toronto Public Library Board, established in 1884, maintains the Central Library, twenty-one branch libraries throughout the City, and public libraries in six hospitals and seventeen primary schools. It provides two basic types of service to the whole area: a large reference collection, which cannot be duplicated, and a lending service. Most of the other area library boards have been set up since 1944 and some have attained high standards. Per capita expenditure on libraries ranged in 1963 from $1.27 in Swansea to $4.52 in Leaside. The figure for Toronto was $4.02.

Under an amendment to the Metro Act, enacted in 1958, the Metropolitan Council is empowered to make grants in aid of capital or current expenditures to any public library board in an area municipality which, in the opinion of Council, provides library services to residents of any other municipality. With its Central Library serving the whole area as a reference library, the Toronto Public Library Board alone has received an annual grant from Metro. The amount of the grant was $25,000 in 1958 and 1959, $100,000 in 1960 and 1961, $250,000 in 1962 and 1963, and $300,000 in 1964.

To aid it in apportioning grants to area library boards and to establish guide lines for the development of higher standards of library services, Metro Council, in 1958, authorized the Council of Library Trustees of Toronto and District to engage Dr. Ralph Shaw, Dean of the Library School at Rutgers University, to conduct a survey of library services in Metropolitan Toronto. Dr. Shaw reported in June 1960. He found a wide disparity in quantity and quality of library service in the area but did not believe that centralization would automatically solve the problems of equalization. His basic recommendation was the establishment of a Metropolitan Library Board to coordinate the activities of the local library boards and to help overcome the obstacles to a steady improvement in library services throughout the area presented by the differences in size and resources of the municipalities. The report recommended the development of the library service in terms of three types of units, namely, a central library, regional libraries and neighbourhood libraries, with funds provided by both Metro and the area municipalities in relation to their respective interests.

In its brief to the Commission, the Toronto Public Library Board submitted that "the system of 13 independent public library boards operating under the present Public Libraries Act is unsuited to the public library requirements in Metropolitan Toronto". It recommended a consolidation of library services in a scheme of central and district organization with appropriate changes in financial arrangements. Some municipalities favoured a metropolitan board to coordinate the activities of local boards but not to supplant them. Others urged retention of the existing system of independent boards.

I find that with thirteen independent library boards the disparity in services in the area is too wide. Complete centralization, however, appears both unnecessary and undesirable. In the words of the Shaw Report, "local participation and responsibility for the development of library services is one of the keystones in developing effective library service". In my opinion, the desired improvements in service could be effected under a consolidation of municipalities, the operation of libraries remaining a local responsibility with coordination by a Metropolitan Library Board.

More specifically, I agree with the recommendations of Report No. 1 (1962) of the Special Committee on Library Services appointed by the Metropolitan Council to study and report on the Shaw Report. The Committee's recommendations are, inter alia, as follows:

(1) Organization:

The Special Committee recommends that the operation of libraries in Metropolitan Toronto continue to be the responsibility of local library boards but that a Metropolitan Library Board be established to encourage and coordinate the raising of library standards throughout the area.

The Special Committee also recommends:

(a) That the Metropolitan Library Board be composed of nine members as follows:

Five members who are Trustees or who have been Trustees of Area Library Boards within Metropolitan Toronto,
Two members representing the Metropolitan Council,
One member representing the Metropolitan School Board,
One member representing the Metropolitan Separate School Board;

provided that not fewer than four members shall be residents of the City of Toronto and not fewer than four members shall be residents of the Suburban Area Municipalities; . . . .

(2) Expansion of Library Facilities:
   (a) Capital Costs:

   The Special Committee recommends:
   (i) that the Metropolitan Library Board assume the function of coordinating the expansion and construction of library facilities throughout the Metropolitan area;
   (ii) that the Metropolitan Library Board pay the full costs of any additions or relocation approved for the central reference library facilities; pay the basic cost of construction and equipping a network of regional libraries according to basic standards approved by the Metropolitan Council; and cooperate with local library boards in the planning and siting of neighbourhood libraries; and
   (iii) that the Metropolitan Library Board assume responsibility for payment of any existing debenture debt as it applies to the central reference library and other existing libraries, or such portions thereof, as may be approved for designation as regional libraries.

   (b) Operating Costs:

   The Special Committee recommends that the Metropolitan Library Board be authorized to contribute from a budget approved by the Metropolitan Council towards the operating costs of local library boards as follows:
   (i) An amount, to be determined each year, to be paid toward the cost of providing the central reference library services, and an amount to be determined each year to be paid to the local library boards to encourage compliance with standards of reference service in regional libraries;
   (ii) The cost of authorized research projects.

(3) General:

   The Special Committee recommends that the Metropolitan Library Board establish salary standards for professional staff, co-ordinate the research programs of the local library boards, encourage interloan activities, establish a union catalogue, provide a centralized cataloguing service, and work towards the development of a single library card for eligible Metropolitan users.

   For these purposes, the Special Committee also recommends that the Metropolitan Library Board be authorized to employ a chief librarian and such other staff as may be required to carry out the foregoing functions.

15. AIR POLLUTION CONTROL

In 1957 the Metro Act was amended to add air pollution control to the responsibilities of the Metropolitan Corporation. The Air Pollution Control Division of the Metropolitan Works Department carries out surveys to establish the nature and degree of pollution, analyzes air samples, conducts pollen counts and tests traffic gases on the main urban arteries. It checks fuel-burning and incinerating equipment and grants permits for the installation of equipment after inspection for conformity with the requirements of the Metro air pollution by-law.

While progress has been made in coping with the problem, the potential sources of pollution are increasing with population growth, the accompanying industrial development and increasing motor vehicle density. The proposed Metro Official Plan envisages controls to reduce the general level of air pollution.

16. CONCLUSION

This chapter has examined the development and operation of services assigned by the Metro Act to the Metropolitan Corporation and the performance by the area municipalities of local services of metropolitan interest. Education, planning, assessment and finance are discussed below.

While I find that the division of responsibilities under the Metro Act has in most respects satisfied the needs of municipal government in the area, I have suggested a number of changes which the experience of the past ten years shows to be necessary. These include additional responsibilities which should be assumed by the Metropolitan Corporation affecting public housing, libraries, an emergency ambulance service, waterfront development for park and recreational purposes, traffic engineering, parking, major local arterial roads, boundary roads and access to metropolitan roads, waste disposal and financial participation in sewer renewal programmes and redevelopment in the core area. Contractual arrangements between the Metropolitan Corporation and the City of Toronto are suggested under which the City would operate the parking and emergency ambulance services.

I find that the Transit Commission should continue to be the authority for the provision of public transportation but suggest a more formal coordination between Metro Council and the Commission.

I also find that the police function should continue to be an exclusive metropolitan responsibility under the Board of Commissioners of Police which, however, should take steps to improve relationships with the municipalities.

In respect of services administered by the area municipalities, there are some, such as street cleaning, street lighting, sidewalk repairs, snow removal and garbage collection, where the standards of service are mainly of local concern. There are others, such as the personal health and welfare services, where, having regard to the interdependence of the people of the area and to their mobility, the standards are of wider concern. With thirteen municipalities varying so greatly in size, in resources and in the composition of their population, disparities in the standards and in the range of health and welfare services are inevitable. I have suggested that these disparities could be appreciably reduced by a consolidation of some of the municipalities which would enlarge the area of service and spread the costs over the larger area with its larger resources.

Fire protection is another service of more than local interest. Since, under the proposed consolidation, the area municipalities would all be economic units for the provision of the standards of service required in a metropolitan area, unification of the fire protection services is not necessary. However, a centralized communications system is essential. This should be operated under contract by the City of Toronto, which, by arrangement, could also centralize the training of personnel.

In the matter of licensing, I have recommended that the licensing of local businesses which are tied to a specific location should be assumed by the consolidated area municipalities. The Metropolitan Licensing Commission should continue to license metropolitan-wide businesses and activities, but the law should require approval by Metropolitan Council of license fees adopted by the Commission.

CHAPTER VI

METROPOLITAN PLANNING

The Metropolitan Corporation is the designated municipality, within the meaning of The Planning Act, for the Metropolitan Planning Area—an area of 720 square miles which covers the thirteen municipalities in the Metropolitan Area and thirteen fringe municipalities. Twenty-two of the municipalities have planning boards and eighteen, of which eight are in Metro, have official plans. Under section 219(4) of the Metro Act, all planning areas established before April 2, 1953, which are included in the Metropolitan Toronto Planning Area, are "subsidiary planning areas within the said planning area".

1. THE LEGISLATION

The Act declares the Metropolitan Corporation to be a municipality for the purposes of The Planning Act, but not in respect of redevelopment, subdivision control, zoning (except adjacent to metropolitan roads), and building by-laws. Upon approval of a Metro official plan by the Minister of Municipal Affairs, any official plan in a subsidiary planning area is to be amended to conform with it and no official plan of a subsidiary area is to be adopted that does not so conform. No public work is to be undertaken and no by-law passed by any municipality or local board in the Metropolitan Planning Area that does not conform with the Metro official plan.

Under section 221 of the Act, the "scope and general purpose of the official plan" for the Metropolitan Planning Area includes:

(a) land uses and consideration generally of industrial, agricultural, residential and commercial areas;
(b) ways of communication;
(c) sanitation;
(d) green belts and park areas;
(e) public transportation; and such other matters as the Minister of Municipal Affairs may from time to time define under The Planning Act.

While the responsibility for planning is shared by Metro and the municipalities in the Planning Area and Metro has not been granted development control powers of zoning and sub-division control, it is the clear intent of the legislation that, on approval of an official plan by the Minister, the Metropolitan Corporation is to be the superior authority. The plan is the instrument through which it is to direct the general physical development of the area. This conforms with the recommendation of the Cumming Report that:

> The Metropolitan Council should be given adequate powers to direct and control in a general way the physical development of the entire metro-

politan area and to require local development plans and land use regulations to conform to a comprehensive plan of metropolitan development prepared by a Metropolitan Planning Board and finally adopted by the Metropolitan Council in conformity with the provisions of the Planning Act.

2. The "Unofficial Official Plan"

The Metropolitan Planning Commissioner completed a draft official plan in 1960, which was revised in December 1964, but no official plan has as yet been adopted. There has been considerable opposition to the proposed plan by municipalities which fear interference with their traditional autonomy in these matters. Accordingly, the requirement that local plans conform with a Metro official plan is not enforceable and the correlation of planning has had to be effected by procedural arrangements under which the Metropolitan Planning Board is consulted by and advises provincial agencies and the local municipalities on matters affecting zoning, sub-divisions and official plans. Notwithstanding resultant uncertainties, the Metropolitan Planning Commissioner, in his brief to the Commission, stated that:

> The planning machinery in the Metropolitan Planning Area has operated fairly effectively over the past ten years, in the sense that the extent of urban development has been reasonably controlled to forestall "sprawl", that generally adequate development standards have been maintained, and that a satisfactory level of public services has been provided. This has occurred through a reasonable level of co-operation between the local planning agencies, the Metropolitan Planning Board and the Provincial agencies concerned.

The Planning Commissioner submits as one reason for the failure to adopt an official plan "the fact that most of the basic policies governing area development have been adopted by the Metropolitan Council or the local Councils in one form or another". Since the staff of the Metropolitan Planning Board helped to prepare or to modify local official plans, these reflect many of the basic principles underlying the proposed Metro official plan. Metro has in effect been operating with an "unofficial official plan". In the circumstances, however, its planning authority is not clear and it must rely on persuasion to achieve implementation of its policies by the local municipalities. This is not enough to curtail further "urban sprawl" in the fringe area and to ensure orderly development of the region as a whole.

3. Need for an Official Plan

While some briefs submitted to the Commission were critical of details of the draft plan, all briefs which dealt with planning called for adoption of a Metropolitan Official Plan. These included briefs from area municipalities, from fringe municipalities, and from bodies primarily concerned with urban development.

The report on "Planning and Development Procedures and Controls", made by McDonald, Currie & Co., in December 1963, for the Township of North York and filed with the Commission by the Township, says:

> We are mindful of the myriad of plans that may result if municipalities within the Metropolitan Toronto Planning Area are not careful to dovetail their documents into a general agreed scheme for the whole area. For instance, it is possible that the Township of Scarborough will find itself with a Metropolitan Toronto Official Plan, several Metropolitan Toronto District Plans, a Scarborough Overall Official Plan, a series of Scarborough Secondary Plans and a series of Scarborough Tertiary Plans, in total a somewhat terrifying prospect if an amendment of significance is contemplated.
>
> Secondly, North York Township is not a planning unit. It is a political unit made up of a number of districts, or parts of districts which overlap into adjacent political units. Don Mills, for example, has little in common with Downsview from a land use, servicing or transportation point of view except that they are both parts of the Metropolitan Toronto complex. How valid, then, is an overall plan which ties those two areas together except that it be a Metropolitan Plan?
>
> We, therefore, recommend that the present, inadequate Official Plan be retained only until the Metropolitan Toronto Official Plan is in force, at which time, the former should be repealed, and the latter accepted as the overall Plan for North York.
>
> In the meantime, the long-range planning staff should undertake, vigorously, the preparation of a series of District Plans, which, as they are progressively completed will provide detailed development proposals for the whole of the Township.

The Central Ontario Chapter of the Town Planning Institute of Canada says, in its brief to the Commission:

> The first draft Metropolitan Plan has now been substantially revised and may be completed for consideration by the Metropolitan and Subsidiary Boards soon. It is to be hoped that agreement, on the Plan, by the area municipalities will be forthcoming. Although several parts of the area have Official Plans, approved by the Provincial Minister responsible at the time of application, none of them can be considered a sound guide for present and future policy in respect to the development, redevelopment, maintenance or conservation of the municipality.

The brief recommends, inter alia:

> That legislation require the implementation of a Metropolitan Official Plan by district plans and subsequently zoning by-laws within two to three years of the adoption of a Metropolitan Official Plan.

The brief of the Ontario Division of the Urban Development Institute says:

> For the developer, the chief disadvantage of the multiplicity of jurisdictions is the confusion which flows from the differences in the types of development controls exercised by the local municipalities, and from their methods of administering them.

For example, some 16 of the local municipalities have Official Plans. All differ in content, format, and terminology. Their approval by the Province notwithstanding, few of these local Plans have any value whatever as guides to future development. While it is true that the Metropolitan Toronto Official Plan, when completed, will provide for the first time a meaningful guide to the manner and sequence of development for the whole urban area, that Plan will be necessarily broad-brush in its proposals. Detailed plans covering Districts will be required to supplement the general proposals of the overall Plan. Unless these District Plans are in harmony with, or preferably, unless they replace the local Official Plans, conflicts, delays and confusion are certainties.

The practice of "planning by assessment" or "fiscal zoning" was criticized in a number of submissions. To strengthen their assessment base, municipalities are competing for the construction of high-rise apartments by allowing increasing densities without regard to the proper location of projects and the availability of services. For example, faced with restrictions on permitted uses of land under Toronto's comprehensive zoning by-law, developers gravitate to suburbs where higher permitted densities offer a greater economic return. This is not orderly development. In a decision of September 28, 1964, rejecting an application by the Township of York to zone an area for high-rise apartments, the Ontario Municipal Board said:

> It is evident that the effect of the Township increasing permitted densities has been to attract developers from other Metro municipalities. It would seem inevitable that other municipalities will feel compelled to lower their standards in order to compete effectively with the Township of York and that therefore unless the Board is prepared to exercise its power to impose some order in the Metro area, a chaotic planning situation is bound to result. The difficulties in this connection are of course compounded because of the absence of any Metro Official Plan.

Orderly development is also impeded by the diversity in zoning standards, as well as in building codes and engineering design standards, in the area. In the words of the Urban Development Institute, the zoning by-laws of the various municipalities "differ in almost every conceivable way. There is no uniformity in the definitions of uses, in the numbers and types of zoning categories, in the uses permitted in each category, or in the regulations which pertain thereto". The Metropolitan Planning Commissioner said:

> The variations in standards are particularly noteworthy in the case of apartment buildings. For example, North York and Scarborough permit a maximum density of about 60 units per acre, Etobicoke 35 units per acre, East York about 100 to 110 units per acre, Toronto generally 130 to 150 units per acre, and York permits apartments, under certain conditions, with no maximum density limit of any kind.

> Minimum front setbacks show equal variation; 20 feet in York and East York, 25 feet in North York and Etobicoke, and 30 feet in Scarborough. East York requires a minimum of 25% landscaped open space, Toronto 35%, and North York an amount equivalent to 2/9 of gross floor space. Etobicoke requires 60% of the lot area to be free of buildings. Toronto,

Etobicoke and Scarborough require 125% parking; York and East York 100%; and North York's requirement ranges between 100% and 150% depending on the size of building. North York and East York have no height limitation; Etobicoke 45 feet (with many exceptions); and Toronto and York limit height on the basis of day-lighting angles.

4. THE PLANNING AREA

The Metropolitan Planning Area, as has been shown, covers a geographic area twice as large as Metro. The Cumming Report, foreseeing the spread of urbanization to and beyond Metro's boundaries, considered it "essential in the interests of the entire area, that the Metropolitan Council should be given a reasonable degree of planning control over the so-called 'fringe areas' otherwise beyond its jurisdiction".

In their briefs to the Commission, no municipality, whether in Metro or in the fringe, complained of the size of the Planning Area or asked to be excluded from it. There appeared to be general acceptance of the principle that regional planning should not be restricted by municipal boundaries.

The Township of Toronto, for example, in its brief to the Commission, says:

> (1) The Township of Toronto has no objection to the principle of a "super" planning agency—similar to the present Metropolitan Toronto Planning Board—having jurisdiction over, and responsibility for, coordination of planning matters in Toronto and its fringe areas.
>
> (2) The physical area of jurisdiction for this agency should be increased to include other rapidly urbanizing areas, such as Brampton and the southern part of Chinguacousy Township, which logically form part of the Fringe Area for planning matters.

At the hearings of the Commission, Mr. R. W. Speck, Reeve of Toronto Township, said (Proceedings, pp. 954-955):

> *Mr. Speck:* We have been a member of the Metropolitan Toronto Planning Area, being one of the fringe municipalities, since its beginning in 1953. I have sat as the western district member for Port Credit and Streetsville and the Township of Toronto for the last five years. We think this type of planning is good. It has certainly, I think, been an advantage for the Township of Toronto and we have had no disagreement with it.
>
> *The Commissioner:* You don't feel it has held you back?
>
> *Mr. Speck:* No, it has not. I don't think it has held us back any. I think in fact it has indicated the manner in which you should develop without this hodge-podge jumping from here and there. It is more on a regulated basis and we accept this and we think it is right economically and proper.

The County of York, with six of its municipalities included in the Planning Area—Vaughan Township, Woodbridge, Markham Township, Markham Village, Stouffville and Richmond Hill—recommended in its brief:

> . . . that the legislative basis for planning in the Metropolitan Area remain substantially as presently enacted. It is the County's view that a

combination of the geographical extent of the Metropolitan Planning Area and the scope of the Metropolitan Official Plan combined with the proposed County planning organization will provide for effective future planning of the area.

The extension of the Planning Area was suggested by the Ontario Municipal Board in a decision of February 29, 1960, on an application by the Town of Brampton for annexation of parts of Chinguacousy Township. The Board said:

> The evidence before the Board indicates clearly that the pressure for development in Brampton and vicinity is caused in very large measure by the proximity of Metropolitan Toronto. The same is undoubtedly true of other areas outside the boundaries of the Metropolitan Toronto Planning Area. In view of this it appears that the time has come to consider the need to enlarge the Metropolitan Toronto Planning Area and include a larger region which would embrace the Town of Brampton and vicinity, as well as other localities where strong pressure for urban development is now being exerted as a result of the relative proximity of Metropolitan Toronto.

The Metropolitan Toronto and Region Conservation Authority also recommended the enlargment of the Planning Area to include Brampton, Chinguacousy and other municipalities lying within the drainage basins which affect the Area.

With the Planning Area extending considerably beyond the borders of the Metropolitan Area, the adoption of a Metro Official Plan would confer powers on Metropolitan Council to regulate development outside Metro's boundaries in municipalities which are not represented on the Council and, in most cases, represented only indirectly on the Metropolitan Planning Board. Accordingly, while accepting the Planning Area as it is, some fringe municipalities, like Ajax and Richmond Hill, asked for direct representation on the Planning Board, and Ajax also requested a voice on Metro Council when matters relating to the Town are under consideration. Toronto Township suggested that requests by fringe municipalities for changes affecting the Metro Official Plan should be dealt with directly by the Minister of Municipal Affairs rather than the Metropolitan Council.

5. CONCLUSIONS

i. *The Metro Official Plan*

The proposed Metro Official Plan, as revised in December 1964, covers the metropolitan aspects of planning: it establishes a general land use pattern, an overall distribution of population and density of residential development, a basic transportation pattern, basic servicing policies, and policies for the regulation of urban development. Such an overall plan should be adopted without undue delay. Adoption of the Metro plan should be followed by the preparation, jointly with the local municipalities, of more detailed district plans, and the enactment of the necessary changes in zoning by-laws. The plans should be subject to periodic review.

ii. *Metro's Planning Powers*

Metro's planning function should be clarified and expanded. The metropolitan planning authority, like Metro itself, is unique in Ontario; it is intermediary between the local municipalities and the Provincial Government. This fact has not been adequately recognized. The Community Planning Branch of the Department of Municipal Affairs does not appear to accept the existence of two levels of government in the Metropolitan Area; presumably, in the absence of a Metro Official Plan, the provincial agency cannot accept the superior authority in planning envisaged for Metro by the Metro Act. Metro is consulted on development control in the area, as are many other bodies, but without recognition of the fact that it was itself established to exercise a form of supervisory control over development through an official plan.

In respect of redevelopment, which vitally affects the core area, the powers conferred on municipalities by The Planning Act were not granted to Metro. But the problem of redevelopment is of metropolitan concern. This was set out in the Cumming Report, as follows:

> In the field of redevelopment it is the opinion of the board that the metropolitan area as a whole, in addition to making adequate provision for the outward extension of municipal services in keeping with the urban expansion of the area, must also protect its sources of tax revenue from fully serviced land in the older central areas. It cannot ignore the economic waste involved in the continued existence of large blighted areas. Fundamentally these areas of blight are a product of the same economy which has produced the attractive new residential and commercial developments in the rapidly expanding suburbs, and the net municipal cost of redevelopment should be considered a responsibility of the whole area.

I recommend that the Metro Act should be amended to declare more explicitly the responsibility of the Metropolitan Corporation, as the designated municipality, for the general direction of the physical development of the Metropolitan Planning Area, with powers:

(a) to establish basic zoning standards and categories;

(b) to participate with an area municipality in redevelopment and urban renewal;

(c) to enact a uniform building by-law and to establish uniform engineering design standards;

(d) to review development applications and proposals and to make recommendations thereon to the provincial agency;

(e) to secure the conformity of local official plans and zoning by-laws in the Metropolitan Planning Area with the Metro Official Plan, reserving to the municipalities a right of appeal to the Ontario Municipal Board. The procedures to ensure conformity of plans should be prescribed by regulations under the Metro Act.

iii. *Local Planning Authorities*

If the foregoing changes are made, local development would continue to be regulated by the local municipality through the established development control instruments but within the standards set by Metro and in conformity with the Metro Official Plan. I suggest that The Planning Act should be amended to permit municipalities to transfer the functions now vested in local planning boards to a Planning Committee of Council with power to co-opt. In any circumstances, the planning staff in area municipalities should be constituted a civic planning department.

iv. *The Metropolitan Planning Board*

There should be provision for a representative of a municipality, which is not otherwise directly represented on the Metropolitan Planning Board, to attend and to be heard when matters originating from, applying to or of particular concern to such municipality are under consideration.

If Brampton and Chinguacousy Township are added to the Planning Area, they should constitute a fringe district entitled to a representative on the Board.

v. *Extension of Metropolitan Planning Area*

With respect to extension of the Metropolitan Planning Area, reference has been made to recommendations by the Metropolitan Toronto and Region Conservation Authority and by Toronto Township that the Town of Brampton and part of Chinguacousy Township and vicinity, on the outskirts of the Planning Area, should be added to it. This was also suggested by the Ontario Municipal Board in its decision on the application by Brampton for annexation of parts of the Township. Considering the potential impact of further development in Brampton and Chinguacousy, which would require the extension of water and sewer services from Lake Ontario through Toronto Township, I am of the opinion that, in the absence of other regional planning machinery, the area covered by Brampton and its vicinity should be included in the Metropolitan Planning Area.

CHAPTER VII

THE TAX BASE

The taxation of real property and business provides the bulk of the revenue for municipal and school purposes in the Metropolitan Area. The tax base is the assessed valuation of real property. To assure a uniform basis of assessment, the Metro Act assigns the assessment function to the Metropolitan Corporation and the Metropolitan Assessment Commissioner is deemed to be the assessment commissioner of each area municipality. For a number of reasons, the Commissioner continues to base assessments on 1940 values.

1. ASSESSED VALUATION, 1954-1964

The growth in taxable assessment between 1954 and 1964 is shown in Table 11. The total tax base increased by 80 per cent, rising from $2.4 billion to $4.4 billion, with an average annual increase of $195.3 million. More than two-thirds of the annual growth occurred in the three outer suburbs. In the ten-year period taxable assessment increased by 288 per cent in North York, with an average annual increase of $58.3 million; 282 per cent in Scarborough, with an average annual increase of $35.2 million; and 252 per cent in Etobicoke, with an average annual increase of $38.5 million. In the same period, the City of Toronto showed an increase of 28 per cent, with an average annual growth of $41.8 million. In the inner ring of suburbs the increases ranged from 36 per cent in Swansea to 88 per cent in Mimico, with the two largest units, York and East York, showing 45 per cent and 37 per cent, respectively. York showed an average annual increase of $7 million and East York, $3.5 million.

Reflecting the much higher rate of growth in the three outer suburbs, the following table shows the changes in the percentage distribution of Metro's total taxable assessment by groups of municipalities between 1954 and 1964:

PER CENT OF METRO'S
TOTAL TAXABLE ASSESSMENT

	1954 %	1964 %
Toronto	62.0	43.9
Three outer suburbs	19.7	41.1
Nine inner suburbs	18.3	15.0

In dollar terms, the taxable assessment of the area was distributed in 1954 and 1964, respectively, as follows:

TAXABLE ASSESSMENT

	1954	1964
Toronto	$1,507,690,000	$1,925,532,000
Three outer suburbs	480,342,000	1,800,398,000
Nine inner suburbs	443,561,000	658,437,000
Total	$2,431,593,000	$4,384,367,000

Table 11

Taxable Assessment, 1954 and 1964[1]

Municipality	1954				1964				Average Annual Increase	Per Cent Increase 1954 to 1964
	Real Property	Business Assessment	Total Taxable Assessment	Per Cent of Metro	Real Property	Business Assessment	Total Taxable Assessment	Per Cent of Metro		
	$000	$000	$000	%	$000	$000	$000	%	$000	%
Toronto	1,263,294	244,396	1,507,690	62.0	1,608,555	316,977	1,925,532	43.9	41,784	27.7
North York	193,478	9,204	202,682	8.3	721,248	64,869	786,117	17.9	58,344	287.9
Scarborough	114,982	10,026	125,008	5.1	436,407	40,499	476,906	10.9	35,190	281.5
Etobicoke	142,357	10,295	152,652	6.3	476,450	60,925	537,375	12.3	38,472	252.0
York	145,593	13,237	158,830	6.5	208,575	20,939	229,514	5.2	7,068	44.5
East York	88,154	4,728	92,882	3.8	119,566	8,069	127,635	2.9	3,475	37.4
Forest Hill	48,571	1,101	49,672	2.1	72,039	1,499	73,538	1.7	2,387	48.0
Leaside	41,335	7,867	49,202	2.0	65,944	11,129	77,073	1.8	2,787	56.6
Mimico	17,771	1,188	18,959	.8	32,994	2,559	35,552	.8	1,659	87.5
New Toronto	21,897	6,625	28,522	1.2	33,356	10,617	43,973	1.0	1,545	54.2
Long Branch	10,711	1,055	11,766	.5	18,915	1,894	20,809	.5	904	76.9
Weston	14,618	1,798	16,416	.7	23,571	3,193	26,764	.6	1,035	63.1
Swansea	16,347	966	17,313	.7	22,223	1,355	23,578	.5	627	36.2
Metro[2]	2,119,108	312,485	2,431,593	100.0	3,839,845	544,522	4,384,367	100.0	195,277	80.3

[1]Assessments prepared in the years 1953 and 1963.
[2]Totals may not add due to rounding of figures.
Source: Metropolitan Toronto Assessment Department.

The figures show that, whereas in 1954 the assessed valuation of the three outer suburbs was only eight per cent higher than that of the nine inner suburbs, in 1964 it was almost three times that of the inner suburbs and very close to the taxable assessment of the City.

Relating taxable assessment to population, Table 12 shows an increase of $540 or 26 per cent in per capita assessment for Metro as a whole between 1954 and 1964, the figure rising from $2,073 to $2,613. There are wide disparities, however, between municipalities. The range in 1964 was from $1,794 in East York to $4,178 in Leaside, as compared with a range from $1,287 in Long Branch to $3,093 in Leaside in 1954. The figure for Toronto was $2,265 in 1954 and $2,990 in 1964, an increase of 32 per cent.

In 1954 per capita assessment was below the Metro average in North York, Scarborough, York, East York, Mimico, Long Branch and Weston. In 1964 all of these municipalities, except Weston, were still below the Metro average, but North York was close to it, as was Swansea, which had dropped somewhat below the average. As compared with a per capita increase of $540 for Metro as a whole between 1954 and 1964, Leaside showed an increase of $1,085, Etobicoke $824, Toronto $725 and North York $689, the range in the remaining municipalities being from $221 in York to $658 in Weston.

While the per capita figures for Metro show a considerable improvement since 1953 in the overall taxable resources of the area, the continuing disparities between area municipalities show wide inequalities in taxable capacity. In 1964 per capita assessments were more than $500 below the Metro average of $2,613 in five municipalities: Scarborough, York, East York, Mimico and Long Branch. Figures for Leaside were more than $1,500 above the average, for Forest Hill and New Toronto, more than $800, and for Toronto and Etobicoke, $400 above the Metro average.

2. RESIDENTIAL AND NON-RESIDENTIAL ASSESSMENT

Commercial and industrial assessment constituted approximately 47 per cent of the total taxable assessment of the area in 1964, as in 1954, but, as shown in Table 13, its distribution among the municipalities is uneven. The ratio of non-residential assessment to total assessment in 1964, excluding Forest Hill, ranged from 23 per cent in East York to 71 per cent in New Toronto. The ratio in Toronto was 62 per cent, in Leaside, 49.5 per cent, and in Weston, 46 per cent. Forest Hill is an exceptional case; with non-residential assessment representing less than 10 per cent of the total, it has the second highest per capita assessment in the area because of the high value of its residential property.

The total non-residential assessment rose by $897 million, from $1,145 million in 1954 to $2,042 million in 1964. Almost 60 per cent of the growth took place in the three outer suburbs. The ratio increased from 18.7 per cent to 31.6 per cent in North York, from 24.9 per cent to 41.6 per cent in Etobicoke, and from 24.4 per cent to 33.7 per cent in Scarborough. Notwithstanding some

Table 12

TAXABLE ASSESSMENT PER CAPITA, 1954 AND 1964[1]

Municipality	1954	1964	Per Capita Increase	Per Cent Increase
	$	$	$	%
Toronto	2,265	2,990	725	32.0
North York	1,830	2,519	689	37.7
Scarborough	1,586	1,969	383	24.1
Etobicoke	2,174	2,998	824	37.9
York	1,581	1,802	221	14.0
East York	1,413	1,794	381	27.0
Forest Hill	2,803	3,432	629	22.4
Leaside	3,093	4,178	1,085	35.1
Mimico	1,541	1,947	406	26.3
New Toronto	2,927	3,435	508	17.4
Long Branch	1,287	1,873	586	45.5
Weston	1,960	2,618	658	33.6
Swansea	2,075	2,519	444	21.4
Metro	2,073	2,613	540	26.0

[1]Assessments prepared in 1953 and 1963. Population as shown by Metropolitan Assessment Department.
Source: Metropolitan Toronto Assessment Department.

Table 13

NON-RESIDENTIAL TAXABLE ASSESSMENT, 1954 AND 1964[1]

Municipality	1954		1964	
	Non-Residential	Per Cent of Total Taxable Assessment	Non-Residential	Per Cent of Total Taxable Assessment
	$000	%	$000	%
Toronto	910,645	60.40	1,196,693	62.15
North York	37,902	18.70	248,248	31.58
Scarborough	30,502	24.40	160,793	33.72
Etobicoke	38,010	24.90	223,627	41.61
York	45,902	28.90	73,062	31.83
East York	16,719	18.00	29,813	23.36
Forest Hill	4,669	9.40	7,056	9.60
Leaside	24,208	49.20	38,124	49.46
Mimico	4,171	22.00	8,695	24.46
New Toronto	19,309	67.70	31,103	70.73
Long Branch	4,153	35.31	6,945	33.37
Weston	6,501	39.61	12,370	46.22
Swansea	3,134	18.10	5,570	23.62
Metro	1,145,824	47.12	2,042,099	46.58

[1]Assessments prepared in 1953 and 1963, including business assessment.
Source: Metropolitan Toronto Assessment Department.

loss of industry, the City of Toronto, with the development of high-rise commercial properties, increased its ratio from 60.4 per cent in 1954 to 62.2 per cent in 1964. Almost all the suburbs in the inner ring also showed an increase.

The marked improvement in the ratio shown by the three large outer suburbs was made possible by Metro, which, by pooling the financial resources of the area, provided the basic physical services necessary for commercial and industrial development. Metro has thereby achieved a more equitable distribution of taxable resources. Nevertheless, there are continued wide disparities because of the uneven spread of assessment growth and differences between municipalities in types of housing development and of commercial and industrial development.

The uneven distribution of taxable resources has led to "planning by assessment" or "fiscal zoning". To strengthen their tax base, municipalities adopt zoning policies directed to secure commercial and industrial assessment and the construction of expensive homes and high-rise apartments. Moderate-cost homes and low-density multiple dwellings are "zoned out". It is particularly to high-rise apartments that area municipalities now look to improve their tax base.

Table 14 shows the marked trend to apartment living in the Toronto area. In the two years immediately preceding Metro, 19,000 dwelling units were built, of which 12,000 or 63 per cent were single family homes. A shift to multiple units was noticeable in the first year of Metro; out of a total of 16,250 dwelling units built in 1954 only 9,600 or 52 per cent were single family homes.[1] During the period from 1954 to 1963, the number of dwelling units built totalled 174,125, of which 89,660 or 51.5 per cent were single family.

The City, with 31 per cent, and North York, with 26 per cent, accounted for almost 60 per cent of the total number of multiple apartment units built during Metro's first ten years. Scarborough accounted for 11 per cent, Etobicoke for 9 per cent and York for 7 per cent. In the older and more fully developed area municipalities, multiple apartment units represented the vast bulk of housing construction in the ten-year period; the proportion ranged from 74.5 per cent of all dwelling units built in Swansea to 97.4 per cent in Leaside. Of the single family units built during this period, 95 per cent were located in the three large outer suburbs; 41 per cent in Scarborough, 26 per cent in Etobicoke and 28 per cent in North York.

These differences between municipalities in types of housing development, combined with the uneven spread of commercial and industrial assessment, are reflected in the disparities in their taxable resources. In this respect, Leaside and Scarborough present extremes. Leaside, with a taxable assessment divided equally between industrial plants and dwelling units of above average values, is in

---

[1]Statistical Supplement to "Market for New Housing, Metropolitan Toronto, 1962", Central Mortgage and Housing Corporation. These figures include duplexes and semi-detached dwellings.

Table 14
Dwelling Units Completed, 1954 to 1963

Municipality	Single Family[1]			Multiple Family[2]			Total Dwelling Units	
	Number	Per Cent of All Dwelling Units Built in Each Municipality	Per Cent of All Single Family Units Built in Metro	Number	Per Cent of All Dwelling Units Built in Each Municipality	Per Cent of All Multiple Family Units Built in Metro	Number	Per Cent of Metro
		%	%		%	%		%
Toronto	1,200	4.5	1.4	26,086	95.5	30.9	27,306	15.7
North York	25,100	53.3	28.0	22,018	46.7	26.1	47,118	27.1
Scarborough	36,950	80.1	41.2	9,191	19.9	10.9	46,141	26.5
Etobicoke	23,295	75.7	26.0	7,478	24.3	8.9	30,773	17.7
York	1,543	20.7	1.7	5,906	79.3	7.0	7,449	4.3
East York	358	8.7	.4	3,738	91.3	4.4	4,096	2.4
Forest Hill	187	7.1	.2	2,438	92.9	2.9	2,625	1.5
Leaside	38	2.6	Neg.	1,450	97.4	1.7	1,488	.9
Mimico	276	9.3	.3	2,700	90.7	3.2	2,976	1.7
New Toronto	124	11.0	.1	1,004	89.0	1.2	1,128	.6
Long Branch	226	20.0	.3	906	80.0	1.0	1,132	.6
Weston	144	12.9	.2	970	87.1	1.1	1,114	.6
Swansea	199	25.5	.2	580	74.5	.7	779	.4
Metro	89,660	51.5	100.0	84,465	48.5	100.0	174,125	100.0

[1]Includes semi-detached and duplex dwellings.
[2]Includes row housing and all apartments of 3 units and more.
Source: Central Mortgage and Housing Corporation.

the most favoured position, with a per capita assessment of $4,178. Scarborough, where one-third of the taxable assessment is non-residential and two-thirds is composed to a large extent of low cost single family homes, shows a per capita assessment of $1,969. The relative capacity to finance municipal and, particularly, school costs is also affected by differences in the nature of population growth: for example, children under 15 years of age constitute 18.7 per cent of the population of Leaside, but in Scarborough they form 37 per cent of the population.

3. TAX-EXEMPT PROPERTIES

Property exempt from general municipal taxation includes properties owned by the federal and provincial governments, municipal governments, churches, hospitals, and educational and charitable institutions. Table 15 shows that the assessed value of tax-exempt property in the Metropolitan Area rose from $332 million, or 13.5 per cent of the assessed value of all real property in 1954, to $782 million, or 17 per cent of the total in 1964, distributed as follows:

TAX-EXEMPT PROPERTIES, 1964

	Assessed Value $	Per Cent of Total %
Federal	56,625,000	7.2
Provincial	89,994,000	11.5
Municipal	198,562,000	25.4
Educational, Religious, Charitable, and Other	437,024,000	55.9
Total	782,205,000	100.0

Sixty per cent of the exempt property in the area is in the City, representing 22.5 per cent of the local real property assessment. In 1954 more than 70 per cent was in the City. The suburbs' share of the total rose from $97.5 million, or 29 per cent in 1954, to $315.4 million, or 40 per cent of the total in 1964, with 15 per cent in North York and 8 per cent each in Scarborough and Etobicoke.

While Crown property is exempt under the British North America Act, payments in lieu of taxes are made on some properties. In a study of municipal tax exemptions, made in April 1963, the Bureau of Municipal Research showed that 96 per cent of all federal property in Metro and 39 per cent of provincial property were eligible for such payments. In the City, the federal government made payments on approximately 100 per cent of its properties, while the Province paid on 34 per cent; in the suburbs, the proportions were 93 per cent and 52 per cent, respectively. Federal grants do not cover business taxes and provincial grants generally do not include payments in lieu of school taxes.

About 56 per cent of the tax-exempt property in Metro represents educational, religious, charitable and other institutions. Many of these institutions, located in the City, which is the cultural centre, serve a wider area than Metro. By virtue of their exemption from taxation, the costs of providing municipal services to them are borne entirely by the Toronto taxpayers.

Table 15

TAX-EXEMPT PROPERTY, 1954 AND 1964[1]

	1954				1964			
Municipality	Real Property Assessment	Exempt Real Property Assessment	Per Cent of Local Real Property Assessment	Per Cent of Metro Exempt Real Property Assessment	Real Property Assessment	Exempt Real Property Assessment	Per Cent of Local Real Property Assessment	Per Cent of Metro Exempt Real Property Assessment
	$000	$000	%	%	$000	$000	%	%
Toronto	1,497,901	234,606	15.7	70.6	2,075,335	466,780	22.5	59.7
North York	236,998	43,520	18.4	13.1	837,317	116,069	13.9	14.8
Scarborough	125,068	10,086	8.1	3.0	501,531	65,124	13.0	8.3
Etobicoke	154,857	12,500	8.1	3.8	540,234	63,785	11.8	8.2
York	156,076	10,483	6.7	3.2	233,891	25,315	10.8	3.2
East York	95,136	6,982	7.3	2.1	136,108	16,541	12.2	2.1
Forest Hill	52,304	3,734	7.1	1.1	79,332	7,293	9.2	.9
Leaside	44,318	2,982	6.7	.9	70,870	4,925	6.9	.6
Mimico	18,791	1,020	5.4	.3	35,303	2,309	6.5	.3
New Toronto	25,135	3,239	12.9	1.0	40,773	7,416	18.2	.9
Long Branch	11,320	609	5.4	.2	20,932	2,016	9.6	.3
Weston	16,336	1,718	10.5	.5	27,102	3,531	13.0	.5
Swansea	17,000	653	3.8	.2	23,323	1,100	4.7	.1
Total[2]	2,451,239	332,131	13.5	100.0	4,622,051	782,206	16.9	100.0

[1]Assessments prepared in 1953 and 1963; exemptions exclude partial exemptions on dwellings in Toronto and New Toronto.
[2]Totals may not add due to rounding of figures.
Source: Metropolitan Toronto Assessment Department.

The figures on exemptions which have been cited do not include the partial exemption of dwellings assessed up to $4,000 in Toronto and New Toronto. The exemption, which is applicable to expenditures for general purposes but not for education or welfare, is 50 per cent up to an assessed value of $2,000 and decreases by 10 per cent for each increase of $500 in valuation. The provision of The Assessment Act authorizing such exemption was repealed in 1955, with the proviso that any by-law passed under it and still in force was to continue in effect until repealed. In 1963 this exempt assessment amounted to approximately $46 million in Toronto and $1.2 million in New Toronto.

4. CONCLUSIONS

The substantial growth in taxable assessment between 1954 and 1964 improved the overall taxable capacity of the Metropolitan Area. By providing adequate basic physical services, Metro has facilitated the spread of residential, industrial and commercial development over the area.

While Metro has achieved a more equitable distribution of taxable resources, the municipalities continue to show wide inequalities because of the uneven spread of non-residential development and differences in the types of residential and industrial and commercial development which they have experienced.

CHAPTER VIII

MUNICIPAL CURRENT EXPENDITURES

Variations in the level of expenditures on municipal services reflect differences in taxable resources, in the characteristics and needs of the area municipalities, and in the quantity and quality of services provided. The size of the unit, its stage of development, population density, incomes, types of dwelling unit, the nature and extent of industrial development, and the rate of growth, are all factors which affect taxable capacity and the level of municipal spending.

1. GROSS CURRENT EXPENDITURES

Table 16 shows for Metro and the area municipalities that general and school gross current expenditures rose from $143.7 million in 1954 to $406.6 million in 1963.

Table 16

GENERAL AND SCHOOL GROSS CURRENT EXPENDITURE, 1954 AND 1963[1]

Municipality	1954			1963		
	Actual[2]	Per Capita	Per $1000 of Taxable Assessment	Actual[2]	Per Capita	Per $1000 of Taxable Assessment
	$	$	$	$	$	$
Toronto	83,559,324	122	58	161,982,371	257	87
North York	12,757,244	98	63	65,030,032	211	91
Scarborough	9,194,422	96	72	51,721,215	215	115
Etobicoke	8,421,039	101	55	40,245,918	227	81
York	9,731,735	92	61	19,204,450	152	85
East York	5,290,923	77	56	10,284,280	147	81
Forest Hill	2,304,269	125	46	4,168,271	197	58
Leaside	2,184,270	129	44	4,467,804	242	59
Mimico	925,882	75	49	2,307,505	127	66
New Toronto	1,671,511	170	60	3,299,244	280	77
Long Branch	692,750	75	59	1,474,345	132	74
Weston	1,351,700	158	82	2,711,593	272	106
Swansea	661,218	76	38	1,283,371	137	55
Metro	55,141,065	44	23	218,971,681	133	53
Area Total	143,695,804[3]	115	61	406,604,856[3]	246	98

[1]Excludes surplus for current year and deficit from prior years.
[2]Gross expenditures for area municipalities include own share of Metro general levy and recoverable debt charges other than education.
[3]Excludes inter-municipal transactions re Metropolitan tax levies and assumed debt.
Sources: Annual Reports of Municipal Statistics, Province of Ontario, 1954 and 1963; Financial Statements of Area School Boards, 1954 and 1963.

The increase was distributed as follows:

GENERAL AND SCHOOL GROSS CURRENT EXPENDITURES

	1954 $	1963 $	Per Cent Increase %
Metro	55,141,000	218,971,000	297.3
City of Toronto	83,559,000	161,982,000	93.7
Three outer suburbs	30,372,000	156,997,000	416.9
Nine inner suburbs	24,814,000	49,200,000	98.3

These figures reflect the development and extension of metropolitan services since 1954 and the much higher rate of growth of the outer suburbs, whose total gross current expenditures almost equalled those of Toronto in 1963. The area as a whole showed an increase in per capita spending from $115 in 1954 to $246 in 1963. The range of spending was from $75 in Mimico and Long Branch to $170 in New Toronto, in 1954, and from $127 in Mimico to $280 in New Toronto, in 1963.

In relating expenditures to assessment it should be noted that while expenditures are expressed in current dollars, assessments in Metro are made in terms of 1940 dollars. A comparison of gross expenditures per $1,000 of taxable assessment with gross expenditures per capita reflects inequalities in the distribution of taxable resources. Some municipalities are able to spend considerably more per capita with a smaller tax effort than others. Municipal gross current expenditures in 1963 ranged from $55 per $1,000 of taxable assessment in Swansea to $115 in Scarborough. With expenditures of $59 per $1,000 of assessment, Leaside spent $242 per capita, while Scarborough, with expenditures of $115 per $1,000 of assessment, spent $215 per capita. Expenditures of $81 per $1,000 of assessment provided a level of $227 per capita in Etobicoke but only $147 in East York. With $77 per $1,000 of assessment, New Toronto was able to spend $280 per capita, but in Long Branch, $74 per $1,000 of assessment meant only $132 per capita.

Gross current expenditures, excluding debt charges, on the main categories of municipal services are shown in Tables 17 to 23. They show trends in expenditures from 1954 to 1963 and the relative position of the different municipalities. Gross expenditures are a measure of the standard of service provided but, since no allowance is made for provincial grants and other offsetting factors, they are not a measure of the actual burden borne by the municipalities in providing the service.

2. GENERAL GOVERNMENT (TABLE 17)

For the area as a whole, per capita gross current expenditures on general administration rose from $7.75 in 1954 to $11.53 in 1963. In the latter year the range in the area municipalities was from $4.11 in North York to $13.20 in Toronto, and the figure for the Metropolitan Corporation was $2.89 per capita.

Table 17

MUNICIPAL GROSS CURRENT EXPENDITURE, 1954 AND 1963
GENERAL GOVERNMENT[1]

Municipality	1954			1963		
	Actual	Per Capita	Per $1000 of Taxable Assessment	Actual	Per Capita	Per $1000 of Taxable Assessment
	$	$	$	$	$	$
Toronto	5,229,111	7.66	3.64	8,323,454	13.20	4.49
North York	376,347	2.88	1.86	1,264,993	4.11	1.77
Scarborough	533,078	5.57	4.19	1,607,887	6.69	3.59
Etobicoke	395,059	4.75	2.59	1,206,305	6.79	2.42
York	241,618	2.28	1.52	681,548	5.40	3.01
East York	132,476	1.93	1.41	350,401	4.99	2.75
Forest Hill	92,457	5.03	1.86	178,849	8.47	2.50
Leaside	60,093	3.56	1.22	169,700	9.20	2.22
Mimico	57,423	4.65	3.03	100,073	5.51	2.87
New Toronto	62,998	6.42	2.27	105,957	8.99	2.49
Long Branch	40,120	4.32	3.41	69,452	6.24	3.49
Weston	62,677	7.31	3.82	112,895	11.31	4.40
Swansea	34,576	3.97	2.00	103,498	11.04	4.44
Metro	2,373,435	1.90	1.01	4,771,819	2.89	1.15
Area Total	9,691,468	7.75	4.10	19,046,831	11.53	4.57

[1]Excluding debt charges.
Source: Annual Reports of Municipal Statistics, Province of Ontario, 1954 and 1963.

When related to assessment, the increase for the area as a whole was comparatively small: the expenditures per $1,000 of assessment rose from $4.10 in 1954 to $4.57 in 1963. On this basis, Metro's costs increased only by 14 cents, from $1.01 to $1.15.

In the ten-year period, the number of employees in general administration in Metro and the area municipalities rose from 955 to 1,580. The increase was distributed as follows:

GENERAL GOVERNMENT: NUMBER OF EMPLOYEES

	1954	1963	Increase
Metro	251	544	293
City of Toronto	418	518	100
Three outer suburbs	169	362	193
Nine inner suburbs	117	156	39
Total	955	1,580	625

Source: Personnel or Clerks' Departments.

Considering Metro's responsibilities and that more than one-half of its expenditures on general administration covers the costs of assessing property for all the area municipalities, it follows that, at a cost which has ranged from $1.01 to $1.15 per $1,000 of taxable assessment, Metro has not added any appreciable burden to the costs of administering local government in the area.

3. PUBLIC WORKS (TABLE 18)

Gross current expenditures, excluding debt charges, on roads, sidewalks and other public works rose from $8.09 in 1954 to $12.93 per capita in 1963. When related to the tax base, gross expenditures per $1,000 of assessment increased from $4.29 to $5.13 for the area as a whole. Metro's share rose from $2.09 to $3.27 per capita and from $1.11 to $1.30 per $1,000 of taxable assessment.

The area municipalities presented a varied picture in 1963, with per capita gross expenditures ranging from $3.44 in Long Branch to $18.02 in New Toronto and expenditures per $1,000 of assessment, from $1.69 in Leaside to $6.50 in North York. While, in terms of expenditures per $1,000 of assessment, the burdens were heaviest in Scarborough and North York in both 1954 and 1963, the gap between the highest and lowest spending municipalities has been considerably narrowed by Metro's assumption of metropolitan roads. The assumption of additional major local arterial roads would afford further relief to the larger municipalities.

4. PROTECTION TO PERSONS AND PROPERTY (TABLE 19)

From 1954 to 1963, gross current expenditures on protection to persons and property over the area as a whole rose from $16.05 to $29.28 per capita and from $8.50 to $11.61 per $1,000 of taxable assessment. During this period Metro assumed responsibility for the police force and for licensing. Accordingly, it showed an increase in costs per capita from $1.29 to $17.17 and from 69 cents to $6.81 in expenditures per $1,000 of assessment. In 1954 the City of Toronto bore 65.5 per cent of the area's total protection costs; by 1963 Metro's share was 58.7 per cent, while that of the City had declined to 22.3 per cent. The City, of course, pays a large proportion of Metro's costs through the metropolitan levy.

In 1963 the protection expenditures of the area municipalities, being largely the costs of fire protection, ranged from $5.43 per capita in Mimico to $17.12 in Toronto and from $2.27 per $1,000 of assessment in Swansea to $5.86 in Weston. The figures point to differences in standards of a basic service affecting the public safety.

5. RECREATION AND COMMUNITY SERVICES (TABLE 20)

Gross current expenditures on parks, municipal libraries, museums and community halls rose over the area as a whole from $4.8 million or $3.87 per capita in 1954 to $16.8 million or $10.16 per capita in 1963. Expenditures per $1,000 of assessment increased from $2.05 to $4.03 in the same period. In 1954 the City's proportion of total expenditures on these services was more than 84 per cent, while the three outer suburbs accounted for only four per cent. In 1963, with Metro, which is responsible for metropolitan parks, spending 14 per cent and the outer suburbs 26 per cent, Toronto's share of the total declined to 48 per cent.

Table 18

MUNICIPAL GROSS CURRENT EXPENDITURE, 1954 AND 1963
PUBLIC WORKS[1]

Municipality	1954			1963		
	Actual	Per Capita	Per $1000 of Taxable Assessment	Actual	Per Capita	Per $1000 of Taxable Assessment
	$	$	$	$	$	$
Toronto	2,103,246	3.08	1.47	4,175,012	6.62	2.25
North York	1,943,636	14.86	9.59	4,644,814	15.10	6.50
Scarborough	1,552,184	16.22	12.19	2,715,788	11.30	6.06
Etobicoke	811,171	9.75	5.32	2,196,534	12.37	4.41
York	361,396	3.41	2.28	737,506	5.84	3.26
East York	154,617	2.25	1.65	382,517	5.45	3.01
Forest Hill	206,550	11.24	4.16	319,833	15.14	4.47
Leaside	65,245	3.87	1.33	128,645	6.97	1.69
Mimico	75,115	6.08	3.96	193,036	10.64	5.53
New Toronto	34,422	3.51	1.24	212,369	18.02	4.99
Long Branch	57,342	6.18	4.87	38,284	3.44	1.93
Weston	100,093	11.68	6.10	109,105	10.93	4.25
Swansea	38,421	4.41	2.22	95,346	10.17	4.09
Metro	2,615,004	2.09	1.11	5,409,476	3.27	1.30
Area Total	10,118,442	8.09	4.29	21,358,265	12.93	5.13

[1]Excluding debt charges.
Source: Annual Reports of Municipal Statistics, Province of Ontario, 1954 and 1963.

Table 19

MUNICIPAL GROSS CURRENT EXPENDITURE, 1954 AND 1963
PROTECTION TO PERSONS AND PROPERTY[1]

Municipality	1954			1963		
	Actual	Per Capita	Per $1000 of Taxable Assessment	Actual	Per Capita	Per $1000 of Taxable Assessment
	$	$	$	$	$	$
Toronto	13,161,835	19.29	9.17	10,792,334	17.12	5.82
North York	1,129,170	8.63	5.57	2,564,840	8.34	3.59
Scarborough	885,752	9.25	6.96	2,048,860	8.52	4.57
Etobicoke	820,945	9.87	5.38	1,751,589	9.87	3.52
York	896,902	8.46	5.65	1,096,967	8.68	4.84
East York	527,941	7.68	5.63	624,130	8.89	4.90
Forest Hill	331,627	18.05	6.68	265,729	12.58	3.71
Leaside	169,144	10.02	3.44	290,171	15.72	3.80
Mimico	94,969	7.69	5.01	98,511	5.43	2.82
New Toronto	166,889	17.00	6.00	172,958	14.68	4.06
Long Branch	80,815	8.71	6.87	86,506	7.77	4.35
Weston	127,795	14.91	7.79	150,523	15.08	5.86
Swansea	67,677	7.76	3.91	52,957	5.65	2.27
Metro	1,618,318	1.29	.69	28,376,433	17.17	6.81
Area Total	20,079,779	16.05	8.50	48,372,508	29.28	11.61

[1]Excluding debt charges.
Source: Annual Reports of Municipal Statistics, Province of Ontario, 1954 and 1963.

Table 20

MUNICIPAL GROSS CURRENT EXPENDITURE, 1954 AND 1963

Recreation and Community Services[1]

Municipality	1954			1963		
	Actual	Per Capita	Per $1000 of Taxable Assessment	Actual	Per Capita	Per $1000 of Taxable Assessment
	$	$	$	$	$	$
Toronto	4,077,242	5.97	2.84	8,032,562	12.74	4.33
North York	122,465	.94	.60	2,102,200	6.83	2.94
Scarborough	63,283	.66	.50	1,069,443	4.45	2.39
Etobicoke	14,090	.17	.09	1,236,066	6.96	2.48
York	261,375	2.47	1.65	667,440	5.28	2.95
East York	101,907	1.48	1.09	621,430	8.86	4.88
Forest Hill	23,445	1.28	.46	122,853	5.82	1.72
Leaside	54,690	3.24	1.11	159,165	8.63	2.09
Mimico	25,276	2.05	1.33	94,378	5.20	2.70
New Toronto	28,757	2.93	1.03	127,327	10.80	2.99
Long Branch	14,892	1.60	1.27	61,583	5.53	3.10
Weston	33,745	3.94	2.06	67,692	6.78	2.64
Swansea	18,024	2.07	1.04	67,702	7.22	2.91
Metro	Nil	—	—	2,359,738	1.43	.57
Area Total	4,839,191	3.87	2.05	16,789,579	10.16	4.03

[1]Excluding debt charges.
Source: Annual Reports of Municipal Statistics, Province of Ontario, 1954 and 1963.

Expenditures on recreation and community services in the area municipalities ranged from $4.45 in Scarborough to $12.74 per capita in Toronto, in 1963. They included public library costs which ranged from $1.26 in Swansea to $4.52 per capita in Leaside.

6. PUBLIC WELFARE (TABLE 21)

The local burden of welfare costs is substantially reduced by provincial grants. Accordingly, while gross current expenditures reflect relative needs and the relative range of services provided, they do not measure the actual burden.

Gross current welfare expenditures in the area rose from $7.8 million in 1954 to almost $21 million in 1963—an increase of 168 per cent—and on a per capita basis, from $6.26 to $12.69. In 1954 the range was from 10 cents per capita in Leaside to $6.02 in Toronto, and, in 1963, from 91 cents per capita in Leaside to $19.34 in Toronto. In 1964 Toronto was afforded relief by Metro's assumption of the municipal share (20 per cent) of the cost of mandatory welfare services. Applied to 1963 expenditures, this would have reduced the City's per capita gross cost by $3.01 and its costs per $1,000 of taxable assessment by $1.02, while Metro's share would have risen by $2.3 million.

Table 21

MUNICIPAL GROSS CURRENT EXPENDITURE, 1954 AND 1963

Public Welfare[1]

Municipality	1954			1963		
	Actual	Per Capita	Per $1000 of Taxable Assessment	Actual	Per Capita	Per $1000 of Taxable Assessment
	$	$	$	$	$	$
Toronto	4,105,879	6.02	2.86	12,193,434	19.34	6.57
North York	104,876	.80	.52	686,810	2.23	.96
Scarborough	81,986	.86	.64	595,435	2.48	1.33
Etobicoke	37,165	.45	.24	257,410	1.45	.52
York	97,449	.92	.61	443,880	3.51	1.96
East York	27,374	.40	.29	140,773	2.01	1.11
Forest Hill	4.986	.27	.10	31,096	1.47	.43
Leaside	1,756	.10	.04	16,729	.91	.22
Mimico	5,795	.47	.31	88,205	4.86	2.53
New Toronto	8,402	.86	.30	137,947	11.71	3.24
Long Branch	7,574	.82	.64	50,473	4.54	2.54
Weston	2,785	.32	.17	23,835	2.39	.93
Swansea	1,835	.21	.11	28,043	2.99	1.20
Metro	3,337,475	2.67	1.41	6,267,358	3.79	1.50
Area Total	7,825,247	6.26	3.31	20,961,428	12.69	5.03

[1]Excluding debt charges.
Source: Annual Reports of Municipal Statistics, Province of Ontario, 1954 and 1963.

The variations in per capita gross welfare expenditures among the municipalities reflect differences in needs but also differences in the range and standards of service provided where there is need. As the core city of the area, Toronto, with the largest case load, necessarily provides the most comprehensive program, including mandatory and optional services. The expenditures shown for the other area municipalities are almost exclusively for the provision of services which are mandatory under provincial legislation.

7. HEALTH (TABLE 22)

Metro's main responsibility in the field of health services is payment of the hospitalization costs of indigent patients. With the introduction of hospital insurance in 1959, this responsibility has been greatly reduced. Accordingly, Metro's gross current health expenditures, which are largely offset by provincial grants, declined from $3.4 million, or $2.71 per capita, in 1954, to $968,000, or 59 cents per capita, in 1963. During the same period, the expenditures of the area municipalities, which are responsible for the basic health services, rose from $4.4 million to $5.6 million. The figures show a small decline for the City but an increase from $374,000 to $1.3 million for the three outer suburbs.

Table 22

MUNICIPAL GROSS CURRENT EXPENDITURE, 1954 AND 1963

Conservation of Health[1]

Municipality	1954			1963		
	Actual	Per Capita	Per $1000 of Taxable Assessment	Actual	Per Capita	Per $1000 of Taxable Assessment
	$	$	$	$	$	$
Toronto	3,706,234	5.43	2.58	3,619,675	5.74	1.95
North York	162,402	1.24	.80	609,023	1.98	.85
Scarborough	99,058	1.03	.78	449,127	1.87	1.00
Etobicoke	112,971	1.36	.74	289,617	1.63	.58
York	115,952	1.09	.73	315,641	2.50	1.39
East York	88,180	1.28	.94	147,666	2.10	1.16
Forest Hill	18,138	.99	.36	38,529	1.82	.54
Leaside	17,119	1.01	.35	32,641	1.77	.43
Mimico	6,212	.50	.33	11,922	.66	.34
New Toronto	9,163	.93	.33	12,495	1.06	.29
Long Branch	6,628	.71	.56	4,595	.41	.23
Weston	16,103	1.88	.98	18,181	1.82	.71
Swansea	7,803	.90	.45	11,216	1.20	.48
Metro	3,394,055	2.71	1.44	967,897	.59	.23
Area Total	7,760,018	6.20	3.29	6,528,225	3.95	1.57

[1]Excluding debt charges.
Source: Annual Reports of Municipal Statistics, Province of Ontario, 1954 and 1963.

On a per capita basis, gross current expenditures on health services ranged, in 1963, from 41 cents in Long Branch to $5.74 in Toronto, and, in terms of expenditures per $1,000 of assessment, from 23 cents in Long Branch to $1.95 in Toronto. The number of persons employed in the health services of each municipality in 1963 was as follows:

HEALTH SERVICES: NUMBER OF EMPLOYEES, 1963

Toronto	538	Forest Hill	12
North York	138	Mimico[2]	½
Scarborough	78	New Toronto[2]	3⅓
Etobicoke	44	Long Branch	1
York	48	Weston	5
East York and Leaside[1]	41	Swansea[2]	1½

[1]Joint Health Unit.
[2]Fractions indicate part time permanent staff.
Source: Personnel or Clerks' Departments.

These figures reflect a range from the very limited services available in some small municipalities to the comprehensive programme of the City of Toronto.

8. SANITATION AND WASTE REMOVAL (TABLE 23)

Gross current expenditures on the operation and maintenance of sewers, sewage treatment and garbage collection and disposal rose from $9.5 million or $7.61 per capita in 1954 to $18.8 million or $11.40 per capita in 1963. The responsibilities in this field are divided between Metro, which is responsible for all permanent sewage treatment plants and trunk sewers and may operate sites for waste disposal, and the area municipalities, which are responsible for local sewage and storm water collection systems and for garbage collection and disposal.

Between 1954 and 1963, the City's proportion of the total area costs for these services declined from 56.8 per cent to 39.8 per cent and that of the inner ring from 12.5 per cent to 9.8 per cent, while the share of the three outer suburbs, reflecting their high rate of growth, rose from 15 per cent to 31 per cent of the total. Metro's share rose from 15.8 per cent in 1954 to 19.6 per cent in 1963. It must be noted, however, that debt charges, which have not been included in the gross expenditure figures, form a very large part of Metro's expenditures on sanitation and that these charges increased from a little more than one million dollars in 1954 to approximately $5.9 million in 1963.

Table 23

MUNICIPAL GROSS CURRENT EXPENDITURE, 1954 AND 1963

Sanitation and Waste Removal[1]

Municipality	1954			1963		
	Actual	Per Capita	Per $1000 of Taxable Assessment	Actual	Per Capita	Per $1000 of Taxable Assessment
	$	$	$	$	$	$
Toronto	5,404,608	7.92	3.77	7,495,896	11.89	4.04
North York	456,118	3.49	2.25	2,413,918	7.85	3.38
Scarborough[2]	328,663	3.43	2.58	1,900,690	7.90	4.24
Etobicoke	637,448	7.66	4.18	1,491,345	8.40	2.99
York	582,993	5.50	3.67	935,746	7.41	4.13
East York	227,727	3.31	2.43	304,084	4.33	2.39
Forest Hill	37,557	2.04	.76	62,420	2.95	.87
Leaside	64,454	3.82	1.31	90,695	4.91	1.19
Mimico	81,261	6.58	4.29	134,395	7.40	3.85
New Toronto	81,988	8.35	2.95	129,741	11.01	3.05
Long Branch	27,316	2.94	2.32	66,158	5.94	3.33
Weston	46,708	5.45	2.85	56,872	5.70	2.22
Swansea	37,072	4.25	2.14	66,479	7.09	2.85
Metro	1,505,613	1.20	.64	3,682,651	2.23	.88
Area Total	9,519,526	7.61	4.03	18,831,090	11.40	4.52

[1]Excluding debt charges.
[2]Excluding debt charges for sewer areas included in source statistics amounting to $222,895 in 1954 and $1,477,812 in 1963.
Source: Annual Reports of Municipal Statistics, Province of Ontario, 1954 and 1963.

9. CONCLUSIONS

This review of expenditures on each of the main categories of municipal services is based on gross current expenditures, excluding debt charges. The figures indicate how the total resources available are spent, but do not measure the actual burden imposed on the local taxpayer because no allowance is made for provincial grants and other offsetting receipts.

Comparative expenditures point to variations in the range and standards of some of the basic services provided by the area municipalities. By assuming responsibility for area-wide services, Metro has prevented wider variations from developing.

Variations in the provision of services are, in part, a reflection of differences in the characteristics of municipalities, and uniform standards are not required in respect of all services. I find, however, that the citizens of the different parts of Metro are entitled to a greater degree of equality in the standards of some of the basic services than can be provided with the division of responsibility among thirteen municipalities of varying size and resources.

CHAPTER IX

TAXATION AND OTHER REVENUES

The Metro Act empowers the Metropolitan Council to levy for its requirements annually against the area municipalities, the amount to be apportioned among the latter in the same proportion as the assessment of the taxable property of each for Metro purposes bears to the total assessment of such property in the Metropolitan Area. The Metropolitan Corporation has no power to collect taxes directly; its levy is added to the local tax bill and collected by the area municipalities. Real property and business taxation provide the bulk of the revenue, with provincial grants as the second largest source. Together, they yielded 85 per cent of total gross revenue in 1963.

1. TAX REVENUES

Table 24 shows that total gross current revenue of Metro and the area municipalities for municipal and school purposes rose from $145.8 million in 1954 to $410.1 million in 1964, an increase of 181.3 per cent. Real property and business taxation yielded $102.5 million or 70.4 per cent of the total in 1954, and $275.3 million or 67.1 per cent of the total in 1964. The increase of 168 per cent in tax revenue compared with an increase of 80 per cent in total taxable assessment, but, since this is a comparison between revenues expressed in current dollars and assessments made in terms of 1940 dollars, the increase is exaggerated. Over the period, the municipal share of the tax levy declined from 63 per cent to 56.5 per cent, with a corresponding rise in the share for school purposes.

Since 1957 tax revenue has included the proceeds of area-wide levies imposed by Metro for capital purposes to relieve debenture borrowing. A levy equivalent to two mills, initially imposed in 1957 for general municipal purposes, has been applied since 1959 to reduction of Metro's share of financing subway construction. Its total yield to the end of 1964 was $61.7 million, of which $47.5 million was applied to subway costs. To reduce debenture borrowing for school purposes, levies equivalent to one-half mill have been imposed on Metro's elementary school assessment and on its secondary school assessment since 1959, yielding $23.3 million to the end of 1964.

2. PROVINCIAL GRANTS

While taxation provided 67 per cent of the gross current revenue of the area in 1963, provincial grants, the other major source, yielded about 18 per cent, as compared with 15 per cent in 1954. Grants for schools, roads, health and

Table 24

METROPOLITAN TORONTO AND AREA MUNICIPALITIES
GENERAL AND SCHOOL GROSS CURRENT REVENUE, 1954 AND 1963

Revenue Source	1954				1963				Per Cent Increase
	$000	$000	Total $000	Per Cent of Total Revenue %	$000	$000	Total $000	Per Cent of Total Revenue %	%
Real Property and Business Taxation:									
General Purposes (including owners' share of local improvement charges)		64,426		44.19		155,546		37.93	141.4
School Purposes		38,131		26.16		119,739		29.20	214.0
Total Taxation Revenue			102,557	70.35			275,285	67.13	168.4
Grants and Subsidies:									
Federal		229		.16		3,363		.82	1,368.6
Federal-Provincial (re vocational schools construction)						10,426		2.54	
Provincial									
Education	9,412				36,634				
Municipal	7,808				14,736				
Roads	3,562				9,405				
Health and Welfare	1,338				12,112				
Total		22,120		15.17		72,887		17.77	229.5
Other Municipalities		140		.09		451		.11	222.1
Total Grants and Subsidies			22,489	15.42			87,127	21.24	287.4
Licences and Permits			1,546	1.06			2,875	.70	86.0
Debt Charges Recoverable			7,332	5.03			19,772	4.82	169.7
Miscellaneous			11,863	8.14			25,058	6.11	111.23
Total Municipal and School Gross Current Revenue			145,787	100.00			410,117	100.00	181.31

Sources: Annual Reports of Municipal Statistics, Province of Ontario, 1954 and 1963; Financial Statements of Area School Boards, 1954 and 1963.

welfare and general municipal purposes rose from $22 million to $72.9 million, or by approximately 230 per cent, as follows:

PROVINCIAL GRANTS

	1954 $	1963 $
Municipal	7,808,000	14,736,000
Roads	3,562,000	9,405,000
Health and Welfare	1,338,000	12,112,000
Schools	9,412,000	36,634,000
Total	22,120,000	72,887,000

The municipal grants include the unconditional grant, as well as provincial payments in lieu of taxes, the municipal share of fees and fines under The Liquor Control Act and The Liquor License Act and payments under the winter works programme. The unconditional grant is paid on a per capita basis at a rate varying with the status and population of the municipality. The grant ranges from $3.00 per capita in towns, villages and townships of less than 2,000 inhabitants to $5.50 per capita in metropolitan municipalities or cities. For the Toronto Metropolitan Area the grant is paid to Metro at the rate of $5.50 per capita. The fringe municipalities in the Planning Area receive their grants at the rate applicable in each case.

In 1963 provincial road grants were equivalent to 44 per cent of gross current expenditures on public works in the area. The grants are paid directly to the municipality responsible for the work on the following basis: to counties, townships, non-separated towns and villages, 50 per cent of the approved costs of road construction and maintenance and 80 per cent of bridge and culvert construction and maintenance; to Metropolitan Toronto, 50 per cent of road and bridge construction and maintenance; and to cities and separated towns, $33\frac{1}{3}$ per cent of road, bridge and culvert construction and maintenance. The Townships of York and East York are considered as cities for the purposes of road grants and, with Toronto, receive $33\frac{1}{3}$ per cent of the costs, while the three outer townships and the towns and villages in the Metropolitan Area qualify for 50 per cent of the costs of roads and 80 per cent for bridges and culverts.

In 1963 provincial health and welfare grants financed 44 per cent of the area's gross current expenditures on these services. The grants for health services include payments toward the cost of school dental services, psychiatric hospital accommodation and treatment, diagnostic public health services and the establishment and maintenance of health units. Welfare grants include assistance toward the cost of child welfare, homes for the aged, homemaker and nursing services and assistance to heads of families or single persons in needy circumstances. The bulk of the grants for optional welfare services are paid to the City of Toronto which alone has a comprehensive programme covering both mandatory and optional services.

The legislative grants for schools, which in 1963 represented one-half of the total of provincial grants, are paid to the Metropolitan School Board, except for small grants of a special nature which are paid directly to the local boards. School grants are based on a number of factors intended to reflect the ability of local taxpayers to pay for school costs. In 1963 the grants yielded the equivalent of 31 per cent of the total tax levy for public schools.

3. METRO AND LOCAL TAX LEVIES

Under The Municipal Unconditional Grants Act, as amended in 1957, the grant must be applied to reduction of the general tax levy on residential and farm property only. Accordingly, the metropolitan general levy is divided into two levies, a levy on residential assessment and a levy on non-residential assessment. In 1963 the division was as follows:

METROPOLITAN GENERAL LEVY, 1963

	Assessment $	Levy before deduction of Per Capita Grant $	Less Per Capita Grant[1] $	Net General Levy $
Residential..	2,430,276,378	38,121,532	9,046,301	29,075,231
Commercial.	1,896,734,914	29,752,353	....	29,752,353
Total...	4,327,011,292	67,873,885	9,046,301	58,827,584

[1]Including adjustment from previous year.

The net general Metro levy on residential assessment is divided among the area municipalities in the same proportion as the residential assessment of each bears to the total residential assessment of the area. The levy on non-residential assessment is distributed on a similar basis. The distribution of the metropolitan general levy among the area municipalities in 1963 is shown in Table 25. By areas, it was distributed as follows: Toronto, 47.3 per cent; three outer suburbs, 38.2 per cent; nine inner suburbs, 14.5 per cent.

In their briefs to the Commission, the City of Toronto and the Township of Scarborough submitted that they are prejudiced by Metro's method of distribution of the benefits from the unconditional grant. While the grant to Metro is based on population, it is distributed among the area municipalities in the proportion that their residential assessment bears to Metro's total residential assessment and not in relation to population. If the 1963 levy of $38.1 million on residential assessment had first been divided among the area municipalities according to their proportion of the total residential assessment and the amount of the grant deducted from the resulting levy in each case

Table 25

DISTRIBUTION OF METROPOLITAN GENERAL LEVY, 1963[1]

Municipality	Residential Properties			Non-Residential Properties			Total General Levy	
	Assessment	Levy	Per Cent of Total	Assessment	Levy	Per Cent of Total	Amount	Per Cent of Total
	$	$	%	$	$	%	$	%
Toronto	806,163,352	9,644,741	33.17	1,158,061,831	18,165,461	61.06	27,810,202	47.27
North York	531,452,595	6,358,168	21.87	210,262,684	3,298,200	11.08	9,656,368	16.42
Scarborough	319,419,312	3,821,455	13.14	135,983,953	2,133,057	7.17	5,954,512	10.12
Etobicoke	318,525,098	3,810,756	13.11	195,933,506	3,073,431	10.33	6,884,187	11.70
York	160,394,631	1,918,922	6.60	66,487,226	1,042,924	3.50	2,961,846	5.04
East York	100,087,745	1,197,425	4.12	27,188,709	426,485	1.43	1,623,910	2.76
Forest Hill	65,314,684	781,409	2.69	6,453,229	101,225	.34	882,634	1.50
Leaside	41,400,847	495,310	1.70	35,973,933	564,290	1.90	1,059,600	1.80
Mimico	27,128,624	324,560	1.11	7,889,439	123,754	.42	448,314	.76
New Toronto	13,619,751	162,943	.56	30,270,403	474,824	1.60	637,767	1.09
Long Branch	13,536,987	161,953	.56	6,331,862	99,322	.33	261,275	.44
Weston	15,012,530	179,607	.62	10,761,763	168,810	.57	348,417	.59
Swansea	18,220,222	217,982	.75	5,136,376	80,570	.27	298,552	.51
Total	2,430,276,378	29,075,231	100.00	1,896,734,914	29,752,353	100.00	58,827,584	100.00

[1]Including supplementary levy of $2,500,000 on May 3, 1963, for T.T.C. purposes.
Source: Annual Report of the Commissioner of Finance, Municipality of Metropolitan Toronto, 1963.

in accordance with their proportion of the total population, the differences in benefits received would have been as follows:

	Gain $	Loss $
Toronto	748,409	
North York		475,167
Scarborough	34,625	
Etobicoke		310,165
York	130,683	
East York	34,028	
Forest Hill		127,833
Leaside		49,391
Mimico	1,260	
New Toronto	16,706	
Long Branch	11,751	
Weston		1,350
Swansea		13,556

I find that, as the unconditional grant is paid to Metro on a per capita basis, the distribution of the grant among the area municipalities should be on the basis of population, and that such distribution would be more equitable in its results.

The metropolitan educational levy is also divided into two parts, the levy for public elementary schools and the levy for secondary schools. The distribution of the levy of $54.3 million among the area municipalities in 1963 is shown in Table 26. By areas, it was distributed as follows: Toronto, 45.3 per cent; three outer suburbs, 39.7 per cent; nine inner suburbs, 15 per cent. It will be noted that the public elementary school assessment was $3,974 million, as compared with the secondary school assessment of $4,289 million. The difference represents the assessed value of property rateable for support of Roman Catholic separate elementary schools, almost all of which are under the jurisdiction of the Metropolitan Separate School Board.

Metro levies for its requirements on the area municipalities. These, in turn, levy for general purposes and for school purposes, respectively, to cover their own and Metro's requirements. The levy for general purposes is divided into two levies, on residential and non-residential assessment, respectively. As Metro's portion of the residential general levy is reduced by the amount of the unconditional grant, the residential general tax rate of an area municipality is in all cases less than the non-residential rate.

The taxable assessment on which the area municipalities levy for elementary school purposes is divided between public and separate elementary school supporters. The secondary school assessment is the sum of the two assessments. Accordingly, the public school tax levied on public school supporters by each area municipality reflects the local and Metro public elementary and secondary school requirements, while the tax on separate school supporters reflects the levy of the separate school board for elementary school purposes plus the local and Metro levy for secondary schools.

Table 26

DISTRIBUTION OF METROPOLITAN EDUCATIONAL LEVY, 1963

Municipality	Public Elementary			Secondary			Total Educational Levy	
	Assessment $	Levy $	Per Cent of Total %	Assessment $	Levy $	Per Cent of Total %	Amount $	Per Cent of Total %
Toronto	1,808,410,437	15,159,038	45.50	1,932,347,565	9,436,190	45.05	24,595,228	45.33
North York	684,590,369	5,738,593	17.23	742,586,671	3,626,257	17.31	9,364,850	17.26
Scarborough	414,484,975	3,474,429	10.43	453,900,275	2,216,521	10.58	5,690,950	10.49
Etobicoke	472,399,813	3,959,901	11.89	510,725,149	2,494,013	11.91	6,453,914	11.90
York	200,992,199	1,684,821	5.06	226,356,651	1,105,363	5.28	2,790,184	5.14
East York	115,335,676	966,804	2.90	126,981,183	620,084	2.96	1,586,888	2.92
Forest Hill	68,641,625	575,390	1.73	71,439,481	348,859	1.67	924,249	1.70
Leaside	73,288,800	614,345	1.84	77,238,837	377,179	1.80	991,524	1.83
Mimico	29,565,339	247,832	.74	34,942,285	170,633	.82	418,455	.77
New Toronto	41,620,453	348,884	1.05	43,696,096	213,380	1.02	562,264	1.04
Long Branch	18,347,285	153,796	.46	19,832,849	96,849	.46	250,645	.46
Weston	24,595,552	206,173	.62	25,740,715	125,699	.60	331,872	.61
Swansea	21,974,769	184,204	.55	23,302,228	113,791	.54	297,995	.55
Total	3,974,247,292	33,314,210	100.00	4,289,089,985	20,944,818	100.00	54,259,028	100.00

Source: Annual Report of the Commissioner of Finance, Municipality of Metropolitan Toronto, 1963.

The local taxable assessment for both public and separate school supporters is further divided into two classifications, covering residential and non-residential property, respectively, so that the school rate levied on residential and farm property will be 90 per cent of the rate levied on non-residential assessment. Differential school tax rates for residential and non-residential properties were the result of direct grants to local school boards under The Residential and Farm School Tax Assistance Grants Act, 1961, which is now repealed. The amount of these grants, since 1964, has been added to the general school grants to Metro, but the differential in rates is continued under section 105 (4) of The Schools Administration Act.

The levies for local municipal and school purposes in 1963 are shown in Table 27. It should be noted that the local taxable assessments, on which the area municipalities levy, differ from the assessment on which Metro uniformly apportions its levies among the municipalities. Under section 230 (9) of the Metro Act, the assessment for purposes of apportionment of the Metro levy includes the valuation of all exempt properties for which payments in lieu of taxes are made by the Crown or its agencies or the Hydro-Electric Power Commission of Ontario. The area municipalities, on the other hand, exclude from their taxable assessments all exempt properties on which grants in lieu of taxes are paid, as well as properties partially or wholly exempt under local by-laws. Accordingly, when expressed as a local tax rate, the uniform Metro levy is different for each area municipality.

Table 27

AREA MUNICIPALITIES

General and School Tax Levies for Local Purposes, 1963[1]

Municipality	General	Schools	Total
	$	$	$
Toronto	49,641,780	28,707,338	78,349,118
North York	11,278,395	11,940,170	23,218,565
Scarborough	10,734,045	7,467,982	18,202,027
Etobicoke	8,026,716	6,825,606	14,852,322
York	4,572,284	3,728,371	8,300,655
East York	2,340,050	2,023,129	4,363,179
Forest Hill	1,026,178	1,016,861	2,043,039
Leaside	901,211	851,834	1,753,045
Mimico	658,995	425,998	1,084,993
New Toronto	709,384	496,772	1,206,156
Long Branch	410,199	231,952	642,151
Weston	559,741	297,961	857,702
Swansea	354,123	220,678	574,801
Total Area Municipalities	91,213,101	64,234,652	155,447,753

[1]Excluding levies for local improvements.
Sources: Annual Report of Municipal Statistics, Province of Ontario, 1963; Audit Report, Municipality of Metropolitan Toronto, 1963.

4. THE TAX BURDEN

With all real property in the Metropolitan Area assessed on a uniform basis, it is possible to compare the burden of real property and business taxation in the area municipalities by comparing their respective mill rates. The general and school mill rates on residential assessment for public school supporters in 1954 and 1964 are shown in Table 28. The rates are for fully serviced areas and do not take account of differentials in rates in some of the suburbs which levy area charges based on the services provided in areas not fully serviced. The mill rates also do not take account of the owners' share of local improvement charges, where the whole or part of the cost of a local improvement is assessed against the land benefiting from the work. In the City of Toronto and in New Toronto the rates reflect the partial graded exemptions on dwellings assessed up to $4,000.

In comparing mill rates, it is necessary to have regard not only to differences in taxable capacity but also to other factors, such as the quantity and quality of services provided and differences in the rates of provincial grants. The relatively high rate in the City of Toronto, for example, pays for a wider range of municipal services of high quality than is provided elsewhere in the area. It has also been shown that provincial road grants pay a smaller share of the costs in Toronto, York and East York than in the other area municipalities.

The figures in Table 28 show that in 1954 the total mill rate ranged from 32 mills in Leaside to 43.83 mills in Scarborough, or a spread of 11.83 mills between the highest and lowest taxed municipalities. In 1964 the range was from 51.37 mills in Leaside to 69.10 mills in Toronto and the spread was 17.73 mills. On the basis of their mill rates, the municipalities ranked as follows, in 1954 and in 1964:

	1954 Mill Rate	*Rank*		*1964 Mill Rate*
Scarborough	43.83	1	Toronto	69.10
Toronto	43.50	2	Scarborough	68.88
Weston	40.00	3	York	65.06
East York	38.50	4	East York	64.03
Forest Hill	37.80	5	North York	60.78
Mimico	37.00	6	Long Branch	60.00
New Toronto	37.00	7	Weston	59.70
North York	36.90	8	Forest Hill	57.90
York	36.54	9	Mimico	57.00
Long Branch	36.00	10	Etobicoke	55.92
Swansea	34.77	11	Swansea	54.95
Etobicoke	33.80	12	New Toronto	54.81
Leaside	32.00	13	Leaside	51.37

The increase over the ten-year period ranged from 17.81 mills in New Toronto to 28.52 mills in York. In all cases, except York, the increase for Metro purposes exceeded that for local purposes. In 1954 Metro's proportion of the total rate ranged from 33.2 per cent in Scarborough to 45.4 per cent in

Table 28

GENERAL AND SCHOOL MILL RATES, 1954 AND 1964
Residential Public School Supporters

Municipality	1954				1964				Increase		
	For Local Purposes	For Metro Purposes	Total	Per Cent of Metro Rate to Total Rate	For Local Purposes	For Metro Purposes	Total	Per Cent of Metro Rate to Total Rate	For Local Purposes	For Metro Purposes	Total
				%				%			
Toronto	28.46	15.04	43.50	34.6	39.75	29.35	69.10	42.5	11.29	14.31	25.60
North York	21.98	14.92	36.90	40.4	31.62	29.16	60.78	48.0	9.64	14.24	23.38
Scarborough	29.97	14.56	43.83	33.2	39.95	28.93	68.88	42.0	10.68	14.37	25.05
Etobicoke	19.28	14.52	33.80	43.0	27.32	28.60	55.92	51.1	8.04	14.08	22.12
York	22.02	14.52	36.54	39.7	36.59	28.47	65.06	43.8	14.57	13.95	28.52
East York	23.84	14.66	38.50	38.1	34.90	29.13	64.03	45.5	11.06	14.47	25.53
Forest Hill	23.28	14.52	37.80	38.4	29.14	28.76	57.90	49.7	5.86	14.24	20.10
Leaside	17.48	14.52	32.00	45.4	23.02	28.35	51.37	55.2	5.54	13.83	19.37
Mimico	22.46	14.54	37.00	39.3	28.46	28.54	57.00	50.1	6.00	14.00	20.00
New Toronto	22.05	14.95	37.00	40.4	25.50	29.31	54.81	53.5	3.45	14.36	17.81
Long Branch	21.46	14.54	36.00	40.4	31.64	28.36	60.00	47.3	10.18	13.82	24.00
Weston	25.48	14.52	40.00	36.3	30.51	29.19	59.70	48.9	5.03	14.67	19.70
Swansea	20.24	14.53	34.77	41.8	25.92	29.03	54.95	52.8	5.68	14.50	20.18

Source: Treasury Department, Municipality of Metropolitan Toronto.

Leaside; in 1964 the range was from 42 per cent in Scarborough to 55.2 per cent in Leaside, with the rate for Metro purposes higher than the rate for local purposes in Leaside, New Toronto, Swansea, Etobicoke and Mimico. Over the period, the small inner suburbs, except Long Branch, either maintained or improved their relative tax position, while Etobicoke maintained its favoured position among the larger municipalities.

5. CONCLUSIONS

As Metro was not designed to produce a completely uniform tax rate for the area, variations in local services and in local tax burdens are to be expected; it was only in respect of area-wide services assumed by Metro that a uniform levy was to apply. By spreading the costs of these services over the area as a whole, Metro has exercised an equalizing influence and has prevented much wider inequalities in tax burdens from developing. Nevertheless, the spread between the lowest and the highest taxed unit has widened since 1954.

Metro's levelling influence has been lessened by the decline in its share of the gross current costs of education from 44.7 per cent to 35.5 per cent. The costs of education should be distributed more equitably over the area. The assumption by Metro of additional responsibilities in respect to other services would further tend to reduce inequalities in burdens, as would the distribution of the unconditional grant among the municipalities on the basis of population.

CHAPTER X

CAPITAL EXPENDITURES AND DEBT

The Cumming Report said "that in the interests of every part of the entire area it is essential that the immense volume of capital expenditures which will be necessary to provide the great variety of costly public works and schools needed throughout the area should be continuously co-ordinated and fitted into a consolidated capital works programme and financed at rates commensurate with the combined credit and resources of all the local municipalities." Accordingly, it recommended that "the Metropolitan Council should clearly have the exclusive right to issue debentures for any purpose", subject to the approval of the Ontario Municipal Board.

The Metro Act gave effect to this recommendation. The power of the area municipalities to issue debentures was terminated as from January 1, 1954, and the Metropolitan Corporation assumed all outstanding debentures issued by them for school purposes and for all works vested in Metro. Since then the Metropolitan Corporation has effected all debenture borrowing for metropolitan general purposes, including the Toronto Transit Commission, for the area municipalities, and for the area public school boards. All such borrowings are, under section 234 (3) of the Metro Act, "direct, joint and several obligations of the Metropolitan Corporation and the area municipalities notwithstanding the fact that the whole or any portion of the rates imposed for the payment thereof may have been levied only against one or more of the area municipalities. . . ."

1. CAPITAL FINANCING, 1954-1963

The provision of capital financing to meet the critical shortages in physical works, such as schools, waterworks, trunk sewers and roads, which faced the area in the early 'fifties, has been one of Metro's greatest achievements. To the end of May 1964, it had issued debentures totalling $877 million, as follows:

$331.6 million for purposes of the Metropolitan Corporation, including $47.5 million for the Toronto Transit Commission;
$303.2 million for the specific capital projects of the area municipalities;
$242.1 million for capital projects of the area boards of education.

The principal and interest charges on approximately $320 million of these debentures are met out of the area-wide Metro general and education levies.

Table 29 shows, by categories of services, the debentures issued by Metro for its own purposes and for the purposes of the area municipalities in the ten-year period 1954-1963. The City of Toronto and the three rapidly growing outer suburbs were the largest borrowers, as shown in Table 30. Without the

Table 29

Debentures Issued by the Municipality of Metropolitan Toronto During the Period 1954-1963, Inclusive, for own Purposes and for the Purposes of the Area Municipalities[1]

	Metropolitan Corporation $	Area Municipalities $	Total Debentures Issued $
General Government.................................	427,000	25,946,056	26,373,056
Protection to Persons and Property			
Administration of Justice........................	8,499,207		8,499,207
Fire Protection.................................		3,649,791	3,649,791
Traffic Engineering.............................	1,573,936		1,573,936
Public Works			
Sanitation and Waste Removal...................	95,522,970	28,948,748	124,471,718
Sewage System.................................	64,424,417	37,164,292	101,588,709
Garbage Disposal...............................			
Conservation of Health...........................	2,225,963	1,238,179	3,464,142
Social Welfare....................................	5,651,115	448,714	6,099,829
Recreation and Community Services			
Libraries......................................	11,150,839	31,995,791	43,146,630
Parks and Recreation...........................		5,277,729	5,277,729
Miscellaneous....................................	10,531,136	26,718,062	37,868,901
Conservation Schemes..........................	5,245,541		5,245,541
B.D.U. Subway (Metro share)...................	5,182,000		5,182,000
Housing and Redevelopment....................		13,058,527	13,058,527
Grants to University of Toronto.................		2,000,000	2,000,000
Market block (bldgs. and land)..................		1,196,319	1,196,319
Miscellaneous..................................	103,595	565,031	668,626
Local Improvement			
Area Municipalities' Share......................		29,282,338	29,282,338
Owners' Share.................................		38,346,341	38,346,341
		67,628,679	67,628,679
Education..	96,187,829	125,659,038	221,846,867
Other..	108,315,585	68,112,576	176,428,161
Waterworks....................................	68,157,585	8,150,685	76,308,270
T.T.C..	40,158,000		40,158,000
Hydro-Electric Systems.........................		39,874,675	39,874,675
Parking Authority..............................		9,925,674	9,925,674
C.N.E..		10,161,542	10,161,542
Totals...	404,509,997	407,611,741	812,121,738

[1]Does not reflect subsequent adjustments during the period 1954-1963, inclusive, between the Metropolitan Corporation and the area municipalities amounting to an assumption by the Metropolitan Corporation of $2,702,051 (net) of debentures issued for the purpose of the area municipalities.
Source: Treasury Department. Municipality of Metropolitan Toronto.

backing of the credit of the area as a whole, it is highly improbable that the three large townships could have raised the sums required to finance their requirements in this period, and such borrowings as they could make would have been at high interest rates. With its area-wide credit rating, Metro has been able to borrow at rates which will save millions of dollars over the lifetime of the debentures. This credit rating has been based in the main on the financial strength and reputation of the City of Toronto.

To set priorities for construction and capital financing a ten-year capital works programme, first established by Metro in 1955, has been reviewed and revised annually for the next following ten-year period. In 1955 Metro also set a limit on annual debenture financing at $60 million, increasing it to $75 million in 1956. The limit was raised to $100 million in 1958, with $40 million allocated to the Metropolitan Corporation, $30 million to the area municipalities and $30 million to the Metropolitan School Board. Metro has adhered fairly closely to this limit since then and the capital works programme for the years 1964 to 1973 indicates that annual capital financing will continue to be governed by the $100 million limit.

The considerations which were said to determine the borrowing limit were annual new assessment, the capacity of the market to absorb debentures at reasonable rates of interest, and the ratio of net debt to assessment. At Council's 1961 inaugural meeting, the chairman said: "I have frequently stated that a ratio of 15% net debt to assessment indicates a satisfactory financial position, that a ratio of 20% should give concern and anything above 20% would indicate trouble." He forecast a 15 per cent ratio by about 1970. It is important to note, however, that the ratio of debt to assessment in the Metropolitan Area is distorted by the fact that assessments are still based on 1940 values. Since the ratio relates debt expressed in terms of current dollars to assessed valuations made in terms of 1940 dollars, it is not in fact a satisfactory measure of Metro's financial position.

While Metro Council fixes an annual borrowing limit, annual capital expenditures are considerably in excess of this limit because of provincial grants, federal loans and the area-wide levies for capital purposes. Over the ten-year period from 1954 to 1963 provincial grants for capital purposes amounted to $107 million, while federal loans in an amount of $14.5 million were approved for elderly persons' housing and $13.7 million for sewage works. In 1961 the Provincial Government undertook to purchase $60 million of Metro debentures to be issued for the Bloor-Danforth-University Subway and, as from April 1964, expenditures for right-of-way construction in respect of this subway became eligible for provincial subsidies which, according to estimates, will amount to $21.4 million. Further financial assistance by the Federal Government became available in 1964, under the Municipal Works Assistance Programme, by way of a loan of $29.5 million allocated to the Metropolitan Corporation and a loan of $21.4 million reserved for the Metropolitan School Board, one-quarter of such loans to be forgiven for projects completed by March 31,

1966. Finally, the Metro levy for capital purposes, imposed annually since 1957, yielded $61.7 million to the end of 1964, while the levy for school capital costs yielded $23.3 million from 1959 to 1964, inclusive. These grants and levies have made it possible for Metro to increase capital expenditures without exceeding its self-imposed limit on annual public debenturing. In 1964, for example, provision was made for total capital expenditures of $210.4 million, of which only $114 million was to be financed by public debentures. For the period from 1964 to 1973, total capital expenditures are estimated at $1,277.7 million and public debenture borrowing at $976.3 million.

In Metro's first five years the larger part of its expenditures on capital projects was allocated to the three outer suburbs where the need for water and sewage facilities was critical. As the urgent needs of these suburbs were met, more funds became available for expressways and subways, with the result that, in the following years, the larger expenditures were made in the City, where 54 per cent of the costs were incurred in the first ten years of Metro. For the ten years 1964-1973 the outer suburbs are again scheduled to receive the largest share. The following table shows the distribution on a cost basis of Metro's capital works (including works constructed by the T.T.C. and the Metropolitan Waterworks System, but excluding works constructed by the area municipalities) for the periods 1954-1958 and 1954-1963, and the forecast for the ten years from 1964 to 1973:

METROPOLITAN CAPITAL WORKS
(INCLUDING T.T.C.)
DISTRIBUTION ON BASIS OF COSTS

	City %	Three Outer Suburbs %	Nine Inner Suburbs %
1954-1958	37.30	53.54	9.16
1954-1963	54.03	38.87	7.10
1964-1973	37.15	52.19	10.66

2. NET DEBT

Table 30 shows the net debenture debt of Metro and the area municipalities for general and school purposes for 1954 and 1963. The total net debt of the area, that is, total debenture debt less self-liquidating debt and less sinking fund, increased by 263 per cent, from $157.4 million in 1954 to $572.5 million in 1963. Metro's share, for which it levies against all area municipalities, rose from $80.6 million to $276 million, while the share for which the area municipalities levy increased from $76.8 million to $296.4 million. Reflecting their exploding growth, the increases shown by the three outer suburbs are spectacular. Compared with an increase of 202 per cent for Toronto and 59 per cent for the nine inner suburbs, the net debt of the three outer suburbs rose by 910 per cent: the increase for North York was 859 per cent, for Scarborough, approximately

1,000 per cent, and for Etobicoke, 878 per cent. In enabling these municipalities to obtain the moneys required to finance their growth, Metro achieved one of its major objectives.

Between 1954 and the end of 1963, Metro's share of the total net debt declined from 51.2 per cent to 48.2 per cent and the share for which the area municipalities are directly responsible increased from 48.8 per cent to 51.8 per cent. The decline in Metro's share largely reflects the decline in its proportion of the total capital costs of schools from 37.9 per cent in 1954 to 22.7 per cent in 1963. As the proportion financed by the Province also declined from 27.1 per cent to 20.5 per cent during this period, the area municipalities' share of school capital financing rose from 35 per cent in 1954 to 56.8 per cent in 1963. This affected the outer suburbs particularly because of their large volume of school construction.

With the assumption, on January 1, 1964, of $49.4 million of T.T.C. debenture debt, which raised total net debt to $621.3 million, Metro's share of the total rose to 52.3 per cent. Metro has also assumed responsibility for the capital costs of all school projects approved after January 1, 1964. The area municipalities continue to be responsible for the outstanding debt of $125.2 million incurred for area school boards between 1954 and 1963, inclusive.

Table 30

NET DEBENTURE DEBT FOR GENERAL AND SCHOOL PURPOSES

as at December 31, 1954 and 1963

Municipality	Amount		Per Cent Change	
	1954	1963	Increase	Decrease
	$	$	%	%
Toronto	46,794,997	141,520,953	202.4	
North York	5,157,197	49,467,811	859.2	
Scarborough	4,115,305	45,239,847	999.3	
Etobicoke	3,309,365	32,377,951	878.4	
York	6,578,234	13,497,063	105.2	
East York	4,901,877	5,234,035	6.8	
Forest Hill	1,531,093	1,502,559		1.9
Leaside	1,862,780	2,533,950	36.0	
Mimico	359,028	540,593	50.6	
New Toronto	743,802	1,427,141	91.9	
Long Branch	547,444	1,502,980	174.5	
Weston	538,559	1,195,986	122.1	
Swansea	389,021	369,032		5.1
Total Area Municipalities	76,828,702	296,409,901	285.8	
Metro[1]	80,618,815	276,057,329	242.4	
Grand Total	157,447,517	572,467,230	263.6	

[1] Levied against all area municipalities.
Source: Annual Reports of the Commissioner of Finance, Municipality of Metropolitan Toronto, 1954 and 1963.

Table 31 shows that net debt per capita for the area as a whole rose by $220.59, from $125.87 in 1954 to $346.46 in 1963. Toronto, with $155.94, showed the largest per capita increase, followed by increases of $145.21 in Scarborough, $142.59 in Etobicoke and $121.39 in North York. In the inner suburbs, which are already built-up, the increases ranged from 69 cents in Mimico to $76.07 in Long Branch. Forest Hill and Swansea showed decreases. In 1954, per capita net debt ranged from $29.07 in Mimico to $110.40 in Leaside; in 1963, the range was much wider—from $29.78 in Mimico to $224.51 in Toronto.

Table 32 shows net debt per $1,000 of taxable assessment. The figures are submitted subject to the qualification that the debt is expressed in terms of current dollars while assessments in Metro are still based on 1940 values.

Net debt per $1,000 of taxable assessment for the area as a whole rose by $70.77, from $66.68 in 1954 to $137.45 in 1963. The increase in respect of the net debt for which the area municipalities are responsible was $38.63 and in respect of Metro's debt, $32.14. The largest increase, $68.70, was in Scarborough, followed by North York, Toronto and Etobicoke, each of which showed an increase of some $43. Five of the inner suburbs—East York, Forest Hill, Swansea, Leaside and Mimico—showed decreases ranging from $3.45 to $11.16. The increases in the remaining four ranged from $6.75 in New Toronto to $29.06 in Long Branch.

Table 31

NET DEBT PER CAPITA FOR GENERAL AND SCHOOL PURPOSES

as at December 31, 1954 and 1963

Municipality	1954	1963	Increase	Decrease
	$	$	$	$
Toronto	68.57	224.51	155.94	
North York	39.44	160.83	121.39	
Scarborough	43.00	188.21	145.21	
Etobicoke	39.79	182.38	142.59	
York	62.06	106.85	44.79	
East York	71.31	74.64	3.33	
Forest Hill	83.33	71.12		12.21
Leaside	110.40	137.32	26.92	
Mimico	29.07	29.78	.69	
New Toronto	75.77	121.10	45.33	
Long Branch	58.98	135.05	76.07	
Weston	62.85	119.80	56.95	
Swansea	44.62	39.38		5.24
Total Area Municipalities	61.42	179.39	117.97	
Metro	64.45	167.07	102.62	
Grand Total	125.87	346.46	220.59	

Sources: Population as shown in the Annual Reports of Municipal Statistics, Province of Ontario, 1954 and 1963. Debenture debt as shown in the Annual Reports of the Commissioner of Finance, Municipality of Metropolitan Toronto, 1954 and 1963.

Table 32

NET DEBT FOR GENERAL AND SCHOOL PURPOSES PER $1000 OF TAXABLE ASSESSMENT

as at December 31, 1954 and 1963

Municipality	1954	1963	Increase	Decrease
	$	$	$	$
Toronto	32.61	76.26	43.65	
North York	25.44	69.19	43.75	
Scarborough	32.31	101.01	68.70	
Etobicoke	21.70	65.01	43.31	
York	41.42	59.58	18.16	
East York	52.29	41.13		11.16
Forest Hill	30.84	20.98		9.86
Leaside	37.86	33.21		4.65
Mimico	18.94	15.49		3.45
New Toronto	26.75	33.50	6.75	
Long Branch	46.54	75.60	29.06	
Weston	32.83	46.59	13.76	
Swansea	22.48	15.84		6.64
Total Area Municipalities	32.54	71.17	38.63	
Metro	34.14	66.28	32.14	
Grand Total	66.68	137.45	70.77	

Sources: Taxable assessment as shown in the Annual Reports of Municipal Statistics, Province of Ontario, 1954 and 1963. Debenture debt as shown in the Annual Reports of the Commissioner of Finance, Municipality of Metropolitan Toronto, 1954 and 1963.

In 1954, net debt per $1,000 of taxable assessment ranged from $18.94 in Mimico to $52.29 in East York; in 1963, the range was from $15.49 in Mimico to $101.01 in Scarborough. The spread had widened very greatly. With a figure of $101.01, Scarborough had by far the highest debt burden in relation to taxable resources; Toronto ranked second with a net debt of $76.26 per $1,000 of taxable assessment. Compared with the City and the outer suburbs, all the inner suburbs, except Long Branch, are in a relatively favourable position: they were not faced with the problems of growth which confronted the outer suburbs or with the special problems of the core city.

3. DEBT CHARGES

Responsibility for the payment of debt charges is divided between the Metropolitan Corporation and the area municipalities. Metro is responsible for charges on debentures issued to finance metropolitan works, including its share of the cost of school projects, and on debentures of the area municipalities, including all school debt, which it assumed on January 1, 1954. These charges are met by metropolitan levies or, where applicable, from the revenues of the T.T.C. and the Metropolitan Waterworks System. The area municipalities are responsible for charges on debentures issued by Metro for their general and school purposes, and on debentures not assumed by Metro on January 1, 1954. The funds are provided by local tax levies and other revenues, including the revenues of local utilities.

Net debt charges for Metro and the area municipalities are shown in Table 33. In addition to interest and principal repayments on debenture debt, the figures include such items as interest on temporary financing, bank charges for debenture redemption, the premium on the purchase of United States funds, and interest and principal repayments on long term loans which have not been debentured.

The figures show that in 1963 the total net debt charges of the area, amounting to $59.7 million, were divided almost equally between Metro and the area municipalities. The charges for which the municipalities were directly responsible were distributed, by areas, as follows:

NET DEBT CHARGES, 1963

	$
Toronto	15,299,864
Three outer suburbs	12,139,182
Nine inner suburbs	2,462,392
Total	29,901,438

York Township was responsible for approximately 50 per cent of the figure for the inner suburbs.

Table 33

NET DEBT CHARGES, 1963

Municipality	General Purposes		Education		Total	
	$	Per Cent of Grand Total %	$	Per Cent of Grand Total %	$	Per Cent of Grand Total %
Toronto	11,326,199	29.26	3,973,665	18.94	15,299,864	25.64
North York	2,440,421	6.31	1,922,858	9.17	4,363,279	7.31
Scarborough	2,402,038[1]	6.21	1,816,855	8.66	4,218,893[1]	7.07
Etobicoke	2,217,207	5.73	1,339,803	6.39	3,557,010	5.96
York	708,652	1.83	476,830	2.27	1,185,482	1.99
East York	260,532	.67	130,966	.62	391,498	.66
Forest Hill	142,126	.37	Nil	—	142,126	.24
Leaside	110,000	.28	34,747	.17	144,747	.24
Mimico	41,205	.11	44,885	.21	86,090	.14
New Toronto	97,233	.25	60,042	.29	157,275	.26
Long Branch	97,632	.25	26,818	.13	124,450	.21
Weston	186,068	.48	7,964	.04	194,032	.32
Swansea	36,692	.09	Nil	—	36,692	.06
Total Area Municipalities	20,066,005	51.84	9,835,433	46.89	29,901,438	50.10
Metro	18,638,625	48.16	11,141,652	53.11	29,780,277	49.90
Grand Total	38,704,630	100.00	20,977,085	100.00	59,681,715	100.00

[1]Inclusive of net debt charges for sewer areas amounting to $1,477,812.
Sources: Annual Report of Municipal Statistics, Province of Ontario, 1963; Audits of Area Municipalities.

Table 34 shows net debt charges per capita and per $1,000 of taxable assessment in 1963. Per capita charges on debt which is the direct responsibility of the area municipalities ranged from $3.92 in Swansea to $24.27 in Toronto. Per $1,000 of taxable assessment, total net debt charges ranged from $1.57 in Swansea to $9.42 in Scarborough; for general purposes, from $1.18 in Mimico to $7.25 in Weston; and for education, from 31 cents in Weston to $4.06 in Scarborough. Forest Hill and Swansea had no direct debt charges for schools.

Table 34

NET DEBT CHARGES, 1963

Per Capita and Per $1000 of Taxable Assessment

Municipality	General Purposes		Education		Total	
	Per Capita	Per $1000 of Taxable Assessment	Per Capita	Per $1000 of Taxable Assessment	Per Capita	Per $1000 of Taxable Assessment
	$	$	$	$	$	$
Toronto	17.97	6.01	6.30	2.14	24.27	8.24
North York	7.93	3.41	6.25	2.69	14.18	6.10
Scarborough	9.99	5.36	7.56	4.06	17.55	9.42
Etobicoke	12.49	4.45	7.55	2.69	20.04	7.14
York	5.61	3.13	3.78	2.10	9.39	5.23
East York	3.71	2.05	1.87	1.03	5.58	3.08
Forest Hill	6.73	1.98	Nil	Nil	6.73	1.98
Leaside	5.96	1.44	1.88	.46	7.84	1.90
Mimico	2.27	1.18	2.47	1.29	4.74	2.47
New Toronto	8.25	2.28	5.09	1.41	13.34	3.69
Long Branch	8.77	4.91	2.41	1.35	11.18	6.26
Weston	18.64	7.25	.80	.31	19.44	7.56
Swansea	3.92	1.57	Nil	Nil	3.92	1.57
Total Area Municipalities	12.14	4.82	5.95	2.36	18.10	7.18
Metro	11.28	4.47	6.74	2.68	18.02	7.15
Grand Total	23.42	9.29	12.69	5.04	36.12	14.33

Sources: Annual Report of Municipal Statistics, Province of Ontario, 1963; Audits of Area Municipalities.

4. CONCLUSIONS

In providing the capital financing to meet the requirements of exploding growth in the area, Metro has succeeded in achieving one of its major purposes.

To protect its credit, Metro has imposed an annual limit on debenture borrowing but provincial grants, federal loans and area-wide levies for capital purposes have allowed capital expenditures to exceed this limit by a considerable margin. As the borrowing limit is self-imposed and not necessarily related to objective criteria, it can and should be varied in any year to meet special needs which may arise.

Reflecting differences among the area municipalities in the stage of development, in the rate and type of growth and in taxable resources, debt burdens are distributed unevenly. These inequalities would now be far greater if there had been no Metro to assume heavy capital costs, which the municipalities would otherwise have had to meet individually, and to borrow for the municipalities at reasonable rates of interest against the credit of the area as a whole.

The assumption by Metro of the capital costs of all school projects approved after January 1, 1964, will prevent wider inequalities in the burdens of school debt from developing. To reduce existing inequalities, Metro should also assume the school debt of the area municipalities incurred from 1954 to the end of 1963.

An analysis of debt and debt charges in the area shows that some of the developed municipalities with favourable tax bases are not bearing their proper share of the costs of capital expenditures from which they derive benefits as parts of a social and economic unit. A consolidation of municipalities would tend to a more equitable distribution of these costs over larger areas.

CHAPTER XI

EDUCATION IN METRO: 1954-1964

Before the creation of Metro, twenty-seven school boards of seven different types were operating in the area. There were rural school boards, union school boards, township school area boards, continuation school boards and boards of education with jurisdiction over one or more municipalities. It was a patchwork pattern which had developed over the years as the City and the surrounding area grew into a metropolitan centre. As a result, there was very considerable variation in the costs and standards of school services provided.

The Cumming Report recommended one board of education responsible for both elementary and secondary school education for each municipality or for groups of municipalities. This change was effected by the Metro Act. The Report also recommended metropolitan participation in planning school facilities and financing education, with the following aim:

> .... Generally speaking, the combined resources of the entire area are to be made available to support education and to overcome the most serious inequities of the present situation where some parts of the area do not have the financial resources required to provide even the bare essentials in the way of education, while others, because of the concentration of non-residential assessment or for other reasons, have taxable resources which in comparison are much greater than their needs.

The recommendations of the Cumming Report, the constitution of the Metropolitan School Board and the powers of the Board are set out in Chapter IV of this report. The Metro Act confers on the Board a coordinating role in capital financing and planning but no powers to force policies on the area boards. It has played an important role in providing a base for joint study of major problems affecting school organization in the area, but has no authority to force joint action.

1. SCHOOL ORGANIZATION

Ontario has two publicly supported elementary school systems: public schools which are open to all, and separate schools open to Roman Catholics who choose separate schools. In 1964 Roman Catholic pupils constituted more than 20 per cent of the public school enrolment. There is only one public secondary school system, to which all secondary school taxes accrue, but the Roman Catholic Church supports a number of private secondary schools.

There are now eleven boards of education operating public schools in Metropolitan Toronto, one in each area municipality except the three Lakeshore municipalities of Mimico, New Toronto and Long Branch, where the Lakeshore District Board of Education, a combined board, has operated since 1951.

School boards are composed of trustees, whose number varies from six in Swansea and East York to twenty in Toronto. Except for the trustees appointed by the Metropolitan Separate School Board, who may act in matters not exclusively affecting public elementary schools, all trustees are elected every two years at the regular municipal elections. For this purpose, the City of Toronto, the three outer townships, and York are divided into wards, while in the other school districts the trustees are elected at large. There are 105 elected trustees on the eleven local boards.

Table 35 shows six types of public elementary school and nine types of secondary school in Metropolitan Toronto. The traditional two-level system, with eight grades of elementary and five grades of secondary education, has been retained only in Scarborough. Swansea has no secondary school. All other school districts have a full or partial three-level system: the first is kindergarten to grade 6; the second is grades 7 and 8, called senior public school, or grades 7, 8 and 9, called junior high school; and the third is the secondary school. The separate elementary schools teach up to grade 8 only, except in five schools where grades 9 and 10 are also taught.

School district boundaries, except in the case of the Lakeshore District, are coterminous with the boundaries of the area municipalities. The districts therefore vary greatly in size, school population and resources. In its brief to the Commission, the Metropolitan School Board said that studies made by it support the conclusion "that a number of school districts recognized under the Metropolitan Act are too small to warrant continuation as separate units in a metropolitan complex." The brief also said:

> When the Metropolitan Act was passed the Toronto Board of Education was the only board which provided a fully diversified program of education from kindergarten to grade 13. The townships of York and East York were almost large enough to support the full program but were dependent upon their neighbours for certain phases of the program. The three large outer townships, Etobicoke, North York, and Scarborough were in an early stage of development.
>
> Over the past ten years two developments have taken place. First, the diversity of the basic program has increased, and, unless a great number of services were assumed by a central authority, both East York and York townships would be scarcely large enough within their present boundaries to offer the complete basic program. Etobicoke, North York and Scarborough, on the other hand, have grown so rapidly that they now rank among the largest urban areas in the Province. It is a fact that if each of these three large suburbs were an urban area, separated by real rather than imaginary boundaries from other urban districts, each could support on its own a fully diversified programme of education. But, as has so often been pointed out and is so clearly manifest in the Metropolitan Act, these areas are not independent urban communities, but are parts of a closely-linked metropolitan complex.

Table 35

TYPES OF SCHOOLS IN METROPOLITAN TORONTO
SEPTEMBER, 1964

ELEMENTARY	Kindergarten to Grade 8	Kindergarten to Grade 6	Technical	Kindergarten to Grade 6 and Senior Public Combined	Senior Public	Junior High School	Special Auxiliary	Total
Toronto........	8	64	2	18	7		1 (Ortho) 1 (Deaf)	99
North York.....	16	74				16		106
Scarborough....	78							78
Etobicoke......		42		7	9			58
York..........	14	5		2	1			22
East York......	1	10				4		15
Forest Hill.....		3				1		4
Leaside........		2		2				4
Lakeshore......	4	3		2				9
Weston........		2			1			3
Swansea.......	1							1
	122	205	2	31	18	21	2	399

SECONDARY	Academic	Commerical	Academic Commercial	Academic Technical	Commercial Technical	Composite	Terminal Vocational	Special Vocational	Total
Toronto........	10	2	1		1	1	1	3	21
North York.....	1		5			6	1	1	13
Scarborough....			6			5			12
Etobicoke......	4		4			3			12
York..........	2		1		1			1¹	5
East York......			1						1
Forest Hill.....	1								1
Leaside........			1						1
Lakeshore......			1	1					2
Weston........						1			1
Swansea.......									
	18	2	20	1	2	16	2	6	69

¹Operated under the Elementary School division.
Source: Metropolitan School Board.

2. GROWTH OF THE PUBLIC SCHOOL SYSTEM

The historical and statistical data on the growth of the public school system during the first ten years of Metro, which are here presented, are in large part based on a study made for the Commission, at its request, by the Metropolitan School Board, entitled "Historical and Statistical Review of Public Education in Metropolitan Toronto, 1953-1963."

i. *Enrolment*

The increase in public school enrolment between 1954 and 1964, shown in Table 36, indicates the magnitude of the problems which have faced school authorities in the area. During this period total public elementary school enrolment rose by 92,760 from 146,392 to 239,152, or 63.4 per cent. Secondary school enrolment increased by 58,200 from 34,465 to 92,665, or 169 per cent. By far the largest growth took place in the three outer suburbs.

Public elementary school enrolment increased by 208 per cent in Scarborough, 160 per cent in North York and 143 per cent in Etobicoke. Toronto showed an increase of 12 per cent; York, 13.6 per cent; the Lakeshore District, 17 per cent; and Swansea, 4.6 per cent. Four inner suburbs showed decreases: Leaside, 29 per cent; Forest Hill, 23.4 per cent; East York, 15.4 per cent; and Weston, 6 per cent.

Table 36

PUBLIC SCHOOL ENROLMENT

September 1954 and 1964

Area Board	Elementary			Secondary		
	1954	1964	Per Cent Change	1954	1964	Per Cent Change
Toronto	64,934	72,849	+12.2	18,225	30,125	+65.3
North York	21,237	55,237	+160.1	2,735	19,658	+618.8
Scarborough	15,608	48,095	+208.1	2,141	15,066	+603.7
Etobicoke	12,921	31,366	+142.8	2,117	13,195	+523.3
York	12,779	14,521	+13.6	3,375	5,729	+69.7
East York	8,256	6,982	−15.4	1,761	2,828	+60.6
Forest Hill	2,207	1,691	−23.4	914	1,225	+34.0
Leaside	2,295	1,626	−29.2	788	1,148	+45.7
Lakeshore[1]	4,013	4,690	+16.9	1,104	2,133	+93.2
Weston	1,358	1,275	−6.1	1,305	1,558	+19.4
Swansea	784	820	+4.6	[2]	[2]	—
Area Total	146,392	239,152	+63.4	34,465	92,665	+168.9

[1]Mimico, New Toronto and Long Branch.
[2]Students attend Toronto schools.
Source: Metropolitan School Board.

The change in public elementary school enrolment by areas in Metro was as follows:

PUBLIC ELEMENTARY SCHOOL ENROLMENT, 1954 AND 1964

	1954	1964	Increase
Toronto	64,934	72,849	7,915
Three outer suburbs	49,766	134,698	84,932
Nine inner suburbs	31,692	31,605	−87
Area Total	146,392	239,152	92,760

The three outer suburbs experienced 91.5 per cent of the total increase, while Scarborough and North York each show an increase which is greater than the total enrolment in the nine inner suburbs.

The percentage increase in secondary school enrolment, as shown in Table 36, was much greater than the corresponding figure for the elementary schools. Again, the bulk of the growth was in the three outer suburbs: North York showed a rise of 618.8 per cent; Scarborough, 603.7 per cent; and Etobicoke, 523 per cent. The increase in Toronto was 65 per cent, and in the remaining municipalities ranged from 19.4 per cent in Weston to 93 per cent in the Lakeshore District.

The increase in secondary school enrolment by areas was as follows:

SECONDARY SCHOOL ENROLMENT, 1954 AND 1964

	1954	1964	Increase
Toronto	18,225	30,125	11,900
Three outer suburbs	6,993	47,919	40,926
Nine inner suburbs	9,247	14,621	5,374
Area Total	34,465	92,665	58,200

With 70 per cent of the growth taking place in the three outer suburbs, their secondary school enrolment, which was one-fifth of the area total in 1954, is now more than one-half. In the same period their proportion of total elementary enrolment rose from 34 per cent to 56 per cent. These figures explain some of the major problems in school finance which the area has faced.

ii. *Number of Schools*

In making possible the expansion of school accommodation and facilities to meet the demands created by the enormous growth of school-age population, the metropolitan system of government in Toronto achieved one of its main purposes. Without Metro's credit base, the school accommodation requirements of the three large and populous outer suburbs, with the bulk of the increased enrolment, could not have been met. This is widely acknowledged. For example, the North York Board of Education, in its brief to the Commission, said:

> During the past ten years, the educational system of North York has exhibited unprecedented development, and is now the third largest local education authority in Canada; this could not have been accomplished without the support of the Metropolitan Government.

For the period from 1954 to 1964, the Metropolitan School Board reports 221 new schools built, 419 additions made and 506 new sites or extensions to sites acquired, at a total capital cost of approximately $372 million. The area was provided with 199,300 new pupil spaces. As shown in Table 37, the largest building programmes were in the three outer suburbs. The number of public elementary schools increased from 48 to 90 in North York, from 32 to 78 in Scarborough and from 21 to 42 in Etobicoke. With no intermediate schools in 1954, North York and Etobicoke now have sixteen each, while the number of secondary schools has multiplied by six in each of the three outer suburbs. Making allowance for changes under the three-level system, under which a number of elementary schools became composite schools or solely intermediate grade schools, and for new school buildings which replaced obsolescent buildings, particularly in Toronto, there was a net increase of 191 schools in the area between 1954 and 1964.

In providing nearly 200,000 new pupil spaces, the school building programme, which is a joint effort of the area school boards, the Metropolitan School Board and the Metropolitan Council, has achieved remarkable results. Nevertheless, there is still a shortage of classrooms and portable classrooms continue to be used.

iii. *Teaching Staff*

From 1954 to 1964 the number of teachers in Metro was doubled, rising from 6,094 to 12,899. Table 38 shows that 75 per cent of the increase was in the three outer suburbs: in Scarborough, the number of teachers rose from 450 to 2,407; in Etobicoke, from 494 to 1,612; and in North York, from 850 to 2,886. Toronto showed an increase of 1,217 teachers.

Table 37

NUMBER OF PUBLIC SCHOOLS, 1954 AND 1964

Area Board	Elementary		Intermediate		Secondary	
	1954	1964	1954	1964	1954	1964
Toronto	86	74	2	25[1]	19	21
North York	48	90	—	16	2	13
Scarborough	32	78	—	—	2	12
Etobicoke	21	42	—	16[1]	2	12
York	19	19	—	3[1]	4	5[2]
East York	13	11	3	4	1	1
Forest Hill	3	3	1	1	1	1
Leaside	3	2	—	2[1]	1	1
Lakeshore	7	7	—	2[1]	2	2
Weston	3	2	—	1	1	1
Swansea	1	1	—	—	—	—
Area Total	236	329	6	70[1]	35	69[2]

[1]Includes composite schools teaching kindergarten to grade 6 and senior public school, grades 7 and 8.
Includes a special vocational school operated under the elementary school division.
Source: Metropolitan School Board.

With more teachers performing tasks of a special nature, the pupil-teacher ratio has declined in every school district. Over the area as a whole, it fell from 29.7 to 25.7. The range in 1954 was from 25.4 in Forest Hill to 39.4 in Scarborough, which was in transition from rural to urban status. In 1964 the ratio ranged from 20 in Forest Hill to 27.6 in Etobicoke. The figure for Toronto is 25. The lowest ratios are 20 in Forest Hill, 21.2 in Leaside and 21.8 in Weston.

Table 38

TEACHERS IN PUBLIC SCHOOL SYSTEM, 1954 AND 1964

Area Board	Number		Pupil-Teacher Ratio	
	1954	1964	1954	1964
Toronto	2,888	4,105	28.8	25.1
North York	850	2,886	28.2	26.0
Scarborough	450	2,407	39.4	26.2
Etobicoke	494	1,612	30.4	27.6
York	532	783	30.4	25.9
East York	320	401	31.3	24.5
Forest Hill	123	146	25.4	20.0
Leaside	118	131	26.1	21.2
Lakeshore	192	264	26.7	25.8
Weston	97	130	27.5	21.8
Swansea	30	34	26.1	24.1
Area Total	6,094	12,899	29.7	25.7

Source: Metropolitan School Board.

The records of the area school boards, as of September 30, 1964, show the percentage distribution of public elementary teachers with university degrees as follows:

PERCENTAGE OF PUBLIC ELEMENTARY (K-8)
SCHOOL TEACHERS WITH UNIVERSITY DEGREE

	%
Forest Hill	33.7
Leaside	29.4
Weston	23.5
Toronto	21.8
York	18.1
Swansea	17.6
East York	16.8
North York	15.6
Etobicoke	15.1
Scarborough	10.0
Lakeshore	8.2

The percentage distribution of secondary school teachers with type "A" specialist certificate is shown as follows:

PERCENTAGE OF SECONDARY SCHOOL (9-13)
TEACHERS WITH TYPE "A" CERTIFICATE

	%
Etobicoke	52.6
Toronto	48.2
Weston	45.9
York	41.5
Leaside	41.0
Forest Hill	37.1
Scarborough	35.4
Lakeshore	30.3
North York	30.2
East York	29.5

It will be noted that Etobicoke has the highest percentage of specialist secondary teachers. The Toronto Board of Education, in its brief to the Commission, criticizing incentives offered by Etobicoke to attract the best teachers, said that Toronto "has been the fascinated spectator at a market where its own offers to teachers are trumped by boards whose resources are swelled by City funds." Etobicoke is one of the "receiving boards" under the system of maintenance assistance payments.

The area boards have for some years co-operated on a voluntary basis through the Metropolitan Salary Coordinating Committee in efforts to co-ordinate salary and hiring policies. The committee, however, lacks the power to enforce its recommendations, with the result that each board remains free to set the salaries of the teachers it wishes to engage. While, in fact, basic salaries are virtually uniform in the area, the shortage of secondary teachers has led to the introduction of special incentives in salary schedules. Etobicoke, in particular, has asserted its autonomy in this regard. A report entitled "The Case for Equalization of Educational Opportunity in Metro Toronto", prepared in 1962 by a special committee of the Metropolitan School Board, described the situation as follows:

> In the highly competitive market for teachers, the boards within the framework of their local autonomy have out-manoeuvred each other in the development of "gimmicks" and special features such as merit plans, double increments at the third and seventh years, an unreasonably large number of department heads, subject chairmen, and so on. These are salary features which the present situation has produced. In retrospect there is little evidence that the public interest has been well served by the effort to preserve autonomy in a matter where autonomy seems impossible of attainment.

On the instruction of a large majority of the area boards, the Metropolitan School Board has from time to time requested an amendment of the Metro Act to provide for uniform teacher salary schedules throughout the area. A special committee of the Board, which reported on school finance in 1963, pointed out that it was difficult for boards which contribute in maintenance assistance payments more than they receive, to become reconciled to the adoption "of higher teachers' salaries in an effort to attract a greater share of the good teachers" by any board benefitting from the metropolitan system of payments.

The majority of the briefs submitted to the Commission were also strongly in favour of uniform salary schedules. Their reasoning, which I find convincing, was summed up by Mr. J. Young, chairman of the York Township Board of Education, when he said at the hearings (Proceedings, pp. 749, 753):

> York has consistently supported the view that a Metropolitan Salary Schedule could be of benefit to the whole area. Such a salary schedule, Mr. Commissioner, could recognize many of the problems facing Boards respecting placement of teachers and, if necessary, provide special allowances for teaching in less centrally located schools, but it would enable the best teachers to be placed where they are needed. The competitive factor would be eliminated from the point of view of one Board vying against another for teacher recruitment. At the same time due recognition could be given to the teachers' legitimate claims for adequate salary standards. . . .
>
> . . . . I would like to say again that I do not consider a uniform salary schedule to be the complete answer to the present teacher problems, neither do I consider that unrestricted competition amongst the limited pool of teachers, experienced teachers that we have available for our area, is an answer.

3. GROWTH OF THE SEPARATE SCHOOL SYSTEM

The separate school system has also experienced a great increase in enrolment. Between September 1953 and September 1964, the number of resident pupils rose by more than 204 per cent, from 18,766 to 57,079. To meet this growth, the Metropolitan Separate School Board provided between 1,000 and 1,100 additional teachers and constructed 55 schools, increasing the number of separate elementary schools in operation to 101. It spent some $21 million on capital plant, but officials estimate that this represented only 50 per cent of requirements. With its limited resources, the Separate School Board does not expect to be able to meet more than 60 per cent of its requirements by 1975.

The constitution and powers of the Metropolitan Separate School Board are set out in Chapter IV of this report.

4. ASSESSMENT AND FINANCE

The Cumming Report regarded the solution of the problem of financing education as "vital to the success of any reform of municipal institutions in the metropolitan area." It found that "the magnitude and urgency of this problem justifies the use of all local financial resources of the area, regardless of their distribution among the existing local municipalities, to provide adequate school accommodation and to give substantial assistance to the education of public and secondary school pupils living in any part of the area."

The basic problem in 1953 was to find an equitable method of financing school costs. The solution proposed in the Cumming Report was to continue the local school boards with "almost all their present powers, duties and responsibilities" and to make available to them "a major source of revenue" from an area-wide levy, with "a corresponding reduction in local levies." In respect of capital costs, the resources of the area as a whole were to be used to provide essential accommodation "up to a reasonable minimum standard only." While these recommendations were implemented in principle by the Metro Act, serious inequalities in financing school costs have not been eliminated.

i. *Assessment Per Pupil*

Assessments per pupil, which are a measure of taxable resources in relation to needs, vary widely over the area. Table 39 shows that the disparities have grown since 1954, when per pupil assessments ranged from $9,900 in Scarborough to $23,900 in Forest Hill. In 1964 the range was from $9,700 in Scarborough to $45,700 in Leaside.

Over the ten-year period, public elementary school assessment per pupil increased in all school districts, except Scarborough. The largest increase by far was in Leaside, where the figure rose by 128.5 per cent, from $20,000 in 1954 to $45,700 in 1964. This is explained by the combination of a decrease of 29 per cent in pupil enrolment and an increase of 35 per cent in per capita taxable assessment. Similar reasons account for an increase of 70 per cent, from $23,900 to $40,600, in per pupil assessment in Forest Hill. Swansea ranked third in 1964, with $27,500, or 32 per cent below the figure for Forest Hill. With an increase of 208 per cent in enrolment and of 24 per cent in per capita taxable assessment, the per pupil assessment in Scarborough declined to $9,700, or 21 per cent of the figure for Leaside.

In order of assessment per public elementary pupil, school districts ranked as follows in 1954 and in 1964:

1954	$	*Rank*	*1964*	$
Forest Hill	23,900	1	Leaside	45,700
Toronto	23,400	2	Forest Hill	40,600
Swansea	21,000	3	Swansea	27,500
Leaside	20,000	4	Toronto	25,800
Lakeshore	14,200	5	Weston	22,800
Etobicoke	13,000	6	Lakeshore	19,300
Weston	12,300	7	Etobicoke	17,400
York	11,700	8	East York	15,300
East York	10,700	9	North York	14,400
North York	10,700	10	York	13,900
Scarborough	9,900	11	Scarborough	9,700
Area Wide	17,200	Average	Area Wide	18,000

Table 39

ASSESSMENT PER RESIDENT PUBLIC SCHOOL PUPIL, 1954 AND 1964[1]

Municipality	Type of School	1954 $	1964 $	Per Cent Increase %	Per Cent Decrease %
Toronto	Elementary	23,400	25,800	10.3	
	Secondary	90,300	78,300		13.3
North York	Elementary	10,700	14,400	34.6	
	Secondary	64,300	44,000		31.6
Scarborough	Elementary	9,900	9,700		2.0
	Secondary	68,200	34,100		50.0
Etobicoke	Elementary	13,000	17,400	33.8	
	Secondary	66,500	46,000		30.8
York	Elementary	11,700	13,900	18.8	
	Secondary	49,200	42,000		14.6
East York	Elementary	10,700	15,300	43.0	
	Secondary	47,000	37,800		19.6
Forest Hill	Elementary	23,900	40,600	69.9	
	Secondary	55,800	51,800		7.2
Leaside	Elementary	20,000	45,700	128.5	
	Secondary	61,800	64,700	4.7	
Lakeshore	Elementary	14,200	19,300	35.9	
	Secondary	56,900	53,800		5.4
Weston	Elementary	12,300	22,800	85.4	
	Secondary	30,600	46,100	50.7	
Swansea	Elementary	21,000	27,500	31.0	
	Secondary	68,700	54,500		20.7
Metro Average	Elementary	17,200	18,000	4.7	
	Secondary	74,300	53,100		28.5

[1]Calculated by dividing the assessments prepared in 1953 and 1963 by the number of resident pupils enrolled as at October 31st, 1953 and 1963.
Source: Metropolitan School Board.

While public elementary school enrolment in the area increased by more than 63 per cent between 1954 and 1964, the corresponding increase in secondary school enrolment was 169 per cent, with the result that secondary school assessment per pupil declined in every school district, except Leaside and Weston. The impact was felt particularly in the three outer suburbs, where secondary school enrolment increased by almost 600 per cent. Accordingly, between 1954 and 1964, secondary school assessment per pupil declined from $68,200 to $34,100, or 50 per cent, in Scarborough; from $64,300 to $44,000, or 31.6 per cent, in North York; and from $66,500 to $46,000 or 30.8 per cent, in Etobicoke. The decline in the other districts ranged from 5.4 per cent in the Lakeshore District to 20.7 per cent in Swansea, while Weston showed an increase of 50.7 per cent and Leaside, an increase of 4.7 per cent.

In order of assessment per secondary school pupil, the rank was as follows in 1954 and in 1964:

	1954 $	Rank		1964 $
Toronto	90,300	1	Toronto	78,300
Swansea	68,700	2	Leaside	64,700
Scarborough	68,200	3	Swansea	54,500
Etobicoke	66,500	4	Lakeshore	53,800
North York	64,300	5	Forest Hill	51,800
Leaside	61,800	6	Weston	46,100
Lakeshore	56,900	7	Etobicoke	46,000
Forest Hill	55,800	8	North York	44,000
York	49,200	9	York	42,000
East York	47,000	10	East York	37,800
Weston	30,600	11	Scarborough	34,100
Area Wide	74,300	Average	Area Wide	53,100

The range in per pupil assessments for both public elementary and secondary schools shows wide inequalities in the ability of different municipalities to finance school costs. Scarborough, with the greatest relative needs, has the smallest relative tax base.

ii. *Maintenance Assistance Payments*

For greater equalization of burdens, the Cumming Report recommended that a portion of the annual costs of public elementary and secondary education should be financed by provincial grants and the proceeds of an area-wide levy. Implementing this proposal, the Metro Act provides that, with minor exceptions, all legislative grants for schools previously paid to the local school boards should henceforth be paid to the Metropolitan School Board and that this Board should make annual "maintenance assistance payments" to each area board in respect of each resident pupil of average daily attendance in elementary, academic secondary, commercial secondary and technical secondary schools. The payments vary according to category of pupil but must be uniform for each category throughout the area. In 1954 and 1955, the first two years of operation, the payments were fixed by the Provincial Government at $150 per elementary pupil, $250 per academic secondary pupil and $300 per vocational secondary pupil. Since 1955 the amounts have been determined by the Metropolitan School Board.

Table 40 shows the increases in maintenance assistance payments since 1955 and relates the payments to the average costs per pupil in each year, excluding Metro debt charges, as reported by the Metropolitan School Board. In 1963 the payments were $205 per elementary pupil, $335 per academic secondary pupil, $380 per commercial secondary pupil, and $535 per technical secondary pupil. For all categories, except technical schools, the payments in

Table 40

SCHOOL MAINTENANCE ASSISTANCE PAYMENTS, 1954 TO 1964

	1955[1]	1956	1957	1958	1959	1960	1961	1962	1963	1964
Elementary										
(1) M.A.P. ($)	150	150	150	180	180	190	190	205	205	250
(2) Unit Cost ($)	251	271	288	313	350	372	384	395	408	
(3) (1) As a percentage of (2) (%)	59.8	55.4	52.1	57.5	51.4	51.1	49.5	51.9	50.2	
Secondary										
Academic:										
(1) M.A.P. ($)	250	250	250	300	300	315	315	335	335	365
(2) Unit Cost ($)	423	437	478	521	609	612	608	605	636	
(3) (1) As a percentage of (2) (%)	59.1	57.2	52.3	57.6	49.3	51.5	51.8	55.4	52.7	
Commercial:										
(1) M.A.P. ($)	300	300	300	350	350	350	350	380	380	420
(2) Unit Cost ($)	464	517	566	585	661	693	669	652	651	
(3) (1) As a percentage of (2) (%)	64.7	58.0	53.0	59.8	53.0	50.5	52.3	58.3	58.4	
Technical:										
(1) M.A.P. ($)	300	400	400	525	525	535	535	535	535	575
(2) Unit Cost ($)	626	721	838	890	940	909	938	1020	1060	
(3) (1) As a percentage of (2) (%)	47.9	55.5	47.7	59.0	55.9	58.9	57.0	52.5	50.5	

[1]Maintenance Assistance Payments were made at the same rate in 1954 and 1955.
Source: Metropolitan School Board.

1963 represented a smaller proportion of average per pupil costs than in 1955, as shown in the following table:

MAINTENANCE ASSISTANCE PAYMENTS
AS PERCENTAGE OF AVERAGE COSTS PER PUPIL

	1955 %	1963 %
Elementary	59.8	50.2
Academic Secondary	59.1	52.7
Commercial Secondary	64.7	58.4
Technical Secondary	47.9	50.5

It is apparent that the increases in the payments did not keep pace with the rising costs of education, except in the case of technical secondary schools. Coupled with the requirement that the amounts in each category must be uniform for all school boards in the area, regardless of circumstances and needs, this has had the effect of reducing the equalizing influence of maintenance assistance payments.

The figures for 1964 show a considerable increase in payments for each category. They now amount to $250 per elementary pupil, $365 per academic secondary pupil, $420 per commercial secondary pupil and $575 per technical secondary pupil. These increases are related to a revision of the provincial school grants system and the repeal of The Residential and Farm School Tax Assistance Grants Act in 1964. Under this Act, school tax assistance grants had been made directly to the area boards; in 1963 the amounts were $20 per elementary pupil, $30 per academic secondary pupil, and $40 per vocational secondary pupil. When the Act was repealed, these direct grants were discontinued and, under the new grant scheme, a corresponding amount was added to the general legislative grant payable to the Metropolitan School Board. The latter then increased its maintenance assistance payments by $45 per elementary pupil, $30 per academic secondary pupil, and $40 per vocational secondary school pupil. In the case of secondary schools, the increases, therefore, merely replaced the Residential and Farm Tax Assistance grants which the area boards had previously received directly from the Province. In respect of elementary school pupils, there was an effective increase of $25 per pupil.

In its brief to the Commission, the Toronto Board of Education described the maintenance assistance payments as "a device by which the wealthier boards, particularly the City of Toronto, subsidized other boards with smaller resources", the principal beneficiaries being the mushrooming three outer suburbs together with York and East York. The City's brief complained that the metropolitan system of school finance has enhanced the schooling available to suburban children by imposing an unfair burden on the City's taxpayers. I find that these complaints are not justified.

One of the main purposes in the creation of Metro was to pool the resources of the area for the provision of certain essential services of area-wide significance. In respect of education, such pooling necessarily means that the municipalities with larger resources, like Toronto, will contribute more in taxes than they receive from metropolitan revenues, while those with smaller resources will receive in metropolitan payments more than they contribute in taxes. There is the further consideration that the growing suburbs, which are "receiving" municipalities, have contributed materially to the favourable assessment ratio and, therefore, larger taxable resources of the City, by providing the homes and schools for the rapidly growing population of the area, which is mainly employed in Toronto. The City could not have maintained so favourable an assessment ratio if it had been called upon to absorb and to provide services for a large influx of people. In the circumstances, it is only fair that it should be called upon to contribute to the support of education in the suburbs whose taxable capacity is largely dependent upon residential assessment.

iii. *Public School Operating Costs*

The operating costs of Metro's public school system increased by 200 per cent between 1954 and 1963, rising from $49.4 million to $149.8 million. On a per pupil basis, the costs vary widely between school districts. Table 41 compares the figures for each area board in 1963 with those for 1957, the earliest year for which comparable figures are available.

In 1957 public elementary costs per pupil per annum ranged from $283 in Weston to $409 in Forest Hill; in 1963 the range was from $378 in Scarborough to $611 in Leaside. The difference between the highest and lowest costs per pupil rose from $126 to $233. The school districts ranked as follows in each of the years:

PUBLIC ELEMENTARY COSTS PER PUPIL PER ANNUM

	1957 $	Rank		1963 $	Rank
Forest Hill	409	1	Leaside	611	1
Leaside	351	2	Forest Hill	589	2
Toronto	337	3	Toronto	523	3
Swansea	324	4	East York	460	4
East York	322	5	AVERAGE	453	—
AVERAGE	319	—	North York	448	5
North York	318	6	Swansea	427	6
Scarborough	311	7	York	426	7
Etobicoke	297	8	Etobicoke	416	8
Lakeshore	289	9	Lakeshore	413	9
York	286	10	Weston	410	10
Weston	283	11	Scarborough	378	11
Range	126		Range	233	

Table 41

PUBLIC ELEMENTARY AND SECONDARY SCHOOL COSTS PER PUPIL, 1957 AND 1963[1]

Municipality	ELEMENTARY			ACADEMIC SECONDARY			COMMERCIAL SECONDARY			TECHNICAL SECONDARY		
	1957	1963	Per Cent Increase	1957	1963	Per Cent Increase	1957	1963	Per Cent Increase	1957	1963	Per Cent Increase
	$	$	%	$	$	%	$	$	%	$	$	%
Toronto	337	523	55	604	768	27	625	640	2	909	1,212	33
North York	318	448	41	585	650	11	711	831	17	1,081	1,078	—
Scarborough	311	378	22	472	670	42	534	728	36	900	1,018	13
Etobicoke	297	416	40	494	663	34	578	818	42	[4]	1,071	—
York	286	426	49	471	621	32	462	618	34	653	860	32
East York	322	460	43	432	590	37	518	677	31	[4]	[4]	—
Forest Hill	409	589	44	605	796	32	[3]	[3]	—	[4]	[4]	—
Leaside	351	611	74	521	680	31	[3]	586	—	[4]	[4]	—
Lakeshore	289	413	43	522	663	27	606	810	34	777	957	23
Weston	283	410	45	372	562	51	453	586	29	804	797	1
Swansea	324	427	32	[2]	[2]	—	[3]	[3]	—	[4]	[4]	—
Average	319	453	42	538	684	27	608	711	17	888	1,111	25

[1] Includes Metro Debt charges and the costs of operating The Metropolitan School Board.
[2] No academic secondary school.
[3] No commercial secondary school.
[4] No technical secondary school.
Source: Metropolitan School Board.

For academic secondary pupils, operating costs ranged from $372 in Weston to $605 in Forest Hill in 1957, and from $562 in Weston to $796 in Forest Hill in 1963. The districts ranked as follows:

ACADEMIC SECONDARY COSTS PER PUPIL PER ANNUM

	1957 $	Rank		1963 $	Rank
Forest Hill	605	1	Forest Hill	796	1
Toronto	604	2	Toronto	768	2
North York	585	3	AVERAGE	684	—
AVERAGE	538	—	Leaside	680	3
Lakeshore	522	4	Scarborough	670	4
Leaside	521	5	Etobicoke	663 ⎫	5
Etobicoke	494	6	Lakeshore	663 ⎭	
Scarborough	472	7	North York	650	7
York	471	8	York	621	8
East York	432	9	East York	590	9
Weston	372	10	Weston	562	10
Range	233		Range	234	

Expenditure per pupil in commercial and technical secondary schools is considerably higher than for academic secondary pupils. The average costs in 1963 were $711 per commercial pupil and $1,111 per technical pupil, compared with $684 per academic pupil. There were no technical secondary schools in Forest Hill, Leaside, East York and Swansea and no commercial secondary schools in Forest Hill and Swansea, which has no secondary school of any type. In 1964 more than 50 per cent of the pupils in the technical schools and 35 per cent of the pupils in the commercial schools of the area were enrolled in the City of Toronto.

Area school boards providing commercial and technical secondary schools ranked by expenditure per pupil, as follows:

COMMERCIAL SECONDARY COSTS PER PUPIL PER ANNUM

	1957 $	Rank		1963 $	Rank
North York	711	1	North York	831	1
Toronto	625	2	Etobicoke	818	2
AVERAGE	608	—	Lakeshore	810	3
Lakeshore	606	3	Scarborough	728	4
Etobicoke	578	4	AVERAGE	711	—
Scarborough	534	5	East York	677	5
East York	518	6	Toronto	640	6
York	462	7	York	618	7
Weston	453	8	Leaside	586 ⎫	8
			Weston	586 ⎭	
Range	258		Range	245	

TECHNICAL SECONDARY COSTS PER PUPIL PER ANNUM

	1957 $	Rank		1963 $	Rank
North York	1,081	1	Toronto	1,212	1
Toronto	909	2	Average	1,111	—
Scarborough	900	3	North York	1,078	2
Average	888	—	Etobicoke	1,071	3
Weston	804	4	Scarborough	1,018	4
Lakeshore	777	5	Lakeshore	957	5
York	653	6	York	860	6
			Weston	797	7
Range	428		Range	415	

School operating costs are influenced by a number of factors which account for some of the variations shown. These are set out concisely in the Gathercole Report[1]:

> In education, the per pupil costs of the school boards are influenced by such factors as the number of pupils per classroom, the academic qualifications and length of service of the teachers, the size of the school units, the extent to which capital expenditures are financed out of revenue and the school building programme. For example, some school boards, particularly those which are supported by a relatively high assessment, are likely to be more selective in the recruitment of teachers and hire not only relatively more teachers with university degrees but more specialists. Furthermore, boards that are experiencing a rapid growth in enrolment tend to have not only higher debt charges but a teaching staff which, on an average, has fewer years of experience and consequently a lower salary per teacher.

The foregoing is confirmed by Table 42, which shows, for each of the area boards, the various components of school operating costs in 1963 in dollars per pupil day, excluding expenditures by Metro on behalf of the boards, such as area-wide debt charges.

Total local operating costs in 1963 ranged from $2.01 per pupil day in Swansea, which has no secondary school, to $3.18 in Forest Hill. The average for the area was $2.49, which, apart from Forest Hill, was only exceeded by Toronto, with $2.98, and Leaside, with $2.95. In the three large outer suburbs, the figures were $2.35 for North York, $2.24 for Etobicoke, and $2.04 for Scarborough.

Table 42 shows that instructional costs per pupil day ranged from $1.32 in Scarborough to $2.38 in Forest Hill. Scarborough has a relatively high pupil-teacher ratio, while the average teaching experience of its teachers is about five

---

[1] A Report on The Metropolitan Toronto System of Government, by the Ontario Department of Economics, November 1961.

Table 42

AREA SCHOOL BOARD OPERATING COSTS PER PUPIL DAY, 1963

School Board	Instructional Costs	Administration	Plant Operation	Plant Maintenance	Local Debt Charges	Capital Out of Current	Miscellaneous[1]	Total Cost
	$	$	$	$	$	$	$	$
Toronto	1.64	.29	.30	.33	.23	.19	Nil	2.98
North York	1.52	.16	.30	.11	.17	.10	−.01	2.35
Scarborough	1.32	.16	.25	.07	.18	.07	−.01	2.04
Etobicoke	1.50	.16	.22	.08	.20	.07	+.01	2.24
York	1.60	.17	.23	.12	.13	.10	Nil	2.35
East York	1.66	.12	.24	.15	.08	.10	−.02	2.33
Forest Hill	2.38	.26	.36	.10	Nil	.09	−.01	3.18
Leaside	2.08	.19	.32	.16	.07	.15	−.02	2.95
Lakeshore	1.67	.10	.26	.08	.11	.18	+.01	2.41
Weston	1.88	.13	.25	.12	.02	.08	−.01	2.47
Swansea	1.47	.05	.31	.18	Nil	.01	−.01	2.01
Area Average	1.56	.20	.27	.17	.18	.12	−.01	2.49

[1]This is a balancing entry including miscellaneous expenditure, less miscellaneous items of revenue such as rent of school halls, milk grants and the local share of the proceeds on sale of capital equipment, etc.
Source: Metropolitan School Board.

and a half years, as compared with about ten and a half years in Toronto. In its brief to the Commission, the Scarborough Board of Education, which has not introduced intermediate schools, showed comparative expenditures on teachers' salaries per pupil in 1962, as follows:

	Elementary	Secondary
	$	$
Toronto	246.08	490.35
North York	232.27	387.03
Etobicoke	230.32	400.53
Scarborough	198.60	357.80

Plant operation costs ranged from 22 cents in Etobicoke to 36 cents in Forest Hill. Maintenance costs were highest in Toronto, with 33 cents per pupil day, as compared with an average of 17 cents for the area. This reflects the age of school plant in Toronto: 13 of its existing public elementary schools were constructed before 1900 and 23 between 1900 and 1915. Toronto, with the widest range of services, had the highest administration costs, and also led in local debt charges per pupil, followed by the three outer suburbs where most of the new schools were built.

It is clear from the foregoing that variations in per pupil costs do not in themselves measure variations in the quality of education provided. Equality of expenditures does not necessarily mean equality of education. There are factors affecting costs over which the school boards have little control and such costs vary from school to school in the same municipality. Nevertheless, while all boards are undoubtedly providing a good basic education, differences of the order of $230 in average costs per pupil per annum point to differences in the range and standards of educational services provided in the area. The Toronto and District Labour Council, in its brief to the Commission, pointed out that:

> In Toronto, a boy in Grade Seven may have the benefits of a science laboratory, music room and library. He can have specialist teachers in art, music, physical training. Dental and psychiatric staffs provide free service to children who need them. In Mimico he would have none of these services except for a library at one school. Weston has no public school libraries, Scarborough has no senior public schools or junior high schools with specialized facilities.

iv. *Taxation*

School operating costs are financed by metropolitan and local tax levies and provincial grants. The proportion contributed by each in 1954 and 1963, excluding levies and grants for capital purposes, was as follows:

FINANCING OF SCHOOL OPERATING COSTS

	1954		1963	
	$000	%	$000	%
Provincial Grants	9,412	19.07	36,634	24.46
Metropolitan Levies	22,050	44.68	53,240	35.55
Local Levies	17,891	36.25	59,882	39.99
Operating Costs	49,353	100.00	149,756	100.00

Source: Financial Statements of Metropolitan and area school boards.

Tax levies financed 81 per cent of the costs in 1954, as compared with 75.5 per cent in 1963, the provincial share rising from 19 per cent to 24.5 per cent of the total in the same period. With a decline in the share financed by area-wide levies from 44.7 per cent to 35.5 per cent, local levies financed 40 per cent of the total in 1963, as compared with 36.2 per cent in 1954.

The nature, amount and distribution of the tax levies for general and school purposes in the Metropolitan Area have been set out in Chapter IX of this report. In this section, the relative tax burden for schools is examined. Table 43 shows school tax rates for residential public school supporters in 1954 and 1964.

In 1954 the rate ranged from 13.38 mills in Weston to 20.49 mills in Scarborough; in 1964 the range was from 24.19 mills in Weston to 31.61 mills in Scarborough. The spread between the lowest and highest rates was 7.11 mills in 1954 and 7.42 mills in 1964. The increase in rates during the period ranged from 7.02 mills in Swansea to 13.57 mills in East York. Toronto's rate rose by 13 mills, from 16.10 to 29.10 mills.

Table 43

SCHOOL MILL RATES, 1954 AND 1964

(Residential Public School Supporters)

School Board	1954	Rank	1964	Rank	Increase
	Mills		Mills		Mills
Toronto	16.10	8	29.10	6	13.00
North York	19.70	2	31.25	2	11.55
Scarborough	20.49	1	31.61	1	11.12
Etobicoke	16.00	9	26.69	7	10.69
York	17.57	5	29.99	5	12.42
East York	17.04	6	30.61	3	13.57
Forest Hill	17.60	4	30.09	4	12.49
Leaside	16.78	7	25.42	8	8.64
Lakeshore	15.60	10	25.22	9	9.62
Weston	13.38	11	24.19	11	10.81
Swansea	18.09	3	25.11	10	7.02

Source: Metropolitan School Board.

When mill rates are related to expenditures per pupil, the continuing inequalities in the financing of school costs become apparent. A few examples will suffice. In 1963:

(a) Leaside, with a tax rate of 22.78 mills, was able to spend $611 per elementary school pupil and $680 per academic secondary pupil.

(b) Forest Hill, with a tax rate of 26.80 mills, was able to spend $589 per elementary school pupil and $796 per academic secondary pupil.

(c) Toronto, with a tax rate of 26.78 mills, was able to spend $523 per elementary school pupil and $768 per academic secondary pupil.

(d) Scarborough, with a tax rate of 28.63 mills, was able to spend only $378 per elementary school pupil and $670 per academic secondary pupil. With the highest tax rate for schools in the area, Scarborough's expenditures per elementary pupil were the lowest.

These differences are explained by the disparities in taxable resources in relation to needs, which have already been described. Table 44 shows the percentage distribution of school population and of school assessment in the area in 1963. Scarborough, with more than 20 per cent of the public elementary school population, had little more than 10 per cent of the assessment; North York, with 22.4 per cent of the elementary school pupils, had 17 per cent of the assessment; Toronto, with 31 per cent of the elementary school population, had 45.5 per cent of the assessment. In respect of secondary schools, Toronto, with 30 per cent of the pupils, had 45 per cent of the assessment; North York, with 22 per cent of the pupils, had 17 per cent of the assessment; Scarborough, with 17 per cent of the pupils, had 10.6 per cent of the assessment. In the circumstances, the different area boards have had to develop their educational programmes on very unequal terms.

Table 44

DISTRIBUTION OF SCHOOL POPULATION
AND SCHOOL ASSESSMENT, 1963

	School Population[1]	School Assessment
	%	%
Public Elementary		
Toronto	30.84	45.50
North York	22.40	17.23
Scarborough	20.07	10.43
Etobicoke	12.66	11.89
York	6.37	5.06
East York	3.30	2.90
Forest Hill	.75	1.73
Leaside	.71	1.84
Lakeshore	2.05	2.25
Weston	.50	.62
Swansea	.35	.55
Total	100.00	100.00
Secondary		
Toronto	29.71	45.05
North York	21.82	17.31
Scarborough	17.08	10.58
Etobicoke	14.22	11.91
York	6.56	5.28
East York	4.03	2.96
Forest Hill	1.69	1.67
Leaside	1.44	1.80
Lakeshore	2.23	2.30
Weston	.70	.60
Swansea	.52	.54
Total	100.00	100.00

[1]Adjusted for non-resident pupils.
Source: Metropolitan School Board.

The situation resulting from these disparities is well stated in the brief submitted by the Metropolitan School Board. Basing its observations on the 1962-63 school year, it pointed out that:

> A mill increase in the Township of Scarborough would yield $9.50 per pupil; the same mill would yield $25.90 in Toronto, $38.10 in Forest Hill and $43.50 in Leaside. Obviously, if these four boards were considering an expansion of the school service involving an expenditure of, say $20 per pupil, it is clearly impossible for Scarborough to compete on anything like equal terms with the other areas mentioned.

v. *Capital Costs*

In the matter of school capital expenditures, the Cumming Report recommended that Metro should finance capital costs of sites, buildings and equipment to an adequate standard, assume all existing school debentures, receive all legislative grants in respect of capital expenditures, and select and purchase school sites. These recommendations were not fully implemented.

Under the Metro Act, the Metropolitan Corporation assumed all debentures for school purposes outstanding on December 31, 1953. In respect of new debt, it was only to assume the amount recognized for legislative grant purposes by the Province, which, in 1954, was limited to construction costs of new public and secondary school buildings up to $20,000 per classroom. Expenditures for construction of administrative facilities, for rehabilitation of existing school buildings, and for purchase of new school sites were not recognized. Any amount in excess of the debt assumed by Metro was to be the responsibility of the area board.

An amendment to the Metro Act in 1958 permitted the Metropolitan Corporation to assume a larger share of the capital debt. In 1959 the legislative grant regulations were amended by increasing the recognized costs in secondary schools from $20,000 to $25,000 per classroom, including general purpose rooms, cafeterias, and shop and home economics classrooms for grant purposes, and making the purchase of school sites eligible in part. Rehabilitation costs, a major problem in the City, continued to be ineligible until 1964.

As school buildings costs rose sharply and relatively static grant formulas restricted Metro's share, the area boards assumed an increasing proportion of the total school debt. In its brief to the Commission, the Metropolitan School Board presented the following figures as an approximation of the amount of school debt shared by the Province, Metro and the area boards, respectively, in the years from 1954 to 1963:

	Province of Ontario	*Metro*	*Area Municipalities*
	%	%	%
1954	27.1	37.9	35.0
1955	26.3	34.1	39.6
1956	17.4	22.6	60.0
1957	17.9	23.5	58.6
1958	18.0	18.1	63.9
1959	24.5	25.5	50.0
1960	18.6	23.1	58.3
1961	21.8	24.3	53.9
1962	21.5	25.6	52.9
1963	20.5	22.7	56.8

The decline shown in the Province's share in 1956 was due to a major school rehabilitation programme undertaken by the Toronto Board of Education. Such expenditures, being then ineligible for legislative grants, were entirely a local responsibility. The increase shown for the Province in 1959 reflected the increase in the grants under amendments to the regulations in that year.

The figures show that with a decline in the provincial share of the debt from 27 per cent in 1954 to 20.5 per cent in 1963, and in Metro's share from 38 per cent to 22.7 per cent, the proportion of the total borne by the area boards rose from 35 per cent to almost 57 per cent.

Under the Federal-Provincial Special Vocational Grant Plan, which came into effect in 1961, the full cost of the construction of vocational facilities was assumed by the federal and provincial governments, the former contributing 75 per cent and the latter 25 per cent of the cost. On April 1, 1963, the federal contribution was reduced to 50 per cent and school boards became responsible for 25 per cent of the cost. Federal and provincial lump sum grants toward vocational school construction costs exceeded $60 million by the end of 1964.

In its letter of approval of Metro's 1963 capital works programme, the Ontario Municipal Board issued the following warning:

> I am directed to bring to the attention of the Metropolitan Council at this time the rise forecast in the local debt of those area municipalities which contain outlying areas still under substantial residential development which latter will occasion large expenditures for new school construction. An examination of the local debt of some of these area municipalities and the anticipated growth of debt at a faster pace percentage-wise than the growth in municipal assessment suggests that some attention and study should be directed now to the possible lessening of this problem by resort to existing statutory provision intended and designed to cope with such a situation when it would arise. Reference is made to Section 145(5)(b) of The Municipality of Metropolitan Toronto Act as amended in 1958.

Section 145(5)(b) of the Metro Act permits Metro to assume a larger share of school debt in an amount to be determined by the Metropolitan School Board "from time to time in accordance with a formula prepared by the School Board and approved by the Metropolitan Council for uniform application in the Metropolitan Area."

Following this warning, Metropolitan Council and the School Board appointed a special committee to consider the matter of school finance. In October 1963, the committee recommended the assumption by Metro of all existing local school debt, that is, all debt incurred by the area municipalities on behalf of local boards since January 1, 1954, and that, effective January 1, 1964, Metro should assume all school debt up to a ceiling cost formula prepared by the School Board and approved by Metro Council. On February 25, 1964, Metro accepted the latter recommendation but did not assume the local debt incurred between 1954 and 1963.

The device of a "ceiling cost formula" to determine the maximum amount which may be debentured for each school project was first adopted in 1955 by agreement among Metro Council, the Metropolitan School Board and the area boards of education. The formula fixes the cost per pupil space for each major classification of school and is re-negotiated annually. Boards desiring to spend beyond this amount must secure the additional amounts from current tax levies. To meet rising construction costs and to cover new facilities, the formula has been revised upwards in each year, as follows:

CEILING COST FORMULA
(PER PUPIL SPACE)

	Elementary (K-6, K-8)	Intermediate	Academic Secondary
	$	$	$
1955-1956	735	1,050	1,350
1957-1958	855	1,178	1,490
1959	890	1,220	1,520
1960	950	1,280	1,600
1961	980	1,340	1,660
1962-1963	995	1,355	1,690
1964	1,108	1,525	1,860

Considering the large annual demands for capital funds for both municipal and school purposes in the area, and the consequent need to negotiate for a proper share of such funds for education, the ceiling cost formula has proved useful in the determination of capital appropriations for schools. The rate of growth of school debt has also been reduced by the area-wide current levy for capital purposes, already described, which yielded $23.3 million from 1959 to the end of 1964. This amount would otherwise have been borrowed.

As of December 31, 1963, the unmatured school debt of Metro and the area municipalities amounted to $216.8 million, of which Metro's share was $91.5 million, or 42.2 per cent. The area municipalities were responsible for 57.8 per cent, or $125.2 million, distributed as follows:

SCHOOL DEBT, 1963

	$ million	%
Toronto	50.4	40.2
Three outer suburbs	64.8	51.8
Nine inner suburbs	10.0	8.0
Total	125.2	100.0

This represents the debt incurred by the area municipalities on behalf of the local boards between January 1, 1954, and December 31, 1963. Metro assumed all existing school debts on January 1, 1954, and is reponsible for all debt incurred up to the ceiling cost formula since January 1, 1964. Considering the inequalities in school burdens and, more particularly, the relatively heavier burdens of the large mushrooming suburbs, I find that Metro should also assume all area school debt outstanding on December 31, 1963.

5. CONCLUSIONS

The major achievement of metropolitan government in public education has been the financing, planning and construction of new school accommodation. The Toronto Board of Education, in its brief, said that "Metropolitan Toronto's record in this respect has the reputation of being among the best in North America." The Toronto Board also acknowledged that in the field of special education, covering both gifted and handicapped children, "Metropolitan co-operation has brought benefits to the entire region." The North York Board of Education said that: "The accomplishments of the Metropolitan form of government and of the Metropolitan School Board have been exceptional. Certainly we in North York realize that by ourselves we could not have carried out our responsibilities in the development of our educational system."

The metropolitan system has not, however, prevented continuing wide disparities in the burden of financing school costs. While, without metropolitan assistance payments, the disparities would be greater, these payments have not succeeded in achieving the degree of equalization which should exist. Under the loose federation for school purposes created by the Metro Act, the payments are uniform per pupil throughout the area without regard to differences in needs and circumstances.

Wide inequalities in burdens and variations in the range and standards of school services are inevitable with eleven independent and autonomous school districts varying greatly in size, population and taxable resources, and with no single authority responsible for developing and maintaining an area-wide standard of education financed by the tax resources of the area as a whole. The Metropolitan School Board, limited in its powers and responsibilities, and on which each suburban board has equal representation regardless of differences in population, is not in a position to resolve the problem. The situation calls for a change in the structure of education in Metro.

CHAPTER XII

EDUCATION: A NEW STRUCTURE

The experience of Metro's first decade establishes the need for change in its educational structure. On this, however, the submissions to the Commission were understandably not unanimous. Tending to reflect local interests, traditions and pride, fear of loss of local autonomy, differences in educational philosophies, and divergent views on the proper municipal structure for Metro, some of the briefs gave little consideration to the overall metropolitan interest.

The small suburban units, except Forest Hill, favoured continuation of the existing system. The Ontario Teachers' Federation also favoured "retaining the status quo . . . with some further equalization of finances over the area and of co-operation in special areas of education." The four largest suburbs recommended varying forms of consolidation of municipalities, with a corresponding reduction in the number of school districts. Both small and large suburbs urged the preservation of local autonomy in school matters, even though seven of the ten suburban boards are in varying degree dependent upon taxes raised in Toronto for financing their schools. The suburbs were united in opposing the recommendation of the Toronto Board of Education that all the school districts should be amalgamated and that the operation of the school system of the whole area be centralized.

The Metropolitan School Board expressed a preference for the coordination of educational finance by a central school authority and the establishment of a uniform tax for education throughout Metro. Forest Hill favoured local districts, each of suitable size to offer complete school services, within a larger school system covering the area as a whole. Under this proposal, the management of the schools would be the responsibility of the districts, while finances would be centralized in a metropolitan school board, which would also coordinate overall policy.

In view of the wide divergence of opinion, and having concluded that changes in the existing structure are necessary, I called upon a group of persons of varied experience and points of view who had been studying proposals advanced in some of the briefs, and each of whom, in one capacity or another, is concerned with the organization of public education, to submit to me their collective judgment as to the best educational structure for Metro. They agreed to serve in their individual capacities, and in due course submitted their proposals. The plan finally drafted by this committee, after discussions with me, is the basis of the new educational structure which I recommend in this chapter.

The following constituted the committee on changes in educational structure:

J. Richard Davidson, Trustee, Ward 9, Toronto
George E. Flower, Director of Graduate Studies, Ontario College of Education
Douglas W. Gilmour, Solicitor, Toronto Board of Education
R. W. B. Jackson, Director, Department of Educational Research, Ontario College of Education
W. J. McCordic, Executive Secretary, The Metropolitan School Board
E. Brock Rideout, Department of Educational Research and Professor, Ontario College of Education
David L. Tough, Superintendent of Secondary Schools, North York Board of Education.

1. INTRODUCTION

The main conflict in briefs to the Commission on the structure of education in Metro was between the advocates of centralization and those who favoured preservation of a decentralized system. It has been shown in this report that, with its highly decentralized system, Metro has not been able to prevent continuing wide inequalities in the burden of financing education in the area. On the other hand, it is noted that large urban centres with centralized school systems, such as New York, Chicago and Detroit, have made efforts in recent years to introduce measures of decentralization, with varying dergees of success. In May 1965 the Acting Superintendent of schools in New York City recommended that the public school system should be subdivided into thirty local districts, each under a district superintendent reporting directly to the Superintendent.

The plan which I recommend for the public school system in Metropolitan Toronto offers a middle course between complete centralization and complete decentralization and is intended to provide flexibility in school administration. It varies from existing patterns of school organization because Metro's position is unique in Ontario. The Metro Act also departed from the accepted pattern when it created the Metropolitan School Board in 1953.

The plan envisages an elected central board, to be called the Metropolitan Toronto Board of Education, with overall responsibility for school finance and for the development of an acceptable and uniformly high metropolitan standard of public education. The administrative responsibilities of this board would be limited to matters related to area-wide policies, to coordination of mutual services, and to the provision of services which can best be provided on a metropolitan basis. Administration and management of the school programme would be decentralized and carried out by a number of local boards to be called District Education Councils. The boundaries of the districts would not be coterminous with municipal boundaries. With centralized finance, the taxable resources of the entire area would be available to all public school districts, while decentralized administration would preserve the initiative of local school staffs and the community interest in the school programme.

2. SCHOOL DISTRICTS

To delineate the districts under the recommended plan, the following criteria were established as basic to the viability of school districts. The districts should be:

(a) approximately uniform in size;
(b) small enough for a district education council to perform efficiently and with understanding most of the traditional functions of a school board (exclusive of functions transferred to the central board);
(c) within the administrative capacity of a superintendent of schools, supported by appropriate staff;
(d) large enough to support a broad programme of public education with the full range of services characteristic of urban centres, each system to be largely self-contained;
(e) large enough to warrant the appointment of a corps of leaders and officials with varied background and experience, with consequent advantages to the district;
(f) large enough to warrant the use of modern methods and equipment in the business operations of the school authority;
(g) so drawn that each district will manifest specific needs and characteristics to which the educational programme can be made responsive;
(h) so drawn as to require minimum alteration in existing school attendance areas;
(i) delineated with due regard for ravine valleys, expressways and railroads that already tend to separate one district from another.

On the basis of these criteria, it is recommended that the Metropolitan Area should be divided into eleven school districts as shown on the map on Plate 5. The proposed district boundaries are set out in an appendix to this chapter.

Statistics on population and school enrolment in each of the proposed districts are shown in Table 45. As Districts 9 and 11 are still in a relatively early stage of development, it is recommended that they be combined initially, the combined district to be divided, as shown on the map, on the first day of January of the next year after the smaller of the two districts reaches an assessed population of 75,000. It is forecast that District 3 will reach the population level of the other districts by 1980 and that District 1 will approximate it soon after.

Since the proposed boundaries are not coterminous with municipal boundaries, it may be feared that this will complicate procedures in taxation and in elections. In my opinion, such fears are unwarranted. Under the recommended centralization of finance, the central board will obtain its local tax funds entirely from the Metropolitan Council. Metro has already assumed responsibility for all new school debt, up to the ceiling cost, as from January 1, 1964. Accordingly, with both current and capital school costs financed on an area-wide basis, there will be no need for continuing the existing relationship between local school boards and municipal councils and for coterminous school district and municipal boundaries.

PLATE 5

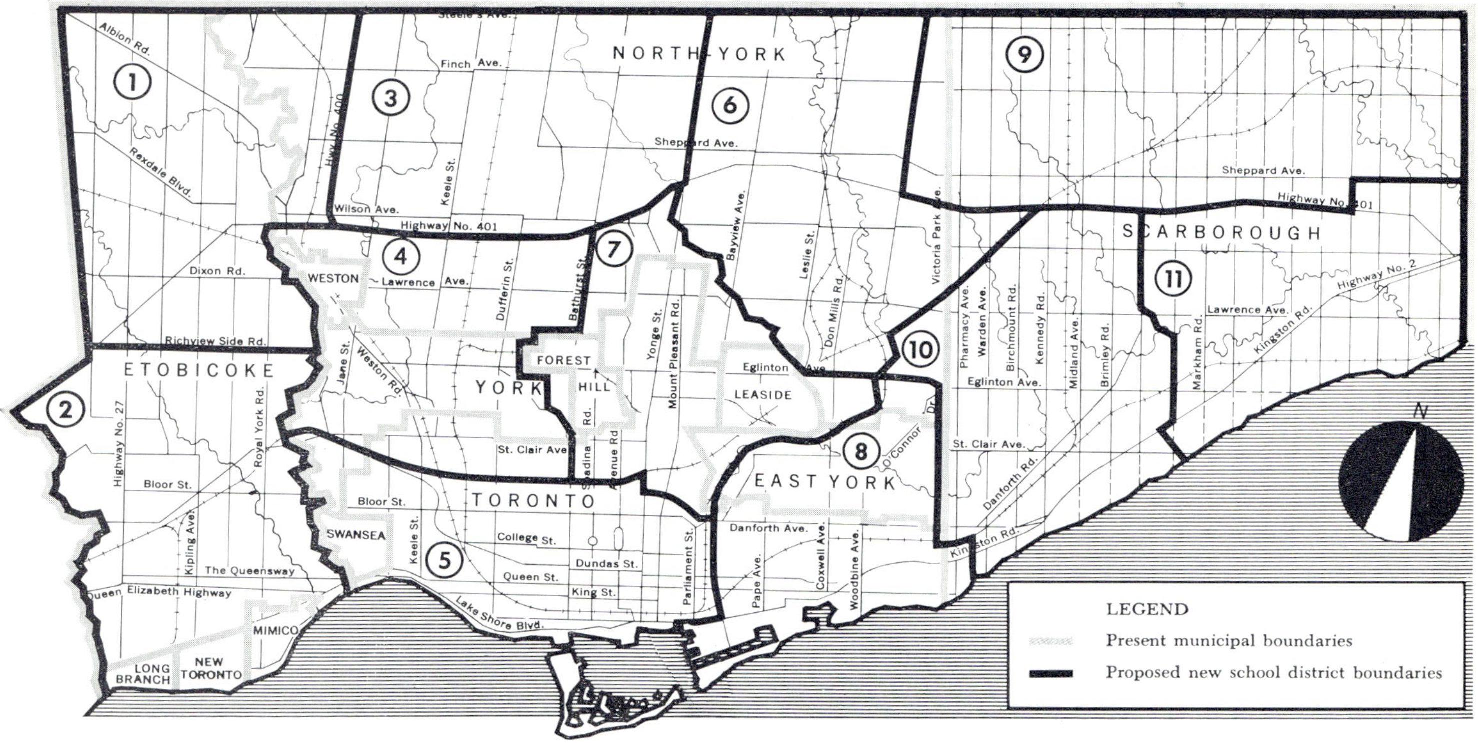

METROPOLITAN TORONTO: PROPOSED SCHOOL DISTRICTS

Table 45

Proposed School Districts:

Population, Enrolment and Schools

District	POPULATION		ENROLMENT		SCHOOLS
	1961	1971 (Est.)	Feb. 1964	1971 (Est.)	1964
1	59,000	106,775	18,891	26,160	31
2	150,000	199,225	32,114	46,818	53
3	93,700	137,100	25,428	33,590	37
4	219,900	245,250	40,058	53,955	56
5	363,100	359,600	51,477	62,930	59
6	78,300	164,473	26,039	41,118	43
7	189,300	233,575	22,711	52,554	37
8	234,100	241,477	38,958	45,881	48
9 & 11	64,400	84,120 (9)	21,327	20,609	40
		97,824 (11)		23,967	
10	144,200	170,581	35,443	41,792	44
Total	1,596,000	2,040,000	312,446	449,374	448

With respect to elections, the existence of two or more school districts in a municipality will call for arrangements similar to the division of municipalities into wards. For districts which cut across municipal boundary lines there are many precedents in the case of school districts in Ontario. It will be necessary, however, that the boundaries of polling subdivisions be so drawn that they do not intersect the boundaries of school districts.

3. THE METROPOLITAN TORONTO BOARD OF EDUCATION

The Metropolitan School Board, as presently constituted, consists of ten members from Toronto, ten from the suburbs, and two Separate School Board representatives. Each suburb is represented by one member: Swansea and Weston, for example, are given the same voice on the Board as North York and Scarborough. Such a degree of inequality in representation, in the words of the York Township Board of Education, is "a most disturbing feature of the present metropolitan organization. . . ." Under the proposed new structure, there would be considerably less variation in the size of the school districts and the central board would have wide authority.

The Metropolitan Toronto Board of Education, under the recommended plan, would consist, initially, of twenty-two trustees, of whom twenty would be elected by the districts and two appointed by the Metropolitan Separate School Board. Two trustees would be elected at large in each school district at elections held on the same day as the regular municipal elections. When the combined Districts 9 and 11 are divided, two additional trustees would be elected. The chairman would be chosen from among the members. For their work to be effective, the term of office of trustees should be three years, which is also my recommendation for municipal office.

Admittedly, with each district electing two members, the Board would not be constituted on an exact basis of representation by population. School districts must satisfy certain basic criteria if they are to be viable administrative units, and each of the proposed districts satisfies to a high degree the criteria which I have listed. The differences in population, which are very much less than under the existing fragmented system and will continue to narrow, would not be such as to prevent the districts from being represented on equal terms on the central board. Equality of status among the districts is essential to the successful operation of the plan.

Elections in large districts, such as District 5 with a population of more than 350,000, may present some problems. Election campaigns are expensive and the maximum remuneration for school trustees in large urban municipalities is now fixed at $1,800. Considering the responsibilities which would be assigned to the Board, and that it would be among the largest business enterprises in Canada, it is important that it should be composed of able and competent persons. It is also desirable that elections be contested; the tendency toward election by acclamation to school boards is not in the public interest. Accordingly, I recommend that the remuneration for members of the Board should be raised to a figure more commensurate with their responsibilities, and that the additional responsibilities of the chairman should be recognized by a higher remuneration, as in the case of mayors and reeves.

To encourage qualified persons to offer their services, I also suggest that consideration should be given to distribution in each district, at public expense, of a pamphlet in which each candidate would be given space to describe his qualifications and platform.

4. DISTRICT EDUCATION COUNCILS

For each school district, I recommend a District Education Council to be composed of the two trustees elected to represent the district on the Metropolitan Toronto Board of Education, one trustee appointed by the Metropolitan Separate School Board, and eight trustees elected in the district, who would be called "District Trustees". The chairman would be elected from among the members.

The district trustees, like the members of the central board, should be elected at large in each district, the election to be held in conjunction with the regular municipal elections. Since the major purpose of decentralization is to encourage and maintain a local interest in school affairs, and as both central and district trustees would be entrusted with the management of public education, it is anticipated that public school supporters in each district will so organize themselves as to ensure the nomination of qualified persons to contest the elections.

5. CENTRAL AND DISTRICT RESPONSIBILITIES

To avoid the problems created by "bigness" in large cities in North America, which are now seeking with much difficulty to decentralize school operations, the plan recommended in this report envisages a high degree of decentralization. The functions of the central board would be restricted to matters of area-wide policy, coordination of mutual services, and the provision of a number of metropolitan services. Detailed administration and management would be the function of the district councils and their staffs. The following division of duties, subject to later review by specialists, is suggested:

Symbols:

- D: a District function
- DC: a District function with some Central coordination
- CD: a Central act taken upon District recommendation
- C: a Central function
- C&D: complementary functioning with each responsible for certain phases

I. THE INSTRUCTIONAL PROGRAMME

Instructional Staff

1. Salary Scales & Policy (incl. fringe benefits) — C
2. Recruitment — DC
3. Appointment & Dismissal — CD
4. Placement — D
5. Duties — D
6. Payment of Salaries — C
7. In-Service Training — C & D
8. Supervision of Instruction — D
9. Inspection — C

Instructional Supplies

1. Textbooks — DC
2. Library Books — D
3. Classroom Supplies — D
4. Equipment — DC
5. Furnishings — DC

Curriculum & Courses of Study

1. Adaptations — D
2. Supplementary — D
3. New — D
4. Experimental — D
5. Teaching Methods — D

Services Ancillary to Instruction

1. Secretarial
   - Selection — D
   - Pre-Service Training — C
2. Libraries — DC
3. Teaching Aids — C & D
4. Radio & Television — C

Services Related to Professional Development

1. Research — C & D
2. Publications — C
3. Local In-Service Training Programmes — C

Services Related to Children

1. Guidance, Psychological Testing, etc. — D
2. Child Adjustment — C
3. Attendance
   - Statistics — C
   - Counselling — D
4. Health Services — DC
5. Transportation — C
6. Food Services — DC

Special Services

1. Schools for Blind, Deaf, Orthopaedically Handicapped — C
2. Classes for Aphasics — C
3. Post-Secondary Schools — C
4. Highly Specialized Secondary Schools (performing arts, plastics, etc.) — C

II. THE MANAGEMENT FUNCTION

Board Activities
1. Area-Wide Policy C
2. Procedures C & D
3. Population Research & Coordination of Plant Expansion C
4. Evaluation & Self Appraisal C

Administrative Functions
1. Secretarial C & D
2. Legal C
3. Personnel
   Recruitment DC
   Promotion & Advancement CD
   Records C
4. Outside Use of Schools D
5. Property Administration C
6. Budget C & D

III. THE BUSINESS FUNCTION

Financial Operations
1. Purchasing & Supply DC
2. Accounting C & D
3. Budget Control C & D
4. Audit C

Plant Maintenance & Operation
1. Custodial D
2. Repairs D
3. Major Maintenance CD

Plant Expansion
1. Planning & Surveys D
2. Sites
   Selection D
   Purchase C
3. Buildings
   Academic Requirements D
   Sketch Plans D
   Construction C
4. Architectural & Engineering C

The foregoing division of responsibilities in the case of the instructional programme shows that, except for the highly specialized services listed, the management and operation of the local schools will be the responsibility of the district education councils and their staffs. This is particularly clear in the matter of curriculum and courses of study. The basic course content in Ontario is prescribed by the Department of Education. In recent years local school authorities have been encouraged to adapt their programmes to local needs; under the proposed structure this would continue to be a district responsibility.

The recommendations on teachers' salaries and recruitment give wider powers to the central board. It would set salary scales and policies, and teachers would officially be under contract to this board. A central personnel office would suggest recruitment procedures and maintain a complete set of staff records. However, actual recruitment, appointment, promotion, and fixing of duties would be responsibilities of the district education councils and the district superintendents. On recommendation of the district council, a teacher would automatically be given an official appointment by the central board. The salary would be fixed in relation to the existing scales and the assignment to specific duties would be made by the local superintendent.

Essentially, the recruitment and deployment of staff in the districts would be quite similar to the present arrangement under which the local board employs staff and assigns their duties. A central personnel office would undertake some coordination of the process to alleviate problems that now develop in the yearly scramble for staff at interview time. Lively competition for the most promising teachers would continue, but it would be based upon factors other than salary gimmicks, availability of parking space, and more lavish buildings, on which the present boards cannot compete on anything like an equal basis.

I am aware that recommendations in favour of metropolitan salary schedules and policies for professional staff will arouse controversy and opposition. There may even be reservations about the limited coordination proposed in the personnel field. As far as placement is concerned, the plan involves little change in the present arrangement because recruitment and deployment would be district responsibilities. With respect to salary scales, however, the variety of competitive features in present schedules is not in the best interests of the provision of education in the area. The trend is toward negotiation of teachers' salaries on some sort of regional basis, and the Metropolitan Area is an appropriate region for such purposes. A metropolitan salary schedule, flexible enough to allow for special area needs, should be negotiated. Under the proposed plan, teachers would bargain collectively with the school authority to which they are under contract and from which they receive their salaries, that is, the Metropolitan Toronto Board of Education. They are well equipped and well organized to negotiate on an area-wide basis.

With the central board assuming overriding financial responsibility for schools, management functions, as listed, would be largely centralized. The business function would be divided between the central board and the district councils.

6. FINANCE

For the effective use of the taxable resources of the area as a whole to meet the needs of education, the plan proposes a high degree of fiscal centralization through coordination of educational finance by the central board and the establishment of a uniform tax for education throughout Metro. The Metropolitan Toronto Board of Education would secure all tax revenue for educational purposes from the Metropolitan Council through a uniform levy. As at present, Metro would also raise the capital funds for school purposes.

i. *Current Expenditures*

The central board would establish procedures for the preparation and submission of their respective budgets by district education councils. Area-wide policies, such as salary scales, pupil-teacher ratios, the number of persons to constitute the establishment for certain functions and services, and the allocation of funds for supplies and equipment would be decided and circulated in advance by the central board.

Local budgets would be prepared by the district superintendents and their staffs for consideration and adoption by the district education councils. They would provide for the on-going needs of the schools, which to a large degree, it would be possible to relate to the metropolitan standard programme. Since requirements vary from school to school and from district to district, each budget would also cover specialized needs for services and facilities beyond the standard programme. These would be identified in the district budgets and the request accompanied by supporting evidence in the submission to the central board.

While the metropolitan standard programme would provide for all the major items of expense, such as salaries, building costs, plant operation and maintenance, equipment, etc., it is probable that some districts would desire to add to their programme through the provision of special equipment or a special service or the undertaking of an educational experiment. In my view, the districts should be free to take such action even though the central board does not include the items in the area-wide budget. To this end, the districts should have some discretionary fiscal powers. These would be applicable only to certain types of expenditures: boards would not be free, for example, to pay higher salaries than authorized or to exceed the ceiling cost formula for school building.

Accordingly, I recommend that, initially, each school district should be allocated a fixed percentage of its total budget for purposes of such special services or equipment or for educational experiments. Districts should be free to spend up to the amount so allocated for such purposes without reference to the central board. If experience shows that it is more desirable to couple financial equalization with some local taxing powers, the system could be changed and districts might, in due course, be authorized to levy a nominal district school tax to cover the cost of expenditures not approved by the central board for inclusion in the metropolitan school budget.

ii. *Capital Expenditures*

The Metro Act already provides for a high degree of coordination in the financing of school capital projects, and there would be little change under the proposed plan. Each district would continue the present practice of the area boards in respect of capital programmes. The districts would prepare their programmes annually for submission to the central board, in two parts: a five-year forecast and a statement of individual projects for the current year. On the basis of the district submissions, the central board would prepare a composite five-year programme and a composite current capital programme for the year for negotiation with the Metropolitan Council. Funds for individual projects would continue to be determined on the basis of a ceiling cost formula approved by the central board and by Metro Council. Since this formula would be flexible and would allow considerable leeway in application, district councils should not be authorized to augment by local taxation the amounts received under the formula.

In respect of school debt, I have pointed out elsewhere in this report that Metro assumed all debt outstanding on December 31, 1953, and all debt incurred after January 1, 1964, up to the ceiling cost formula. I have recommended that Metro should also assume from the area municipalities all area school debt outstanding on December 31, 1963.

7. ADMINISTRATIVE ARRANGEMENTS

The administrative arrangements will be the key to effective operation of the proposed plan, which combines a central policy-making board of education with a high degree of decentralization at the staff and operational level. The arrangements should be such as will ensure that the local school districts will, in fact, accept responsibility for management of the schools in their respective districts. In broad outline, the plan envisages that:

i. A Director of Education will be the chief executive officer of the Metropolitan Toronto Board of Education. The central office staff could be relatively small but should be large enough to perform its primary function of coordination.

ii. The school districts will be relatively self-contained, with a District Superintendent as the principal officer. He will be responsible for all public education services in the district, including both elementary and secondary schools. Since the real work of a school system goes on in the local schools, specialist instructional personnel, as required, will be attached to the district office and be immediately responsible to the District Superintendent. As recommended in the brief submitted by the Forest Hill Board of Education, each district "would be so staffed and structured as to offer complete school services for its area, responsive to its own area, and probably differing in many matters of detail from adjoining area divisions." The District Superintendent will report directly to the Director of Education.

iii. An Administrative Council, consisting of the Director of Education and his central staff and the District Superintendents, will be constituted to advise the central board on policy. The Council will develop standards for the area as a whole and will coordinate the efforts of the districts to achieve these standards.

Under the proposals, district administration would be similar in many respects to the present system in the larger school districts. Apart from the functions and services which can be more efficiently performed on a centralized basis, the district staffs would undertake the same range of activities as now required at the local level. There would, however, be an identification with area-wide needs.

8. CONCLUSIONS

While in many respects the proposed structure for public education would not differ greatly from the typical structure in Ontario, it calls for major changes in the existing system in Metropolitan Toronto which experience since 1953 shows to be necessary. The Cumming Report envisaged the development of an acceptable standard for public education in the area as a whole and the Metro Act provided a plan of financial equalization with a view to assisting the less favoured municipalities in maintaining such a standard. In fact, however, there has been no authority in Metro charged with the responsibility of developing a metropolitan standard of public education, while the measure of financial equalization has been insufficient to prevent wide disparities in the burden of financing education in the area. Under the plan proposed in this report, the Metropolitan Toronto Board of Education would be responsible for developing an acceptable and uniformly high standard consistent with area-wide formulae for most major items of expense, while the local districts would be allowed some discretionary fiscal powers for special purposes, such as experimentation. The varying school rates in the area would be replaced by a uniform tax rate for public schools.

With management of the schools in the hands of district councils, the disadvantages of "bigness," which would flow from amalgamation and complete centralization, should be avoided. The proposed school districts have been recommended on the basis of sound criteria for viable self-contained units. They would replace school districts which now vary greatly in size, population and resources because their boundaries are coterminous with present municipal boundaries. Each of the new districts would have an equal voice on the central board. This would accord more closely with accepted principles of representation than the present system, which gives equal representation to Swansea, Forest Hill, Weston, Leaside, North York, Scarborough, and Etobicoke.

The recommended changes would require many detailed structural adjustments. These could not be made without considerable study and preparatory work. Accordingly, if it is decided to implement my recommendations, provision should be made for a transition period. There is precedent for this in the creation of Metro itself. In 1953 both the original Metropolitan Council and the original Metropolitan School Board were sworn in more than nine months before the effective date for the commencement of their operations. This period was a preparatory stage during which both bodies met frequently, appointed senior officials, determined the size and nature of their establishments, and approved policies. If the changes proposed in this report are to be made, I recommend that a similar procedure should be followed, allowing for a transition period of twelve months during which the terms of office of the present Metropolitan School Board and area boards and the new Metropolitan Toronto Board of Education and district councils will overlap.

APPENDIX

PROPOSED SCHOOL DISTRICT BOUNDARIES

District
1
    N. Steeles Avenue
    E. Highway 400, Highway 401 and the Humber River
    S. Richview Side Road
    W. Etobicoke Township boundary

2
    N. Richview Side Road
    E. Humber River
    S. Lake Ontario
    W. Etobicoke River and Etobicoke Township boundary

District

3
- N. Steeles Avenue
- E. Yonge Street
- S. Highway 401
- W. Highway 400

4
- N. Highway 401
- E. Bathurst Street, boundary between Forest Hill Village and York Township, Winnett Avenue, Vaughan Road and Bathurst Street
- S. C.P.R. Right of Way
- W. Humber River

5
- N. C.P.R. Right of Way, Yonge Street and Rosedale Valley Road
- E. Don Valley Parkway, Gardiner Expressway and Cherry Street
- S. Lake Ontario
- W. Humber River

6
- N. Steeles Avenue
- E. Woodbine Avenue (future Don Valley Parkway), Highway 401, C.P.R. Right of Way and Don River (east branch)
- S. Eglinton Avenue
- W. Don River (west branch), Highway 401 and Yonge Street

7
- N. Highway 401
- E. Don River (west branch), Eglinton Avenue, Don River (east branch), and Don Valley Parkway
- S. Rosedale Valley Road, Yonge Street, and C.P.R. Right of Way
- W. Bathurst Street, Vaughan Road, Winnett Avenue, boundary between Forest Hill Village and York Township and Bathurst Street

8
- N. Eglinton Avenue
- E. Victoria Park Avenue, C.N.R. Right of Way, Cornell and Haig Avenues approximately
- S. Lake Ontario
- W. Cherry Street, Gardiner Expressway, Don Valley Parkway and Don River (east branch)

9
- N. Steeles Avenue
- E. Scarborough Township boundary
- S. Sheppard Avenue, Conlins Road and Highway 401
- W. Woodbine Avenue (future Don Valley Parkway)

10
- N. Highway 401
- E. McCowan Road, branch of the Highland Creek, Bellamy Road and Ravine Drive
- S. Lake Ontario
- W. Haig and Cornell Avenues approximately, C.N.R. Right of Way, Victoria Park Avenue, Eglinton Avenue, Don River (east branch) and C.P.R. Right of Way

11
- N. Highway 401, Conlins Road and Sheppard Avenue
- E. Scarborough Township boundary
- S. Lake Ontario
- W. Ravine Drive, Bellamy Road, branch of the Highland Creek and McCowan Road

CHAPTER XIII

METRO'S BOUNDARIES AND THE FRINGE AREAS

My terms of reference include "the boundaries of the metropolitan area . . . with due regard to probable future urban growth within or beyond the present metropolitan limits and future service requirements." Metro's present limits were recommended by the Ontario Municipal Board in the Cumming Report, which deemed them to be "a temporary boundary only." Taking note of urban development in a number of outside municipalities, the Board, in its recommendations for regional planning, recognized "the need for immediate planning and supervision of that development in the interests of the metropolitan area of the future."

1. URBAN DEVELOPMENT

Metro's boundaries and the thirteen fringe municipalities on its borders, which together with the area municipalities constitute the Metropolitan Planning Area, have been described in Chapter I of this report. The eastern and western boundaries of Metro were determined by the outer limits of the County of York. The fringe municipalities are spread into three counties—York, on the north, Ontario, on the east, and Peel, on the west.

While the boundary areas of Metropolitan Toronto are still largely rural, there are growing extensions of urban development into the fringe. Such development is much more marked on the west of Metro, in Toronto Township, than in Pickering Township, on the east, both of which border on Lake Ontario. Northward, there is a continuous ribbon of urbanization along Yonge Street extending beyond the boundaries of Metro to the far side of Richmond Hill. Further urbanization in the northern fringe is largely dependent upon Metro, which controls access to Lake Ontario for water and sewage facilities.

The proposed Metro Official Plan (Table 5) shows that more than 81 per cent of the land in the fringe areas is now agricultural or vacant, as compared with less than 30 per cent in Metro. The figures for 1963, by areas, were as follows:

FRINGE AREAS: AGRICULTURAL OR VACANT LAND, 1963

	Acres	% of Total
Northern Fringe	132,352	84.9
Eastern Fringe	63,685	84.0
Western Fringe	53,156	70.9
Total Fringe	249,192	81.3

For the four large townships, the figures, as shown in Table 46, are as follows: Pickering, on the east of Metro, 85.3 per cent; Markham and Vaughan, on the north, 91.1 per cent and 81.8 per cent, respectively; and Toronto Township, on the west, reflecting a higher degree of urbanization, 72 per cent.

Under the proposed Metro Official Plan, 64 per cent of the land in the fringe will continue to be held for agricultural use. The plan projects an urban development area "which can be serviced effectively and with due regard for reasonable development standards." Its depth will therefore be limited generally by the effective range of lake-oriented water and sewage facilities. Reflecting the existing pattern and trend of development in southern Ontario, the suitability of the land for residential and industrial development, and the excellent transportation network, the plan emphasizes overall development toward the western section of the area and restricts development at the eastern end to a narrow band extending three or four miles from the lakeshore.

The proposed limit of urban development is shown on Plate 6. It envisages a continuous urban area which, on the east, will include Pickering Township south of Highway 2, the Town of Ajax and Pickering Village; on the west, about two-thirds of Toronto Township, Port Credit and Streetsville; and, on the north, portions of the townships of Markham and Vaughan centering on Yonge Street and extending to the outer limits of Richmond Hill, together with the C.N.R. marshalling yard in Vaughan and adjacent lands designated for industrial use.

2. POPULATION IN THE FRINGE

The population growth of the thirteen fringe municipalities has been described in Chapter II. Between 1953 and 1963 the increase was 96 per cent, as compared with an increase of 40 per cent for Metro. The average annual increase, however, was 48,000 persons in Metro and 8,700 in the whole of the fringe. Toronto Township, with a population of more than 70,000, contained 40 per cent of the total fringe population of 178,000 in 1963. Pickering Township, with 22,000 people, ranked second. Considerable increases have taken place in a number of pockets of urban development, particularly in Richmond Hill. The details are shown in Chapter II, Table 9.

The fringe population was distributed by areas in 1963 as follows:

FRINGE POPULATION, 1963

	Population	*% of Total*
Northern Fringe	63,218	35.3
Eastern Fringe	31,818	17.8
Western Fringe	83,346	46.5
Total	178,382	100.0

Table 46

FRINGE MUNICIPALITIES:
EXISTING LAND USE, 1963

	Residential		Agricultural or Vacant		Other		Total
	Acres	% of Total	Acres	% of Total	Acres	% of Total	Acres
Northern Fringe							
Township of Vaughan..............	3,108	4.6	55,974	81.8	9,312	13.6	68,394
Village of Woodbridge.............	250	39.2	184	28.8	205	32.0	639
Town of Richmond Hill............	1,083	64.5	344	20.5	253	15.0	1,680
Township of Markham.............	2,430	3.7	60,086	91.1	3,424	5.2	65,940
Village of Stouffville..............	334	20.5	1,230	75.3	69	4.2	1,633
Village of Markham...............	566	28.5	1,209	60.8	213	10.7	1,988
Township of Toronto Gore.........	213	1.4	13,325	85.6	2,032	13.0	15,570
Total	7,984	5.1	132,352	84.9	15,508	10.0	155,841
Eastern Fringe							
Township of Pickering............	3,375	4.7	61,575	85.3	7,212	10.0	72,162
Village of Pickering..............	191	31.6	236	38.9	177	29.5	604
Town of Ajax....................	415	13.6	1,874	61.6	754	24.8	3,043
Total	3,981	5.3	63,685	84.0	8,143	10.7	75,809
Western Fringe							
Township of Toronto..............	7,795	10.6	52,812	72.0	12,713	17.4	73,320
Town of Streetsville..............	473	47.8	320	32.5	196	19.7	989
Town of Port Credit..............	400	65.4	24	4.0	187	30.6	611
Total	8,668	11.6	53,156	70.9	13,096	17.5	74,920
Fringe Municipalities Total	20,633	6.7	249,192	81.3	36,745	12.0	306,570

Source: Table 5, Proposed Official Plan, Metropolitan Toronto Planning Board, Dec. 1964.

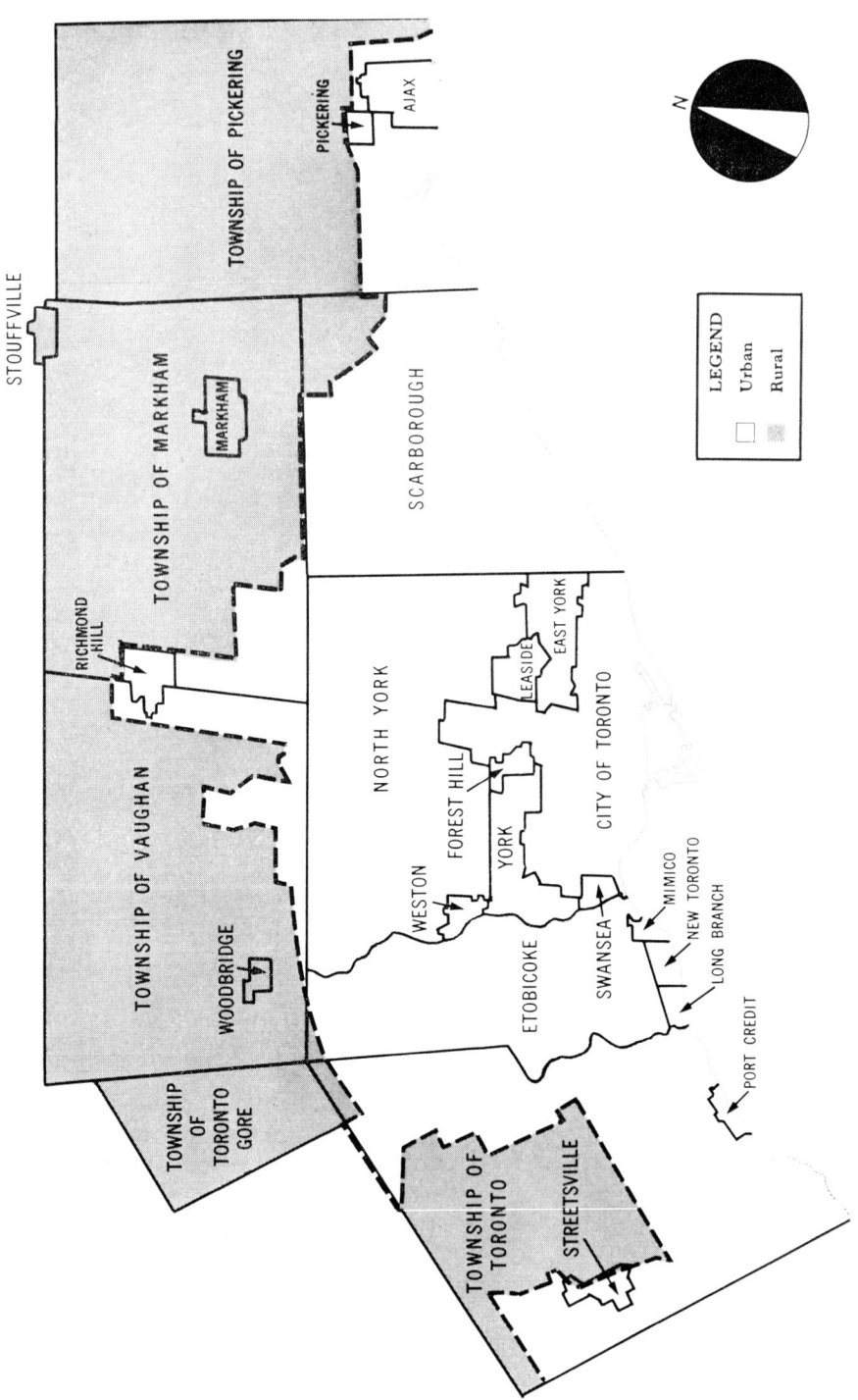

Limit of Urban Development Under Proposed Metropolitan Toronto Official Plan

The Metropolitan Planning Board has projected the fringe population to 1971 and 1980, respectively, as follows:

FRINGE POPULATION PROJECTIONS

	1971	1980
Northern Fringe	78,500	149,500
Eastern Fringe	53,500	85,000
Western Fringe	125,000	265,500
Total	257,000	500,000

The projections forecast a population increase of 180 per cent between 1963 and 1980. For the individual municipalities, Table 47 shows a population of 110,000 in Toronto Township by 1971 and 250,000, or 50 per cent of the whole fringe population, by 1980. Pickering Township ranks second in each of the years, with 37,500 in 1971 and 57,000 in 1980. In the latter year, a population of 55,000 is projected for Vaughan and 50,000 for Markham Township. On the basis of these projections, by 1980 the Township of Toronto alone will have attained a population which would now rank it with Metro's three large outer suburbs.

Table 47

FRINGE MUNICIPALITIES: POPULATION PROJECTIONS
1971 and 1980

Municipality	1971	Per Cent of Total	1980	Per Cent of Total
Northern Fringe				
Township of Vaughan	22,250	8.6	55,000	11.0
Village of Woodbridge	3,750	1.4	3,000	.6
Town of Richmond Hill	19,000	7.4	19,500	3.9
Township of Markham	18,250	7.1	50,000	10.0
Village of Stouffville	5,250	2.0	8,000	1.6
Village of Markham	8,000	3.1	14,000	2.8
Township of Toronto Gore	2,000	.8	(n.a.)	(n.a.)
Total	78,500	30.4	149,500	28.9
Eastern Fringe				
Township of Pickering	37,500	14.6	57,000	11.4
Village of Pickering	3,000	1.2	4,000	.8
Town of Ajax	13,000	5.0	24,000	4.8
Total	53,500	20.8	85,000	17.0
Western Fringe				
Township of Toronto	110,000	42.8	250,000	50.0
Town of Streetsville	7,000	2.7	7,000	1.4
Town of Port Credit	8,000	3.1	8,500	1.7
Total	125,000	48.6	265,500	53.1
Fringe Municipalities—Total	257,000	100.0	500,000	100.0

Source: Metropolitan Toronto Planning Board. (Projections based on existing boundaries).

3. TAXABLE RESOURCES IN THE FRINGE

For purposes of comparing taxable assessments in the fringe areas and between fringe municipalities and area municipalities in Metro, assessments throughout the area have been equalized to the Metro standard by relating the provincial equalization factor for each fringe municipality to the corresponding factor for Metro and applying the resultant factors to the locally reported assessments. Table 48 shows the assessment figures arrived at in this way for the years 1958 and 1963, with corresponding figures for the three outer Metro suburbs. A five year interval has been used because there was no single provincial equalization factor for Metro before 1958.

Table 48

FRINGE MUNICIPALITIES:

Assessment Equalized to the Level of Metropolitan Toronto Assessment

Municipality	1958 Equalized Assessment	1963 Equalized Assessment	Average Annual Increase	Percentage Increase 1958-1963
	$000	$000	$000	%
Northern Fringe				
Township of Vaughan	17,022	27,337	2,063	60.6
Village of Woodbridge	3,377	4,526	230	34.0
Town of Richmond Hill	18,444	26,454	1,602	43.4
Township of Markham	17,007	24,839	1,566	46.0
Village of Stouffville	3,460	4,568	222	32.0
Village of Markham	5,386	8,205	564	52.3
Township of Toronto Gore	1,301	1,612	62	23.9
Total	65,997	97,542	6,309	47.8
Eastern Fringe				
Township of Pickering	14,692	28,835	2,829	96.3
Village of Pickering	1,462	2,243	156	53.4
Town of Ajax	9,257	12,220	593	32.0
Total	25,411	43,298	3,577	70.4
Western Fringe				
Township of Toronto	96,095	149,382	10,657	55.5
Town of Streetsville	4,671	7,305	527	56.4
Town of Port Credit	10,866	15,213	869	40.0
Total	111,632	171,899	12,053	54.0
Fringe Municipalities Total	203,040	312,738	21,940	54.0
Three Outer Suburbs				
Township of North York	418,314	714,905	59,318	70.9
Township of Scarborough	284,026	447,894	32,774	57.7
Township of Etobicoke	321,197	498,061	35,373	55.1
Total	1,023,537	1,660,860	127,465	62.3
Metro Toronto	3,200,064	4,164,708	192,927	30.1

Sources: Assessments, Annual Report of Municipal Statistics, Province of Ontario, 1958 and 1963. Assessment Equalization Factors, Assessment Branch, Department of Municipal Affairs. Assessment, Port Credit, Clerk's Return, 1963. Streetsville, Clerk's Return, 1958.

The table shows an increase of 54 per cent in the equalized assessment of the fringe between 1958 and 1963, as compared with 62 per cent for Metro's three outer suburbs and 30 per cent for Metro as a whole. The following figures compare changes in fringe areas with changes in the adjoining Metro municipalities:

	1963 Equalized Assessment $000	Per Cent Increase 1958-1963 %
Township of North York	714,905	70.9
Northern Fringe	97,542	47.8
Township of Scarborough	447,894	57.7
Eastern Fringe	43,298	70.4
Township of Etobicoke	498,061	55.1
Western Fringe	171,899	54.0

In 1963 population and equalized assessment in the fringe were distributed as follows:

	% of Total Population %	% of Total Assessment %
Northern Fringe	35.4	31.2
Eastern Fringe	17.8	13.8
Western Fringe	46.7	55.0

The Township of Toronto, with approximately 40 per cent of the population, contained almost 48 per cent of the total equalized assessment of the fringe.

Per capita equalized assessments in 1958 and 1963 are shown in Table 49, with corresponding figures for the three outer suburbs. The figures compare as follows:

PER CAPITA EQUALIZED ASSESSMENT, 1963

	$
Township of North York	2,324
Northern Fringe	1,543
Township of Scarborough	1,863
Eastern Fringe	1,361
Township of Etobicoke	2,805
Western Fringe	2,062

The difference of $701 between the eastern and western fringes reflects the differences in the degree of urban development. Toronto Township, with $2,108 per capita, is at a metropolitan level, while Pickering Township, with $1,317, shows the lowest figure in the area. In its brief to the Commission,

Pickering pointed to its assessment ratio of 88.43 per cent residential to 11.57 per cent commercial and industrial in 1963. The Township of Toronto showed a ratio of 56.47 per cent residential to 43.53 per cent commercial and industrial.

Table 49

FRINGE MUNICIPALITIES:

Per Capita Assessment Equalized to the Level of Metropolitan Toronto Assessment

Municipality	1958 Equalized Assessment	1963 Equalized Assessment	Percentage Increase 1958-1963
	$	$	%
Northern Fringe			
Township of Vaughan	1,125	1,563	38.9
Village of Woodbridge	1,586	1,853	16.8
Town of Richmond Hill	1,300	1,422	9.4
Township of Markham	1,314	1,678	27.7
Village of Stouffville	1,305	1,321	1.2
Village of Markham	1,350	1,558	15.4
Township of Toronto Gore	1,261	1,397	10.8
Total	1,267	1,543	21.8
Eastern Fringe			
Township of Pickering	934	1,317	41.0
Village of Pickering	910	1,235	35.7
Town of Ajax	1,160	1,507	29.9
Total	1,004	1,361	35.6
Western Fringe			
Township of Toronto	1,806	2,108	16.7
Town of Streetsville	1,056	1,368	29.5
Town of Port Credit	1,711	2,129	24.4
Total	1,744	2,062	18.2
Fringe Municipalities Total	1,436	1,753	22.1
Three Outer Suburbs			
Township of North York	2,118	2,324	9.7
Township of Scarborough	1,688	1,863	10.4
Township of Etobicoke	2,649	2,805	5.9
Total	2,101	2,289	8.9
Metro Toronto	2,266	2,521	11.3

Sources: Population and Assessment, as shown in Annual Report of Municipal Statistics, Province of Ontario, 1958 and 1963, and Clerk's Return, Village of Streetsville.

The three counties through which the fringe municipalities are spread are dependent on these municipalities to a large degree for the funds to finance county services. The levy is based on a county equalized assessment. Table 50 shows that in 1963 the three municipalities of the eastern fringe provided 38.2 per cent of the levy in Ontario County; the six southern municipalities of York County provided 51.8 per cent of its levy; and the four municipalities in

Peel County paid 71.5 per cent of the levy, Toronto Township alone contributing 62 per cent. The proportions are significant, particularly in the counties of Peel and York.

Table 50

COUNTY LEVIES:
Fringe Municipalities' Share

County of York
Total County Levy 1963....... $1,517,532

Municipality	County Levy	% of Total County Levy
	$	%
Township of Vaughan............	227,394	15.0
Village of Woodbridge...........	36,617	2.4
Town of Richmond Hill.........	214,034	14.1
Township of Markham...........	204,517	13.5
Village of Stouffville............	37,850	2.5
Village of Markham.............	65,754	4.3
Total.......................	786,166	51.8

County of Ontario
Total County Levy 1963....... $1,223,195

Municipality	County Levy	% of Total County Levy
	$	%
Township of Pickering..........	308,784	25.2
Village of Pickering............	23,977	2.0
Town of Ajax...................	134,619	11.0
Total.......................	467,380	38.2

County of Peel
Total County Levy 1963..... $1,684,408

Municipality	County Levy	% of Total County Levy
	$	%
Township of Toronto............	1,044,372	62.0
Town of Streetsville............	54,030	3.2
Town of Port Credit............	94,251[1]	5.6
Township of Toronto Gore.......	12,366	.7
Total.......................	1,205,019	71.5

[1]Auditor's Report and Financial Statement, 1963.
Source: Annual Report of Municipal Statistics, Province of Ontario, 1963.

4. METRO AND THE FRINGE

The foregoing analysis shows different rates of growth and varying degrees of urbanization on Metro's fringe, with the largest growth in the western section and the smallest in the east. Projections to 1971 and 1980 indicate a continuation of this pattern, which is reflected in the limits to urban development proposed in the draft Metro Official Plan.

Resulting from the pressure of metropolitan expansion, there is now a continuous urban development from the south-western section of Pickering Township, in the east, to and beyond the outer limits of Toronto Township, in the west, and, in a northerly direction, along Yonge Street to the outer limits of Richmond Hill. The various parts of the area are interdependent. The fringe municipalities are to a large degree dormitory to Metro, where most of their work force is employed. Pickering Township, in its brief to the Commission, estimated that 87 per cent of the residents of School Area No. 2, where most of its people live, derive their income from industry and commerce in Metro. The corresponding estimate by Richmond Hill was 65 per cent. The brief of the southern six municipalities of York County showed that at least 55 per cent of their working residents are employed outside their boundaries.

There is also interdependence in respect of the provision of basic urban services, such as roads, water, sewers and planning. This applies particularly to development on the north. The eastern and western fringes, bordering on Lake Ontario, are physically in a position to provide basic water and sewage facilities. The Lakeview sewage treatment plant, on the west, is operated jointly by Metro and Toronto Township. The northern fringe, however, cannot secure a sufficient water supply to sustain growth except by obtaining it from Metro. It is also dependent upon Metro for sewage outlets and metropolitan sewer services are already being supplied to a small part of the area north of Steeles Avenue.

Considering the interdependence of this continuous urban area and its forecast growth, it has been suggested that Metro's boundaries should now be extended to include all or some of the fringe municipalities, or parts thereof. The suggestion has merit in regard to certain areas but it also poses problems. It is admittedly important to avoid a repetition of the critical situation which developed in the outer suburbs before the creation of Metro. Distance from the lake and consequent water and sewage problems in North York and Scarborough were a major cause of the crisis. Without effective controls and some integration of services, this situation could well recur on the northern fringe, where development pressures are increasing and will increase more sharply with the construction of new north-south expressways. It is also argued that, as the large open spaces of North York and Scarborough are developed, Metro will need room for expansion; by adding the six southern municipalities of York County to Metro now, metropolitan services could be integrated to meet prospective requirements.

While the situation on the northern outskirts of Metro presents similarities to that which faced North York and Scarborough in the post-war years, the overall situation is different. The development pattern has been relatively well controlled, as a result, in part at least, of the ability of the Metropolitan Planning

Board and the Province to withstand the pressure for widespread septic tank development. As stated in the brief submitted by the County of York:

> Many things have happened since 1953 which can and do act as effective substitutes for expansion of political territories. The existence of the Metropolitan Toronto Planning Area, the powers contained in the Metropolitan Act with respect to the Official Plan, the active and coordinated programmes of the Conservation Authority and the role of the Ontario Water Resources Commission all combine to produce the basis for physical, policy and financial planning which did not exist previously. The case of certain services illustrates this point. A definite and long-range plan is in existence for serving the future urban areas in the southern part of the County with metropolitan services, in part, being extended to the limit of their capacity on a simple contractual basis and with the balance of the area being served by a limited system of local facilities, so located and controlled as to provide adequate local services and at the same time not causing difficulties for the residents of Metropolitan Toronto.

Accordingly, continued orderly development appears possible without extending Metro's northern boundaries at this time. The need for the adoption and implementation of a Metro Official Plan covering the wide Metropolitan Planning Area has been dealt with in Chapter VI of this report. The plan will delineate the limits of urban development and project a desirable rate of growth, which should, in turn, determine the programme for the provision of urban services. Water and sewage facilities required on the northern fringe can and should be provided on an agreed basis by the Metropolitan Corporation in co-operation with the Ontario Water Resources Commission. Metro now has authority to enter into contracts to supply water to any municipality outside its jurisdiction.

In considering the need for an extension of Metro's boundaries, it is relevant to note that in 1963, according to Table 5 of the proposed Metro Official Plan, agricultural or vacant land represented a large proportion of the areas of Metro's three outer suburbs: 21,000 acres or almost 47 per cent of the area of Scarborough; more than 14,000 acres or 33 per cent of the area of North York; and over 9,000 acres or 32 per cent of the area of Etobicoke. Accordingly, there are still large areas available for development within Metro, and there is also the need for renewal and redevelopment of its older areas. There is the further consideration that the fringe municipalities, except for pockets of urban development, are predominantly rural. It has been shown that 85 per cent of the northern fringe, 84 per cent of the eastern fringe, and 71 per cent of the western fringe is agricultural or vacant land. To incorporate areas which are still so predominantly rural into an urban complex like Metro would create complications. It is significant that the Manitoba Legislature found it necessary to amend The Metropolitan Winnipeg Act in 1964 to exclude substantial rural areas which had been included within the boundaries of Metropolitan Winnipeg under the original legislation of 1960.

Reference has been made to the financial dependence of the counties on the fringe municipalities. The extension of Metro's boundaries to include only the urbanized portions of the fringe would create serious financial problems for the remaining parts of the counties by removing a major portion of their taxable assessment. One result would be pressure for a more balanced tax base and the creation of a new urbanized fringe. In the words of the Provincial Planning Director of Alberta:[1]

> The accumulative result of successive annexations is, of course, more and more urban development at the fringes of the built-up area which, in their turn, produce a new fringe extending a little farther from the centre of the city than before—and so on and so on!

An analysis of the taxable resources of the areas which would be directly affected by an extension of Metro's boundaries shows that only the Township of Toronto has approached a metropolitan level of per capita assessment. Fronting on Lake Ontario and extending north to Steeles Avenue, it has developed and will continue to develop more rapidly than the rest of the fringe. It has a balanced assessment. Its projected population is 110,000 by 1971 and 250,000 by 1980. In its brief to the Commission, the Township, opposing inclusion in Metro, showed that it "has been able to cope with its own problems as far as education is concerned", that it has adequate physical facilities, which can be enlarged, and that it "has been able to maintain a fairly even tax rate for general purposes and believes it can continue to do so because of its policies of controlled development." The brief also referred to negotiations for amalgamation with the towns of Port Credit and Streetsville.

Urban development in the southern section of the Township is part of the urban belt which stretches westward to Hamilton. Toronto Township, although oriented mainly to Metro, also has ties to the west. Adjoining it is the Town of Oakville, where the large Ford automobile plant employs many residents of the Township. "Unless you knew the boundary was there you would not see any difference going from Oakville into Toronto Township and vice versa", said Reeve Speck in his evidence before the Commission. In other words, the urban area continues unbroken well beyond the Township's limits, and if Metro's limits were extended to the outer limits of the Township, the western boundary would still necessarily be an arbitrary line.

The extension of Metro to include the whole or part of Toronto Township would endanger the survival of Peel County which depends upon the Township for 62 per cent of the county levy. The position and functions of the County and alternative forms of regional municipal organization in the area should be examined before considering integration of the Township with Metro. Consideration might well be given to the creation of a smaller "Metro" on the western fringe of Metropolitan Toronto.

Pickering Township, to the east of Metro, with a population of 22,000 in an area of 70,000 acres, is the least urbanized part of the fringe. Its projected population is 37,500 by 1971 and 57,000 in 1980. As a dormitory municipality,

---
[1]The Alberta Municipal Counsellor, February 1964.

with residential property representing almost 90 per cent of its taxable assessment, the Township faces problems in financing rising school budgets and municipal costs.

Both Pickering Township and Richmond Hill, on the north, submitted in their briefs to the Commission that they are entitled to financial assistance from Metro to meet the costs of serving as dormitory municipalities. There is no doubt that the residential development to which they attribute their financial problems is a result of their proximity to Metro. It is equally true that the Metropolitan Corporation was not in a position to force or to prevent the approval of such development by the local councils. The fact remains that proximity to a large urban complex like Metro creates "spill-over" problems in adjacent municipalities. The Provincial Government should give recognition to such special situations through appropriate adjustments in the system of grants to municipalities and school districts, including the municipal unconditional grant.

5. CONCLUSIONS

The area of the Municipality of Metropolitan Toronto is 240 square miles, which, it is estimated, is developed to about two-thirds of its designated urban capacity under the proposed Official Plan. Its population in 1964 was approximately 1,750,000; the projected population is 2,040,000 by 1971 and 2,300,000 by 1980, and the urban capacity is estimated at 2,685,000. The fringe municipalities, with an area of 480 square miles, twice the area of Metro, have a population of about 180,000, with estimated increases to 257,000 by 1971 and 500,000 by 1980. Their estimated urban capacity is 960,000. Accordingly, the combined population of Metro and the fringe, with an area of 720 square miles, is now almost 2,000,000 and, if trends are maintained, will be approaching 3,000,000 by 1980. It is necessary to have regard to these facts and projections in considering an extension of the boundaries of the Metropolitan Area. It is true that Greater London now covers an area of almost 620 square miles, with a population of about 8,000,000, but the United Kingdom is a unitary state whereas Canada is a federation of provinces. In considering the potential size of Metropolitan Toronto, consideration must also be given to its place in the Province of Ontario.

There is no ideal size for a metropolitan area, and the forces contributing to this pattern of urban growth are not abating. It is now more than sixty years since H. G. Wells described the developing problem as follows:[1]

> You will find that many people who once slept and worked and reared their children and worshipped and bought all in one area, are now, as it were, "delocalized"; they have overflowed their containing locality, and they live in one area, they work in another, and they go to shop in a third. And the only way in which you can localize them again is to expand your areas to their new scale.

---

[1] H. G. Wells: "A Paper on Administrative Areas Read Before the Fabian Society," in appendix to "Mankind in the Making". (New York: Charles Scribner's Sons, 1904), p. 379.

I am confident that if Wells had lived to witness "the metropolitan explosion" since 1945, he would have agreed that there are limits to expanding areas "to their new scale".

Metropolitan Toronto and its urban fringe form part of an urban belt which extends eastward to Oshawa and westward to Hamilton. A dividing line might be drawn on the east, but the belt to the west is unbroken; it can be said that the Toronto metropolitan region runs right up to the metropolitan area of Hamilton or that the latter is only a further extension of the former. It is clear that, for political and administrative reasons, Metro's boundaries cannot be extended indefinitely to encompass the extension of urban development. Subject to other regional adjustments in the interval, however, growing urbanization and interdependence point to an extension of Metro's boundaries in due course to include substantial parts of the urbanizing fringe units.

An important test for the delimitation of urban boundaries is the need for the provision of integrated urban services. Accordingly, there would be justification for extending Metro's boundary northward, since urbanization on this boundary is dependent on Metro for water and sewage services. But, as has been shown, the area is still very largely rural and urbanization has been fairly effectively controlled and should continue to be regulated by a Metro Official Plan. On the basis of present projections, it will be some years before the municipalities on the northern fringe, even as a group with an area larger than Metro, would qualify, in terms of population, as a Metro area municipality. Moreover, the removal at this time of all or part of the southern six municipalities for municipal purposes from York County would seriously affect the financial position of the County and its remaining municipalities. Prior consideration should therefore be given to a reorganization of county government. In the meanwhile, the powers and the machinery are available, both at the provincial and the Metro level, to provide the services required for present and planned urban development. The Metro Act confers authority upon the Metropolitan Corporation to enter into agreements with outside municipalities in respect of water supply, sewage disposal and public transit. There are also the powers of the Ontario Water Resources Commission in the matter of water and sewage facilities. However, failing satisfactory arrangements to provide the required facilities, the appropriate built-up area north of Steeles Avenue in Vaughan and Markham townships should be annexed to North York without undue delay, with compensation to the townships and the County of York for loss of assessment, under the provisions of section 14 of The Municipal Act.

Metro's northern boundary should be reviewed from time to time in relation to the progress of urbanization. My recommendations are predicated on the relatively limited urban development envisaged in the proposed Metro Official Plan. If, more extensive urbanization is contemplated, with the consequent need for a wide extension of Metro services, incorporation in some form with Metro will have to receive serious consideration. As stated by Mr.

Murray Jones, formerly Metropolitan Planning Commissioner, in presenting a brief for the County of York, (Proceedings, pp. 845-846):

> .... the basic issue is a question of the timing of further extensive urbanization not presently contemplated ..... Should it become necessary in the future to contemplate another extensive area of urbanization much larger than that now proposed, it would obviously have to result in a change in political organization for the simple reason that it would involve the creation of an extensive new system of "Metropolitan" services.

On the west, the Township of Toronto, with the largest urban growth in the fringe area, resembles more closely the growing area municipalities of Metro. The extension of Metro's boundaries to include the Township would have serious effects on Peel County. Prior consideration should be given to other forms of regional municipal reorganization in the area, such as the creation of a smaller "Metro."

Urbanization in the eastern fringe is still very limited. Pickering Township is experiencing the "spill-over" problems of a dormitory municipality adjacent to a large urban complex. The special situation of such municipalities should be officially recognized by the Provincial Government through appropriate adjustments in grants for municipal and school purposes.

If it were the sole test, the existence of a continuous urban area extending beyond its boundaries would justify extensions of Metro's limits. But, as has been shown, there are other considerations. If Metro's limits are to be extended, it is necessary to assure a viable pattern of municipal organization on its new boundaries. Accordingly, I have recommended that prior consideration should be given to municipal reorganization in the fringe areas.

CHAPTER XIV

REORGANIZATION OF METROPOLITAN TORONTO

In 1953 the Ontario Municipal Board reported that "the basic problem to be solved in the Toronto metropolitan area is indicated in the significant contrast between the underlying social and economic unity of the area on the one hand, and the illogical and inequitable but extremely rigid divisions of political jurisdiction and available taxable resources on the other." As a solution, the Board recommended the establishment of a metropolitan form of government based upon a federation of the thirteen area municipalities with powers divided between the latter and the new central authority.

1. METRO'S ACHIEVEMENTS AND CONTINUING PROBLEMS

The Municipality of Metropolitan Toronto came into being on January 1, 1954. It has realized its objectives in substantial measure. The many briefs submitted to the Commission were unanimous in their praise of Metro's accomplishments and its contribution to the remarkable growth and development of the Toronto area in the past decade. Thus, while proposing a basic change in the system, the City of Toronto, in its brief, said:

> In giving thought to the best form of government for the Toronto metropolitan area, the City of Toronto is well aware of the remarkable record of achievement which has been chalked up throughout the past decade by the Municipality of Metropolitan Toronto. In this brief we have no wish to play down Metro's accomplishments.

Notwithstanding these accomplishments, this report has shown that some of the problems described in the Cumming Report of 1953 persist and have grown. They flow from continuing "illogical and inequitable but extremely rigid divisions of political jurisdiction and available taxable resources." The area is divided into thirteen municipalities ranging from less than one square mile to seventy square miles in size, from 9,000 to 650,000 in population, and from $22 million to $2 billion in taxable assessment. As a result, in an area which is a social and economic unit, there are undue inequalities in the burden of financing essential services and in the range and standards of some of the basic services provided. While the equalizing influence of Metro has prevented far greater inequalities from developing, the spread between the lowest and highest taxed municipalities has tended to widen. Moreover, with population growth concentrated in the outer suburbs, inequalities in representation on the Metropolitan Council have grown to the point that reform is imperative. A system which gives equal representation to Swansea, with 9,300 people, and North York, with 340,000, can no longer be maintained.

In 1961 and 1962 three municipalities proposed changes which would affect the structure of Metro. On December 20, 1961, the Village of Long Branch passed a by-law authorizing an application to the Ontario Municipal Board for amalgamation of the three Lakeshore municipalities. On September 24, 1962, a by-law passed by the Town of New Toronto authorized an application for amalgamation of the Lakeshore municipalities and the Police Village of Malton with the Township of Etobicoke. On October 9, 1962, a by-law of the City of Toronto authorized an application for amalgamation of all the municipalities in the Metropolitan Area. The powers of the Board to hear such applications were rescinded as from April 26, 1963, by an amendment to the Metro Act, following a statement in the Legislature by the Hon. John P. Robarts, Prime Minister, that the Government of Ontario had decided to appoint a Commission to inquire into the structure and organization of Metropolitan Toronto.

The need for change was recognized in most briefs to the Commission, but no brief suggested a return to the pre-Metro forms of municipal organization in the area. The City of Toronto submitted that:

> Despite the weaknesses of Metro, its critics have not proposed turning back the clock. The degree of metropolitan unification which has been attained should in the opinion of all responsible observers be preserved. It is generally recognized that Metro has proven, as the Ontario Municipal Board had hoped, "a forward step in the solution of an extremely difficult problem" ..... *Change ought therefore to consolidate gains and build upon them* .....

On changes in the Metro structure, the area municipalities were understandably divided. Most of the smaller units, while recognizing that some changes are necessary, urged that they be made within a continuing metropolitan federation of thirteen municipalities. The larger suburbs also favoured continuation of the metropolitan system but with the area municipalities consolidated into a small number of "boroughs". The City of Toronto alone recommended amalgamation of the whole area into one city.

2. Maintenance of the Status Quo

The arguments of the smaller municipalities in favour of the status quo are twofold. There is, first, the sentimental desire to preserve their local identity, with emphasis on the values of the neighbourhood area and community feeling, of citizen interest and the responsiveness of local government. Secondly, it is argued that the smaller units now provide a level of services which reflects the needs and desires of the local residents whereas under any form of merger these residents would have to pay higher taxes for a uniform level of services over a wider area.

The desire to preserve local identity for its own sake is understandable. In some cases it is naturally fortified by financial, economic and other advantages which attach to the unit as a separate political entity. A local patriotism develops and local boundaries are considered as fixed and permanent. The resulting situation has been fittingly described by Dr. Luther H. Gulick, a noted authority on municipal government and former City Administrator of New York:[1]

> Finally, a fixed political boundary serves as the mediaeval wall behind which the employees of the governmental unit, including the local politicians, are deployed, not only to perform their services, but to defend "their town" and themselves against the outside world; and this they do in all sincerity. Fixed boundaries thus create their own protection by raising up powerful political defenses, patriotic loyalties, fiscal rigidities, and bureaucratic mercenaries.

There is considerable nostalgia in the arguments for the preservation of all existing local boundaries in the Metro area. The submissions bring to mind the days before the widespread use of motor cars and the rapid spread of urbanization, when municipal boundaries were more realistic and each town was a clearly recognizable entity, separate and distinct from its rural hinterland. The neighbourhood, the local area in which each inhabitant knows a large number of the others and is conscious of a considerable community of interest with them, was the unit of local government. In areas which are largely rural, this is still true. But in large integrated urban areas where the people are economically interdependent, working in one municipality and living and paying taxes in another, with large numbers moving from one unit to another every few years, the old concept of the neighbourhood as the unit of local government scarcely applies. This is the price of mobility. The nostalgic arguments for the preservation of all artificial boundaries in an urban complex such as Metropolitan Toronto have been largely invalidated by social and economic change.

It does not follow that with a change of boundaries a sense of community is or should be lost. It is an asset which can be preserved. The local neighbourhood does not disappear with the extension of municipal boundaries, nor should the patriotism which attaches to it. The brief of the City of Toronto says, with effect, that:

> When a former self-contained town or village is swept up in a metropolitan expansion, part of its character is lost whether or not it is stripped of its independent municipal status; and part of it remains even if its corporate entity has disappeared. Toronto people still talk of Yorkville, which was annexed in 1883, of Riverdale, which was absorbed a year later, of Rosedale, of the Annex, Sunnyside and Parkdale, each of which became part of the City of Toronto before 1890. The history of Toronto annexations contains many another familiar name including Deer Park, Wychwood, West Toronto, Balmy Beach, Dovercourt, North Toronto and Moore Park. The two latest were added to the City in 1912!

Having been "swept up in a metropolitan expansion", the Toronto area municipalities are, as such, no longer distinct and separate neighbourhoods but interdependent parts of a geographic, social and economic unit. It is in this

---
[1] Luther Halsey Gulick: The Metropolitan Problem and American Ideas. (New York: Alfred A. Knopf, 1962), p. 50.

context that we must look at the thirteen municipalities into which this integrated urban area is divided, the great variations in their size, population and resources, and the consequent disparities in their financial burdens and in the range and standards of some of the basic municipal services which they provide.

Reeve Edwin J. Pivnick, of Forest Hill, in his evidence before the Commission, acknowledged that (Proceedings, p. 329):

> . . . . . co-operative action between component members of an amalgamated or federated system can be diminished significantly if the members are separated by fundamental disparities in economic resources.

Co-operative action is also impeded by the gross inequality in representation on the Metropolitan Council inherent in the present structure which calls for one representative from each suburb regardless of differences in population.

It has been argued that to minimize the effects of an uneven distribution of resources more responsibilities should be assigned to Metro. This argument has merit; I have recommended an extension of metropolitan responsibilities in respect of education and certain other matters. But I have also recommended that important functions be left to the area municipalities, provided that the municipalities are regrouped into larger units which would make a fuller range of basic local services more widely and more equally available than is possible under the existing system. The alternative is to transfer responsibility for an increasing number of services to the Metropolitan Corporation. If this process is carried much further, however, it will be difficult to justify the continued existence of the individual municipalities. There will not be much left for them to do. In the words of W. A. Robson, Professor of Public Administration in the University of London:[1]

> Those who cling too tenaciously to the preservation of "historic" areas in a world where the traditional boundaries have become irrelevant can achieve their object only at the cost of depriving the "historic" areas of all administrative significance and vitality.

Having considered the submissions and the facts of the situation, I find that the case for the maintenance of the status quo in Metropolitan Toronto is not valid.

3. AMALGAMATION

The City of Toronto recommended amalgamation of the Metropolitan Area into one big city. While this recommendation was supported by a number of other briefs, it was opposed by the large bulk of the submissions to the Commission. The other area municipalities were of course unanimous in their opposition.

The history of the City's policy on annexation has been outlined in Chapter III of this report. Having expanded over a period of thirty years by absorbing newly built-up areas, Toronto, after the first World War, adopted a policy of

---
[1] W. A. Robson, in "A Century of Municipal Progress." (London: George Allen & Unwin Ltd., 1936), p. 458.

"no further annexations". It was only in 1950 that it reversed its position by applying to the Ontario Municipal Board for an order amalgamating the City with the surrounding municipalities. The Board dismissed the application and recommended a form of metropolitan government for the area. In 1962 a City by-law authorized a new application for amalgamation.

The case submitted by Toronto to the Commission is based on three main grounds: that amalgamation "offers the most complete and direct cure to current problems of taxation, representation and organization"; that "an outright merger is the simplest and most logical governmental arrangement, offering the best prospects for continuing achievement"; and that such a merger "is entirely practical and readily attainable." The brief submits that, with the elimination of thirteen municipal councils and the related boards, commissions and departments, substantial savings in administrative costs would be effected, although it admits that additional expenditures would be necessary "to eliminate differences in service standards that could not be tolerated within an amalgamated municipality." It alleges that the Metro system involves duplication of effort and "adds to the cost of administering local government services"; one big city could introduce economies of scale. With respect to its own position in the area, Toronto complains that the creation of Metro has locked it "inside its existing boundaries with no opportunity to expand but a responsibility to assist the suburban municipalities with their expansion"; that it "is bearing more than its fair share of the cost of services as a consequence of its central location"; and that, as a result of "planning by assessment" in the suburbs, it is subject to unfair competition for high-grade commercial and residential development. The City maintains that amalgamation, with centralized control and uniform tax rates, would eliminate city-suburban tensions and consolidate the gains flowing from the degree of unification already attained under Metro.

There is much that appeals in the case for amalgamation. With local government shared by Metro and thirteen municipalities, the area is highly over-governed, and the variations in size and resources of the units are reflected in wide disparities in tax burdens and in services. Amalgamation offers a solution which would eliminate thirteen local governments, equalize tax rates, consolidate administration, and prepare the way for uniformity of services. To many persons this is a simple straightforward answer to Metro's problems. But "neat and tidy" solutions to complex problems of government are not necessarily applicable or practical.

The City's case assumes that municipal services and tax rates should be equal throughout the 240 square miles of the Metro area. This assumption fails to recognize that there are differences between the inner ring of developed municipalities with high population densities and the three developing outer townships with large areas of agricultural and vacant land and relatively low density of population. I have said in this report that the citizens of the thirteen municipalities are entitled to more equality in the range and standards of basic services than the present fragmented system of government permits, but this does not mean that there must be complete equality in respect of all services regardless of the different requirements of developed and developing areas. At this stage, there is room for some diversity in services and therefore in tax rates.

The City submits that total amalgamation will mean more efficiency in administration. In relation to administration by thirteen units of varying size and resources, this argument has validity. However, such savings in costs as may be effected would soon be more than offset by the increase in expenditures to raise the standards of services to a common level. In respect of Metro, no proof was submitted of unnecessary duplication of effort or that the metropolitan system has added considerably to the costs of local government. It has been shown in Chapter VIII of this report that Metro's expenditures on general government, including the costs of assessment for all the area municipalities, have ranged from only $1.01 to $1.15 per $1,000 of taxable assessment. Considering the growth of the area and the consequent expansion of municipal services since 1953, costs would have risen whatever system of local government prevailed.

While economy and efficiency in administration are necessary, they should not be the sole test of representative government. The recent report of the Royal Commission on Greater London points out that: "Local government is with us an instance of democracy at work, and no amount of potential administrative efficiency could make up for the loss of active participation in the work by capable, public spirited people elected by, responsible to, and in touch with those who elect them."[1] The report goes on to say, however, that "it is always necessary to bear in mind that unless local authorities are so constituted as to be able to undertake all the functions appropriate to local government there will always be the risk that more and more functions will be taken away from local government and given to ad hoc bodies or to central government."[2] Total amalgamation of the Metro area would mean centralized administration with necessary decentralization of some local services through the establishment of divisional offices responsible to the central office. In my opinion, the requirements of both democracy and administrative efficiency will be better satisfied if the administration of such local services, as distinct from area-wide services, is, as far as possible, in the hands of local officials responsible to local elected representatives in municipalities properly constituted to meet the needs of the Metropolitan Area.

The population of the Metropolitan Area in 1965 is greater than that of seven of the ten provinces of Canada and approximately equal to the population of the eighth, British Columbia. Total amalgamation would therefore create a city with a population of more than 1,750,000 in 1965 and a forecast population of more than 2,000,000 by 1970 and about 2,500,000 in the early 'eighties. On the matter of bigness, the Toronto brief says that in 1963 there were 41 cities, "single municipal entities", which were larger in population than Metro: "The number included five cities in the United States and one in Mexico, nine in

---

[1] Report of the Royal Commission on Local Government in Greater London, op cit., p. 59.
[2] Ibid, p. 61.

Europe, five in South America, two in Australia and the remaining twenty in Asia." This is scarcely a valid argument for total amalgamation in Toronto; I doubt that its citizens would want to pattern their municipality on or face the problems of any of the cities to which the brief has reference. It is relevant to note that the municipal reorganization of Greater London which became effective on April 1, 1965, took the form of a new metropolitan government, with a great reduction in the number of local authorities, and that in Los Angeles, a report in 1961 also recommended a metropolitan government for area-wide functions.[1]

The Toronto brief submits that: "A unique requirement of government at the local level is to accomplish periodic adjustments of the units of government in response to the growth of urban areas." I have said, in Chapter XIII of this report, that increasing urbanization in the fringe areas points to an eventual extension of Metro's boundaries. The City admits that "the extent of urban development which needs to be enclosed may be a factor in deciding which is more practical, amalgamation or federation. If federation should be continued, the most likely way of adding territory would be to take in some further municipalities and to give them the status which now applies or is then assigned to local municipalities within the present boundary line. If we amalgamate, the outer boundary could be extended by adding whole or part municipalities which would thereby be brought into the enlarged city." On this point, I agree with Controller William L. Archer of Toronto, who, in his brief, said:

> ..... The brief from the City of Toronto has raised the question of the location of our outer boundaries. It is my submission that in those cases where it becomes necessary to alter the outer boundaries of Metropolitan Toronto, it can be done more easily through a district system than through a totally amalgamated system. The essential point of our system of government in this area is that we must retain a high degree of flexibility for the future. The rigidity of total amalgamation would place restrictions on the future growth and development of our area and make it difficult, if not impossible, to develop regional government for the urbanized area that exists between Oshawa and Niagara Falls.

Toronto submits that: "It is generally recognized that Metro has proven, as the Ontario Municipal Board had hoped, 'a forward step in the solution of an extremely difficult problem.' *Change ought therefore to consolidate gains and build upon them."* The brief does not prove that consolidation of the gains under Metro calls for the dissolution of the metropolitan system and total amalgamation of the area. Reeve True Davidson, of East York, in her evidence before the Commission, said, with effect, (Proceedings, p. 1567):

> I think that there is no reason to have amalgamation. You don't have to put the baby out with the bath water. There is no reason why we shouldn't retain the Metro system while getting rid of the inequitable—nobody denies the present representation is inequitable, and that there is a wide variation in the tax rate, although I don't object to some variation in the tax rate. I think this is reasonable so that people can have what they want and can pay for.

---
[1]Metropolitan Government for Los Angeles: A Workable Solution. (March 1961).

4. CONSOLIDATION

All briefs submitted to the Commission praised the achievements of Metro and the large majority favoured the continuation of metropolitan government with a consolidation of the area municipalities into a smaller number of units, usually referred to as "boroughs". The number suggested ranged from four to eight.

For the reasons already set out in this report, I have concluded that, notwithstanding the impressive accomplishments of Metro, there are certain continuing problems which call for a reorganization of the municipal structure in the area. Accordingly, I have rejected the maintenance of the status quo. While recognizing some of its advantages, I have also rejected total amalgamation. I do not find that a case has been made for the dissolution of the metropolitan system of government. It is my conclusion that continuation of a metropolitan federation with a consolidation of some of the area municipalities will best meet the requirements of government and of continued growth of the Metropolitan Area.

In recommending a metropolitan government based on the principle of federation, the Ontario Municipal Board, in the Cumming Report of 1953, said that "one of the great virtues of any federal scheme is its flexibility and the comparative ease with which it can be adapted to changed conditions and the realities of a particular situation." In my opinion, the continuing rapid growth of the Metropolitan Area in the 'sixties makes it essential to maintain such flexibility. This must be a basic consideration in a reorganization of the municipal structure of the area.

Having proposed a new form of government which involved many adjustments, the Cumming Report, as a practical consideration, sought to avoid drastic changes which were not immediately necessary. However, it did foresee changes in due course and pointed out that:

> They [the municipalities] are not in the position of sovereign states entering a federation on a contractual basis and the scheme of federation now proposed will not be comparable to a rigid written constitution to be amended only by mutual consent. Necessary changes can and will be made as the need arises by the act of the legislature which is at all times the only source of the powers which are being discussed.

The Board's comments, in 1953, on the existing boundaries of the area municipalities are particularly relevant. The Cumming Report anticipated a regrouping of municipalities when it said that:

> The need of future changes in the boundaries of the city and the twelve suburbs ..... must not be overlooked. In many cases these boundaries have been the result of purely arbitrary decisions or the result of temporary influences and do not now conform to natural or logical divisions of community interest. It is also quite possible that within some of the larger municipalities the process of further division by separate incorporation may continue as in the past.

I have concluded that a regrouping is now necessary.

My recommendations for a consolidation of area municipalities are not based on theories as to the "optimum" size of a municipality in terms of population. Much has been written on this subject and the briefs to the Commission made many references to such writings, but there is no agreement on the "optimum", and the figures vary widely with the criteria applied. I agree with the Royal Commission on Greater London that "there is no special virtue in any one figure". In fact, it cannot be said that there is one optimum size for municipalities. What may be the appropriate size of constituent units of one metropolitan area will not necessarily be appropriate to another with different characteristics derived from its own history, geography, population composition and economic development. The "metropolitan problem" is general, but it must be dealt with on the basis of the facts of each particular situation.

In briefs submitted by area municipalities to justify the preservation of existing units, there was frequent reference to the principles of democracy. I hold that a democratic solution for the problems of a metropolitan area is one which is based on the needs of the larger community rather than on the special interests of particular sections within that community. The situation in Metro must therefore be viewed in the context of one geographic, social and economic unit divided into thirteen municipalities which vary greatly in size and resources, with consequent disparities in tax burdens, in the range and standards of services, and in representation on the Metropolitan Council. There is the core city, fully developed, which is the financial, industrial, commercial and cultural centre, providing services which benefit all parts of the area. There is the inner ring of nine developed suburbs, of which some are not in a position to provide the range and standards of services required in a modern urban complex, while others, with large industrial and high class residential assessment, are able to provide local services with considerably less tax effort than their neighbours. There are, finally, the three large and populous outer suburbs which are still in the stages of development and, therefore, face problems which are different from those confronting the developed City and inner suburbs.

By far the bulk of population growth in Metro's first ten years took place in the three outer townships. This trend is continuing and, according to projections, will continue into the 'eighties, as shown in Table 51. It is forecast, on the basis of existing local boundaries, that by 1980 the proportion of Metro's population residing in the City and the inner ring will have declined as follows:

DISTRIBUTION OF POPULATION IN METRO

Year	City and 9 Inner Suburbs %	3 Outer Suburbs %
1953	77.9	22.1
1963	56.2	43.8
1971 (forecast)	49.3	50.7
1980 (forecast)	44.6	55.4

Table 51

METROPOLITAN TORONTO: POPULATION FORECAST
1971 and 1980

Municipality	1963 Population[1]	Per Cent of Total	1971 Population[2]	Per Cent of Total	1980 Population[2]	Per Cent of Total
		%		%		%
Toronto	630,339	38.1	670,000	32.8	680,000	29.6
North York	307,584	18.6	450,000	22.0	515,000	22.4
Scarborough	240,371	14.5	345,000	16.9	485,000	21.1
Etobicoke	177,537	10.7	240,000	11.8	275,000	11.9
York	126,311	7.6	137,000	6.7	137,000	5.9
East York	70,176	4.2	77,000	3.8	84,000	3.6
Forest Hill	21,126	1.3	25,000	1.2	23,000	1.0
Leaside	18,453	1.1	24,000	1.2	28,000	1.2
Mimico	18,150	1.1	20,000	1.0	20,000	.9
New Toronto	11,785	.7	14,000	.7	15,000	.6
Long Branch	11,129	.7	14,000	.7	14,000	.6
Weston	9,983	.6	13,000	.6	12,000	.5
Swansea	9,371	.6	11,000	.5	12,000	.5
Metro Total	1,652,315	100.0	2,040,000	100.0	2,300,000	100.0

[1]Annual Report of Municipal Statistics, Province of Ontario, 1963.
[2]Metropolitan Toronto Planning Board 1963 (Forecast based on existing boundaries).

Considering the growth and development trends of the area and the problems created by the inequitable division of political jurisdiction and taxable resources, I find that the thirteen diverse municipalities—one city, four towns, three villages and five townships—should be consolidated into four cities.

i. *A Four-City System*

The City of Toronto and the inner suburbs of York Township, Forest Hill, Leaside, East York and Swansea are linked by geography and common interests. They are mature and developed areas, and, except for Forest Hill and Leaside, face common problems of renewal and redevelopment. With each municipality seeking to improve its tax base independently, they compete for development and redevelopment projects, which are accordingly dealt with on a piecemeal basis and without regard to sound planning in the overall interests of the area. The current disputes over the proposed densities of building projects in York Township are an example of the conflict of interest under the existing fragmentation of authority.

The six municipalities are highly interdependent. Leaside, for example, with the highest rate of average annual earnings and the lowest tax rate in the Metro area, derives its economic strength from a high assessment base divided equally between industrial plants and dwelling units of above average values. Located in the heart of the Metropolitan Area, its factories draw their manpower, in the main, from Toronto, East York, and other municipalities. Leaside, therefore, requires a minimum of such services as welfare; the City, East York and the other areas provide most of the employees for its industries and the municipal services for them and their families.

A look at the map shows the artificial boundaries which separate each of the five suburbs from the City of Toronto. Each is a political unit, but in terms of geography and of social and economic interdependence they are all parts of the City. It is only logical that they should be merged with it politically. A consolidation of the five suburbs with the City of Toronto will strengthen the core upon which the strength of the Metropolitan Area as a whole depends. It will make possible the coordination of planning for urban renewal and redevelopment by one planning body operating under one local council. It will also eliminate the unfair disparities in financial burdens and inequalities in the range and standards of services in the area of 54 square miles covered by the six municipalities.

The three outer suburbs are actually three large cities; in fact, they rank in population with the largest cities in Canada. Among Ontario municipalities, North York ranked second, Scarborough fifth and Etobicoke sixth, in 1963. They meet the tests of viable and effective local government in terms of size, population, resources and scale of operations. As urban entities, the municipal status of township is no longer appropriate to them. North York, Scarborough and Etobicoke should continue to be area municipalities of Metro and the status of each should be changed from township to city.

The remaining four suburbs of the inner ring, Weston and the Lakeshore municipalities of Long Branch, New Toronto and Mimico, share the problems of the inner group. However, they are not linked to the City geographically like the others. The geographic ties of the Lakeshore municipalities are with Etobicoke. It is relevant to note that in September 1962, the Town of New Toronto applied for amalgamation of the three municipalities with Etobicoke. I find that such a consolidation is logical and warranted by the existing situation.

Weston is geographically linked with North York and there is a history of inter-municipal agreements between them. For these reasons and in the interests of administrative efficiency, I find that Weston should be consolidated with North York.

Accordingly, I recommend that the area municipalities of Metropolitan Toronto should be consolidated to form four cities, as follows:

The City of Toronto, consolidating the City of Toronto, the Township of York, the Village of Forest Hill, the Town of Leaside, the Township of East York, and the Village of Swansea. (Area: 54 square miles).

The City of North York, consolidating the Township of North York and the Town of Weston. (Area: 69.1 square miles).

The City of Scarborough. (Area: 70 square miles).

The City of Etobicoke, consolidating the Township of Etobicoke, the Village of Long Branch, the Town of New Toronto, and the Town of Mimico. (Area: 47.9 square miles).

PLATE 7

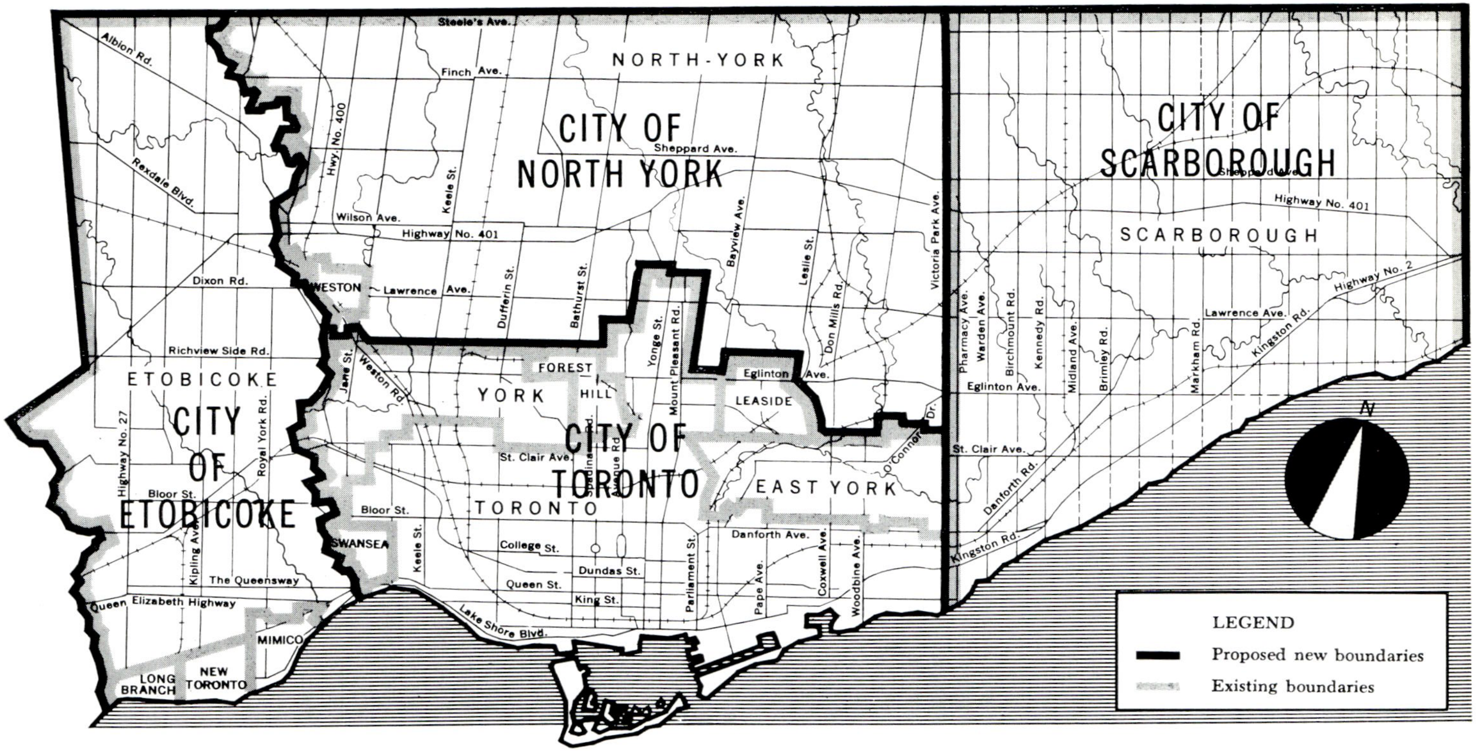

METROPOLITAN TORONTO: PROPOSED FOUR CITIES

Revised population figures for 1964, prepared by the Metropolitan Assessment Department in March 1965, and forecasts for 1971, prepared by the Metropolitan Planning Department on the basis of existing boundaries, show that the population of the four cities would be as follows:

	Population 1964	% of Metro Population	Population 1971	% of Metro Population
Toronto	900,513	51.7	944,000	46.3
North York	351,891	20.2	463,000	22.6
Scarborough	253,292	14.5	345,000	16.9
Etobicoke	238,635	13.6	288,000	14.2
Total	1,744,331	100.0	2,040,000	100.0

Taxable assessment in 1965, on the basis of figures prepared by the Metropolitan Assessment Commissioner in March 1965, would be distributed among the four cities as follows:

	Taxable Assessment 1965 $	% of Total Metro Assessment %
Toronto	2,487,846,569	54.5
North York	893,946,785	19.6
Scarborough	496,713,346	10.9
Etobicoke	684,825,052	15.0
Total	4,563,331,752	100.0

ii. *Financial Implications*

It is not possible to forecast the changes in tax rates which would result from a consolidation which reduces the number of municipalities from thirteen to four. Mill rates are predicated on estimated expenditures and are influenced by factors of a technical and policy nature, and four councils would not necessarily adopt the same policies as the thirteen councils which they replaced. It is possible, however, to illustrate the impact of the redistribution of taxation under a four-city system by comparing net local and Metro expenditures per $1,000 of assessment for each area municipality under the existing system with estimates of the corresponding figures for the proposed four cities adjusted to give effect to the recommendations for a uniform tax rate for schools and distribution of the unconditional grant to the cities on a population basis. This comparison is shown in Table 52 on the basis of 1963 figures, the latest available. It should be noted that no adjustments have been made for possible savings in administrative costs, recommended changes in partial exemptions in Toronto and New Toronto, or for the use of area charges in some of the townships. It has also been assumed that there will be no changes in provincial grants. Accordingly, the figures do not represent tax rates, actual or hypothetical, but serve only to illustrate how the tax position would be influenced by the proposed consolidation.

Table 52

COMPARISON OF NET EXPENDITURES:
Present System and Proposed 4-City System[1]

	Per $1,000 of Metro Assessment			
	Present System[2]		4-City System[3]	
	Residential	Commercial	Residential	Commercial
	$	$	$	$
City of Toronto	—	—	62.06	69.29
Toronto	63.75	70.30	63.55	71.10
Leaside	46.84	53.07	51.67	57.10
East York	59.19	66.08	56.66	63.62
Forest Hill	54.13	60.85	55.41	60.07
Swansea	46.67	52.88	51.19	57.06
York	60.11	66.94	57.63	65.07
City of Etobicoke	—	—	55.70	61.57
Etobicoke	52.87	59.29	55.87	61.52
New Toronto	49.82	56.07	52.11	59.96
Mimico	53.41	59.79	55.71	62.38
Long Branch	55.56	61.91	57.29	64.78
City of North York	—	—	56.12	61.87
North York	57.04	63.90	55.94	61.66
Weston	56.90	63.07	61.15	67.68
City of Scarborough	—	—	62.71	69.44
Scarborough	65.19	72.09	62.71	69.44

[1] Expenditures of area municipalities, including respective shares of Metro expenditures, for general and education purposes, 1963.
[2] Expenditures adjusted for assumption by Metro of 20 per cent mandatory welfare costs.
[3] Expenditures additionally adjusted to reflect a uniform school tax rate and distribution of the Unconditional Per Capita Grant on a population basis, showing effect of these adjustments on basis of (a) present system of 13 municipalities and (b) proposed 4-city system.

Table 52 shows the following range of expenditures per $1,000 of assessment under the existing system:

	Residential	Commercial
	$	$
High	65.19 (Scarborough)	72.09 (Scarborough)
Low	46.67 (Swansea)	52.88 (Swansea)
Spread	18.52	19.21

If the figures are adjusted to give effect to a uniform tax rate for education and the distribution of the unconditional grant on a population basis under the existing system of thirteen municipalities, the spread is reduced as follows:

	Residential	Commercial
	$	$
High	63.55 (Toronto)	71.10 (Toronto)
Low	51.19 (Swansea)	57.06 (Swansea)
Spread	12.36	14.04

Under the four-city system, with expenditures similarly adjusted, the range of expenditures per $1,000 of assessment would be narrowed much further:

	Residential $	Commercial $
High	62.71 (Scarborough)	69.44 (Scarborough)
Low	55.70 (Etobicoke)	61.57 (Etobicoke)
Spread	7.01	7.87

It is clear that the four-city plan would greatly reduce existing inequalities. By widening the areas of service, it would lead to more uniformity in the range and standards of local services. It would not produce uniform tax rates; while the public school rate would be the same throughout the area, the local municipal rate would vary. As urbanization spreads, the rates in the three outer cities are likely to move closer to each other. But, with the elimination of nine municipalities, the existing wide inequalities in financial burdens would be considerably narrowed.

Leaside, Forest Hill and Swansea would necessarily face the largest increases in taxation. While paying their due share of the costs of Metro services, they have been in the privileged position of not having to provide or to share the costs of services which Toronto, in particular, has been compelled to provide and from which the wider area has benefitted. Having regard to the range of rates in the area and to the fact that assessments are still based on 1940 values, the anticipated higher rates would not be abnormal. In case of necessity, the effects of the increases could be cushioned.

The four-city plan would also redistribute local debts more equitably. Table 53 compares net debt per capita and per $1,000 of assessment under the existing system with the corresponding figures under the proposed four-city system after assumption by Metro of local school debts outstanding at the end of 1963.

The figures show that in 1963 net debt per capita ranged from $29.78 in Mimico to $224.51 in Toronto; the spread was $194.73. Under the four-city system, with Metro assuming the local school debts, the spread would be narrowed to $36.12 per capita. On the basis of net debt per $1,000 of taxable assessment, the spread would be reduced from $85.52 to $21.30. The largest increase in debt would be reflected in the existing municipalities which have not had to face the vast problems of development in recent years, but, as geographic parts of the area, have shared with the other municipalities in the benefits from such development.

With respect to the adjustment of assets and liabilities between amalgamating and amalgamated municipalities under the four-city plan, I recommend that the transfer of assets from area municipalities to the amalgamated cities should be effected without adjustment to compensate any area municipality but subject only to the assumption and payment by the amalgamated cities of

Table 53

COMPARISON OF NET DIRECT DEBT:
Present System and Proposed 4-City System
(as at December 31, 1963)

	Per Capita		Per $1,000 of Taxable Assessment	
	Present System	4-City System[1]	Present System	4-City System[1]
	$	$	$	$
City of Toronto.........................	—	129.71	—	47.71
Toronto.............................	224.51		76.26	
York...............................	106.85		59.58	
Leaside............................	137.32		33.21	
East York..........................	74.64		41.13	
Forest Hill.........................	71.12		20.98	
Swansea...........................	39.38		15.84	
City of Etobicoke.......................	—	94.20	—	34.58
Etobicoke..........................	182.38		65.01	
New Toronto.......................	121.10		33.50	
Mimico............................	29.78		15.49	
Long Branch.......................	135.05		75.60	
City of North York......................	—	93.59	—	40.13
North York........................	160.83		69.19	
Weston............................	119.80		46.59	
City of Scarborough.....................	—	104.13	—	55.88
Scarborough.......................	188.21		101.01	
Area Municipalities Total..............	179.39	114.35	71.17	45.37
Metro................................	167.07	232.11	66.28	92.09
Grand Total..........................	346.46	346.46	137.46	137.46

[1]Adjusted for assumption by Metro of net local school debt outstanding on December 31, 1963.
Source: Municipality of Metropolitan Toronto, Debenture Debt Report of the Commissioner of Finance, December 31, 1963.

the relative outstanding capital indebtedness. This was the policy adopted with respect to assets taken over by Metro, and was recommended by the Ontario Municipal Board in the Cumming Report, which said that:

> In the board's opinion, the true nature of these assets is often misunderstood. Although they have been built and financed by the various individual municipalities and their local boards, they are not in a legal sense the property of the residents or ratepayers for the time being resident within the municipality where the assets are located. They are, in every sense of the word, public property and are held in trust for the use and benefit of the present and future residents of the area within the jurisdiction of the local authority. But that area has no fixed and predetermined limits and it may be indefinitely enlarged or included with other areas for the purposes of local government at the will of the legislature. The municipal government is, after all, a government and not a commercial corporation which can wind up

its affairs, sell its assets and distribute the proceeds among its shareholders. For this reason it seems to the board that so long as the residents of the particular area are not deprived of the beneficial use of the assets built or maintained for them by their local government, the management and operation of the asset by a new type of local government which will be, in effect, a new trustee, deprives them of no rights whatever, and entitles them to no individual or collective compensation.

iii. *Provincial Road Grants*

It was pointed out that the estimates in Table 52 assume that the creation of the four-city system would not mean changes in provincial grants paid to the municipalities. Under current policy, as described in Chapter IX, road grants are equal to 50 per cent of approved costs in the case of townships and $33\frac{1}{3}$ per cent in the case of cities; the townships of York and East York are considered to be cities for the purposes of these grants. If the townships of North York, Scarborough and Etobicoke are created cities, as recommended in this report, it is my recommendation that there should be no reduction in the road grants paid to them. The proposed cities of North York, Scarborough and Etobicoke should continue to be considered townships for purposes of such grants.

iv. *Partial Exemption of Dwellings*

Reference has been made to the partial exemption from general purpose taxation of single family dwellings assessed at $4,000 or less in the City of Toronto and the Town of New Toronto. The exemption ranges as follows:

% of Exemption	Assessed Value
50	up to $2,000
40	$2,001 to $2,500
30	$2,501 to $3,000
20	$3,001 to $3,500
10	$3,501 to $4,000

In 1963 the exempt assessment amounted to $46 million in Toronto, representing almost 62,000 properties, and in New Toronto, to $1.2 million. Under the consolidations which I have proposed, such partial exemptions could not be maintained in Toronto and New Toronto alone; they would have to be abolished or, in the alternative, extended throughout the enlarged City of Toronto and the proposed City of Etobicoke.

Introduced in 1921 to assist veterans of the First World War to acquire homes, these exemptions can no longer be said to serve their original purpose. They are difficult to determine and to administer. They increase the general tax rate and create inequalities among taxpayers because the benefit conferred is not related to capacity to pay. There are many home owners enjoying a partial exemption to whom it could not have been intended to apply. For example, 7,494 properties in Toronto's Ward 9 qualified for a partial exemption in 1963, although in each census tract of the 1961 census the median value of the houses ranged from $15,818 to $35,083. It is obvious that if assessed values had been kept closer to market value, a much smaller number of homes would now be eligible for a partial exemption.

I recommend that, with the introduction of the four-city system, the partial exemptions in the City of Toronto and in New Toronto should be abolished in stages over a five-year period by reducing the percentage of exempted assessment by ten percentage points in each year, with provision for assistance in the case of affected owners and tenants who show need.

5. INTEGRATION OF MUNICIPAL STAFFS

Consolidation of the thirteen municipalities into four cities will necessitate the integration of services and of municipal staffs within each city. This should not create formidable problems. I am confident that, once the decision to adopt the four-city plan is made, the problems of adjustment could be solved through joint consultation during the transition period between the enactment of the relevant legislation and the date fixed for the plan to take effect. Ontario municipalities have had considerable experience in making adjustments consequent upon amalgamation.

With respect to those municipal officers and employees whose positions would be affected by the proposed reorganization, I am of the opinion that, with the continuing rapid growth of the area and the necessary expansion of municipal services, the new authorities should not find it difficult to absorb them. In his evidence before the Commission, Mr. Eric Hardy, appearing for the City, pointed out "that Toronto's growth rate corresponds to the addition of a Peterborough or a Brantford year by year." It is obvious, however, that, making allowance for growth, in a reorganization such as is recommended, each civic employee affected by the change could not expect to be guaranteed work equal in responsibility to that which he now performs. While I do not suggest any particular pattern for the integration of staffs, I recommend that:

i. The new authorities should offer employment to all employees who had permanent status on the first day of April in the year preceding the effective date of the reorganization.

ii. The new authorities should assess each employee affected by the change so that each person may be placed in the most responsible post available among those for which he is qualified.

iii. Until an offer of a permanent post is made, an employee should be retained in employment at a level of pay and on terms and conditions of employment no less favourable than those which he enjoyed before the reorganization.

iv. If an employee is transferred to duties reasonably comparable to those which he performed previous to the transfer, his pay, salary scale and terms and conditions of employment should be no less favourable than those which he previously enjoyed.

v. If the employment offered to an employee is at a level of pay and on terms and conditions which are less favourable than those which he previously enjoyed and the employee therefore terminates his employment, he should be entitled to reasonable compensation for loss of employment.

vi. The existing and accrued rights and benefits of each employee in respect of retirement benefits, pensions, group insurance, sick leave credits, vacations, and the like, should be fully protected by the new authorities.

vii. If rights acquired under existing collective agreements are affected by proposed changes, there should be prior consultation with the trade union representing the employees concerned.

viii. Existing wage and employment standards should as far as possible be protected.

In conclusion, I draw attention to the following recommendation in the reports of the Board of Conciliation in the matter of disputes between Metro and Locals 79 and 878 of the Canadian Union of Public Employees, dated October 17, 1964:

> We do have one general recommendation to make, based on our experience this year on the various boards of conciliation in the Metro area. We recommend to the parties and to the Government that consideration be given to a scheme whereby all municipalities in the Metro area (if there are in the future to be a number of such municipalities) would be represented by one bargaining committee and all employees and union represented by one bargaining committee. We understand that such a scheme is in operation in the Vancouver area. The Metro municipalities and the various unions are aware, we are sure, that a duplication over the years of the 1964 experience negating collective bargaining in the conciliation procedure, may well lead to the imposition of compulsory arbitration, an end not desired by either side.

CHAPTER XV

THE METROPOLITAN COUNCIL AND PROPOSED CITY COUNCILS

The constitution of the Metropolitan Council is described in Chapter IV of this report. There are twenty-four councillors, divided equally between representatives of the City of Toronto and representatives of the suburbs. Each of the twelve suburbs is represented by the mayor or reeve, while the representatives of the City are the mayor, the two controllers who received the highest number of votes at the preceding municipal elections, and the alderman from each of the nine wards who received the highest number of votes in the ward. The chairman is elected by the Council which may choose one of its own members "or any other person".

The constitution of the Council thus presents some special features: the members are not elected directly but become Metro councillors by virtue of their election to office in an area municipality; the City and the suburbs, as a group, have equal representation; each City ward and the voters of the City at large are represented; and each suburb, regardless of size and population, is entitled to one representative. These were ingenious features of the Metro Act of 1953; they made for wider acceptability of the new form of government and helped to solidify its political base. Moreover, the system of indirect election was familiar to the people because the members of county councils in Ontario are selected in this way.

The value of the liaison between the area councils and the Metropolitan Council under the existing system was emphasized in the briefs submitted to the Commission by the area municipalities; Metro has not become a rival or alien government. Linking the councils in this way has made it possible for all parts of the metropolitan community to become associated in the solution of area-wide problems. I find that Metro's success is due in no small part to the fact that its Council has been composed of persons who were also members of the councils of the area municipalities. The brief of the City of Toronto pointed out that:

> The arrangement for representation on the Metropolitan Council and School Board has had certain obvious advantages by comparison with the system of direct election which applies to county councillors in London, England, and to metropolitan councillors in Winnipeg. The method we follow has meant that one or more elected representatives in each area municipality has a personal stake in the success of the Metropolitan government. In addition, it has ensured that persons with an intimate knowledge of each area municipality and its problems would bring that knowledge to bear upon the consideration of the metropolitan undertakings.

While the system of indirect election has helped to secure Metro's political base, it is valid to argue that Metro councillors should be elected directly because they have decision-making authority in major matters of area-wide interest and are responsible for a large part of the tax levy in the area. It has been suggested that Metro should be divided on the basis of population into metropolitan electoral districts which disregard local municipal boundaries, as in Metropolitan Winnipeg, and that the councillors should be elected by such districts. This would destroy the formal link between Metro and the area councils, which I find has been one of the great strengths of the Toronto system as compared with other experiments in metropolitan government. To maintain this link, and, at the same time, to have regard to the principles of responsible government, reform of the existing system should combine direct election of councillors with representation of the area municipalities on the Metropolitan Council.

The basis of representation on Council, as set up in 1953, was politic but unequal. With one representative for each of the suburbs and for each Toronto ward, inequalities in representation have been greatly intensified by the wide disparities in the rate of population growth. Swansea, with a population of 9,322 in 1964, and North York, with 341,437, are each represented by one councillor. Seven small suburbs with 104,000 people have 29 per cent of the votes in Council, as compared with 21 per cent for five suburbs with 990,000 people. In Toronto, Ward 3, with a population of 40,738, has the same vote in Metro Council as Ward 6, with a population of 122,900. Toronto, with 56.7 per cent of Metro's population in 1953, was awarded one-half of the seats on the Council; to-day, with less than 38 per cent of Metro's total, it still retains the same representation. It is obvious that the system of representation must be reformed.

1. THE METROPOLITAN COUNCIL

Under the recommended four-city plan, the population of Metropolitan Toronto as has been shown, would be distributed as follows:

	1964	1971
Toronto	900,513	944,000
North York	351,891	463,000
Scarborough	253,292	345,000
Etobicoke	238,635	288,000
Total	1,744,331	2,040,000

This distribution provides a basis for equitable representation on Council within a metropolitan federation.

I reject the suggestion made in a number of briefs that representation should be determined by assessment as well as population. This is a theory which is long outdated. It is incompatible with the principle of representation by population. In modern democracies representatives are elected to represent people, not dollars. As stated by Reeve True Davidson of East York, in her brief, "a democratic belief in the significance of the individual, regardless of his wealth or poverty, forbids acceptance of the theory that financial interest should be regarded as justifying special representation."

Metro Council is now composed of twenty-four members and the chairman. Considering the need to provide reasonable representation for each of the proposed cities, I recommend that the membership of the Metropolitan Council should be set at twenty-six, with the following representation for each of the cities:

City of Toronto	13
City of North York	5
City of Scarborough	4
City of Etobicoke	4
Total	26

On this basis, the representation of each city would reasonably approximate its percentage of the total Metro population, as shown by the following comparisons:

	% of Total Council Membership	% of Total Metro Population	
		1964	1971
	%	%	%
Toronto	50.0	51.7	46.3
North York	19.2	20.2	22.6
Scarborough	15.4	14.5	16.9
Etobicoke	15.4	13.6	14.2

The average population represented per member of Metro Council would be as follows:

	1964	1971
Toronto	69,270	72,615
North York	70,378	92,600
Scarborough	63,323	86,250
Etobicoke	59,658	72,000
Average	67,089	78,461

The overall average should serve as a guide on population and representation when the incorporation of fringe municipalities into Metro is considered.

I recommend that, to maintain reasonable equity, representation on Council should be reviewed every ten years on the basis of the last Census of Canada.

To maintain the link between Metro Council and the area councils, I recommend that the representation of each city on the Metropolitan Council should be composed of the mayor and of metropolitan councillors elected directly by each ward or by a combination of wards, the councillors to serve on both Metro Council and the respective city councils. This proposal is described in more detail below.

2. THE CHAIRMAN OF METROPOLITAN COUNCIL

The Metro Council may elect as chairman one of its own members or any other person. If elected from outside the membership of Council he has no vote "except in the event of an equality of votes"; when elected from Council he "has a second or casting vote". Mr. F. G. Gardiner, Q.C., the first chairman, whose dynamic leadership has become legendary, held no elective office when he was originally appointed by the Lieutenant Governor in Council nor when he was thereafter elected and re-elected by Council. His successor, Mr. W. R. Allen, Q.C., was a member of the Board of Control of Toronto when first elected chairman; he resigned from the Board following his election and held no elective office when re-elected for a second term. It has been urged that the responsibilities of the post call for the election of the chairman by the citizens of Metro at large; alternatively, it has been suggested that, if he is to be elected by the Council, he should be chosen only from among its members.

The chairman is in law and in fact not only the head of Council but also the chief executive officer of the Metropolitan Corporation. He is the only member of Council who is required to devote his full time to Metro. As the head of the government of a federation of municipalities, he must be impartial. He must also be sufficiently independent in relation to local politics to be able to face pressures and to fight on issues where the area-wide interest may conflict with a local interest. There is no doubt that the independence of the chairman has contributed in large measure to the successful operation of metropolitan government in Toronto. I doubt that he could retain his independence if he were required to be elected at large; an election in an area of 240 square miles, with a population of 1,750,000, would have to be financed by large business enterprises or by a political party. The fact that the mayors of big cities in the United States are elected at large is not very relevant; they are as a rule the candidates of a party. Moreover, they are elected as heads of individual municipalities and not as chief executive officers of municipal federations.

While I find more merit in the submission that the chairman should be elected from among the members of the Council, I do not think that the requirements of the office and the experience of Metro justify such a limitation. As briefs to the Commission made frequent reference to English local government, it may be pointed out that municipal councils in England are composed of elected and non-elected persons: councillors, elected by popular vote, and a certain number of aldermen who are chosen by the councillors and not by the electors. The council as a whole elects the chairman, who qualifies if he is a councillor or alderman or is eligible for election as a councillor. The Greater London Council, created by the London Government Act, 1963, following the report of the Royal Commission on Greater London, is composed of one hundred directly elected councillors and sixteen aldermen chosen by the councillors. The chairman, who is chiefly a presiding officer, is elected by the Council but does not have to be a councillor or an alderman himself.

Considering the operation of Metro under its first two chairmen and my recommendation for the direct election of metropolitan councillors, I recommend no change in the provisions of the Metro Act governing election of the chairman of Metropolitan Council. If a metropolitan councillor representing one of the consolidated cities is elected chairman, he should be free to decide whether he is in a position to retain both posts. If, however, the mayor of a city is elected chairman and were to retain both posts, it would be difficult for him to remain impartial in the event of a conflict of interest between his city and Metro. Accordingly, I recommend that the Metro Act should be amended to provide that on the election of the mayor of a city to the office of chairman of the Metropolitan Council, the office of mayor of the city shall become vacant.

3. THE CITY COUNCILS

The municipal councils of the thirteen area municipalities now have a total of 119 members, including the mayor or reeve, deputy reeves, controllers, and aldermen or councillors, as shown in Table 54. Variations in local government in the area reflect variations in the size and municipal status of the units. The City of Toronto and the townships of North York, Scarborough, Etobicoke and York are divided for electoral purposes into wards; in the remaining units, elections are held at large. Toronto, North York and Etobicoke alone have boards of control. The size of council in relation to population varies widely: there is a council of nine members both in Scarborough, with a population of 253,000, and in York, with 128,000, while East York, with 72,000 people, and Weston, with 10,000, have councils of seven members each.

Table 54

COMPOSITION OF MUNICIPAL COUNCILS IN METROPOLITAN TORONTO, 1965

	Wards	Aldermen or Councillors	Controllers	Deputy Reeves	Mayor or Reeve	Total Elected Council
City of Toronto	9	18	4	–	1	23
Township of York	4	4	–	4	1	9
Township of East York	–	6	–	–	1	7
Town of Leaside	–	4	–	1	2[1]	7
Village of Swansea	–	3	–	1	1	5
Village of Forest Hill	–	3	–	1	1	5
Township of North York	12	12	4	–	1	17
Town of Weston	–	6	–	–	1	7
Township of Etobicoke	4	8	2	–	1	11
Town of Mimico	–	6	–	–	1	7
Town of New Toronto	–	6	–	–	1	7
Village of Long Branch	–	3	–	1	1	5
Township of Scarborough	7	7	–	1	1	9
Total		86	10	9	14	119

[1]Leaside has both a mayor and a reeve.

With each area municipality constituted a city under the four-city plan, local government would be organized along more uniform lines. Having regard to the present population and prospective growth of each of the proposed consolidated cities, the need for adequate representation on a council of reasonable size, and the proposal for direct election of metropolitan councillors, who would also be members of the city councils, I recommend that:

i. Each city should be divided into wards, the number of wards to be as follows:

    City of Toronto...................... 12
    City of North York.................. 8
    City of Scarborough................ 6
    City of Etobicoke................... 6

If the wards were divided evenly in terms of population, which is scarcely possible, the average population per ward, based on the Assessment Commissioner's figures for 1964, would be as follows:

    City of Toronto.................. 75,042
    City of North York.............. 43,986
    City of Scarborough............. 42,215
    City of Etobicoke................ 39,772

The present range in population per ward is from 40,738 to 122,894 in Toronto; from 17,975 to 34,826 in North York; from 19,127 to 56,448 in Scarborough; and from 37,426 to 59,187 in Etobicoke.

I recommend that the division into wards should be made by the Ontario Municipal Board, by virtue of its authority under section 13 of The Municipal Act. In determining ward boundaries within each city, the Board should aim at a reasonably approximate equality of population per ward. It should also endeavour, as far as possible, to retain the whole of an amalgamating municipality within a single ward. Thus, in the consolidated City of Toronto, East York might constitute one ward and York, one and a half or two wards, while the Lakeshore municipalities could form one of the wards in the City of Etobicoke.

ii. The city council of each of the cities should be composed of the mayor, who would be elected at large and would be ex officio a representative on Metro Council; aldermen, who would serve only on city council; and metropolitan councillors, who would serve on both Metro and city councils. I recommend that the four city councils should be constituted as follows:

	Mayor	Aldermen	Metropolitan Councillors	Total Council
Toronto...............	1	12	12	25
North York............	1	16	4	21
Scarborough...........	1	12	3	16
Etobicoke.............	1	12	3	16

For the election of aldermen and metropolitan councillors in each city, I recommend as follows:

City of Toronto: one alderman and one metropolitan councillor from each of the twelve wards.

City of North York: two aldermen from each of the eight wards and one metropolitan councillor from each combination of two contiguous wards. For example, one metropolitan councillor would be chosen by Wards 1 and 2 combined, Wards 3 and 4 combined, and so on.

City of Scarborough: two aldermen from each of the six wards and one metropolitan councillor from each combination of two contiguous wards.

City of Etobicoke: two aldermen from each of the six wards and one metropolitan councillor from each combination of two contiguous wards.

If this recommendation is implemented, the total membership of the municipal councils of the area would be reduced from 119 to 78. A council of sixteen members is recommended for Scarborough because it would be more appropriate to a city of 250,000 people than the present council of nine. The larger council proposed for Etobicoke has regard to the recommended consolidation with the Lakeshore municipalities, while, in the case of North York, particular account has been taken of the fact that it is the area of most rapid growth. The proposed increase in the number of wards in Toronto takes account of the recommended consolidation which would increase its population by some 250,000.

iii. Each city council should have an executive committee consisting of the mayor, who should also be the chairman, and four members elected by the council from among its members. The executive committee should exercise the powers conferred by The Municipal Act on a board of control.

The existing boards of control are in effect executive committees of council but they are elected separately and, like the mayor, at large. The history of municipal politics in the Toronto area shows that this system has not tended to produce harmony in council. With both the mayor and the controllers elected at large, there tends to develop a competition for popular support which accentuates division within the board. Relations with council are also affected where the executive and the councillors are elected separately and on a different basis. Election of the executive committee by city council, in addition to reducing unnecessary friction and rivalries, would make the executive more responsive and responsible to the legislative body in conformity with our concept of responsible government.

iv. The municipal franchise in the four cities should be uniform.

Ten of the area municipalities, acting under the provisions of The Municipal Franchise Extension Act, have extended the right to vote to all British subjects of the full age of twenty-one years who have resided in the municipality for at least one year; Scarborough, Swansea and Weston have not done so. The extension of the franchise would apply within the present boundaries of Swansea and Weston if, as recommended, they are consolidated with Toronto and North York, respectively. The franchise should be similarly extended in Scarborough.

v. The term of office of members of the proposed city councils and of the Metropolitan Council should be increased to three years.

The term of municipal office in the area is now two years. It was suggested in a number of briefs that a longer term is warranted by the responsibilities which the elected representatives are called upon to discharge. The Cumming Report in 1953 recommended a term of not less than three years, pointing out that in a major metropolitan area "the elected representatives are expected to formulate wise long-term policies and to control the expenditure of millions of dollars". The argument for a longer term has been strengthened by the tremendous growth which has taken place in the area since the creation of Metro and the consequent increase in the responsibilities of the members of Metro and local councils.

CHAPTER XVI

CONCLUSION

The creation of Metro in 1953 was a bold experiment which has been justified by the accomplishments of more than a decade of operations. To consolidate the gains achieved and to cope with problems which have been accentuated by growth and development, the time has come to move forward again. This, too, calls for bold measures.

I have recommended the continuance of metropolitan government with a consolidation of the thirteen area municipalities into four cities. Having regard to the strong instinct for institutional self-preservation, I know that the suggested elimination of nine municipalities, with a reduction in the membership of municipal councils in the area from 119 to 78, will encounter strong resistance. Changes in governmental structures which affect existing interests and relationships always arouse opposition. Writing on the long resistance to reform in Greater London, Professor W. A. Robson said that:[1]

> ..... From the great county council down to the small parish, they one and all regard the continuance of their own existence not merely as an absolute good in itself, but as something compared with which any scheme of reform intended to benefit the larger metropolitan community is but as dust in the balance.

In the words of Dr. Luther H. Gulick, "among governmental institutions the suicide complex is notably absent."[2]

Notwithstanding powerful resistance, the reform of metropolitan government in Greater London which went into effect on April 1, 1965, consolidated 85 local authorities into 32 boroughs. My proposal for Metropolitan Toronto is therefore not without precedent. While there is no "one way" for solving the problems of diverse metropolitan areas, I hold that, in any circumstances, the solution must be determined by the needs of the larger community and not by the special interests of particular sections within that community. It is on this principle that I have founded my recommendations.

---

[1]William A. Robson: The Government and Misgovernment of London. (London: George Allen & Unwin Ltd., 1939) p. 457.
[2]The Metropolitan Problem and American Ideas, op. cit., p. 36.

CHAPTER XVII

SUMMARY OF RECOMMENDATIONS

1. REORGANIZATION OF METROPOLITAN TORONTO

   i. The system of metropolitan government should be maintained, with a consolidation of the thirteen area municipalities into four cities, as follows:

   The City of Toronto, consolidating the City of Toronto, the Township of York, the Village of Forest Hill, the Town of Leaside, the Township of East York and the Village of Swansea.

   The City of North York, consolidating the Township of North York and the Town of Weston.

   The City of Scarborough.

   The City of Etobicoke, consolidating the Township of Etobicoke, the Village of Long Branch, the Town of New Toronto and the Town of Mimico.

   ii. The transfer of assets from the amalgamating municipalities to the amalgamated cities should be effected without compensation to any area municipality but subject only to the assumption and payment by the amalgamated cities of the relative outstanding capital indebtedness.

   iii. The cities of North York, Scarborough and Etobicoke should continue to be considered townships for the purposes of provincial road grants.

   iv. With the introduction of the four-city system, the partial graded exemptions in Toronto and New Toronto should be abolished in stages over a five-year period by reducing the percentage of exempted assessment by ten percentage points in each year, with provision for assistance in the case of affected owners and tenants who show need.

   v. In integrating municipal staffs, the new authorities should offer employment to all employees who had permanent status on the first day of April in the year preceding the effective date of the reorganization. Existing wage and employment standards should, as far as possible, be protected.

2. THE METROPOLITAN COUNCIL AND PROPOSED CITY COUNCILS

   i. Representation on the Metropolitan Council should combine direct election of metropolitan councillors with representation of the area municipalities.

   ii. The Metropolitan Council should be composed of 26 members, with the following representation for each of the four cities:

Toronto	13
North York	5
Scarborough	4
Etobicoke	4

iii. Each city should be represented on the Metropolitan Council by the mayor and by metropolitan councillors elected directly by each ward or by a combination of wards, the councillors to serve on both Metropolitan Council and the respective city councils.

iv. The existing provisions of The Municipality of Metropolitan Toronto Act governing the election of the chairman of Metropolitan Council should not be changed, except to provide that on the election of the mayor of a city to the office of chairman, the office of mayor of the city shall become vacant.

v. Representation on the Metropolitan Council should be reviewed every ten years on the basis of the last Census of Canada.

vi. The four cities should be divided into the following number of wards:

>   Toronto..................... 12
>   North York.................. 8
>   Scarborough................. 6
>   Etobicoke................... 6

vii. The division into wards should be made by the Ontario Municipal Board, by virtue of its authority under section 13 of The Municipal Act. The Board should aim at a reasonably approximate equality of population per ward and should also endeavour, as far as possible, to retain the whole of an amalgamating municipality within a single ward or within contiguous wards.

viii. Each of the city councils should be composed of the mayor, to be elected at large and to be ex officio a representative on Metropolitan Council; metropolitan councillors, to serve on both Metropolitan Council and city council; and aldermen, to serve only on city council.

ix. Aldermen and metropolitan councillors should be elected on the following basis:

>   *Toronto:* one alderman and one metropolitan councillor from each of the twelve wards.
>   *North York:* two aldermen from each of the eight wards and one metropolitan councillor from each combination of two contiguous wards.
>   *Scarborough:* two aldermen from each of the six wards and one metropolitan councillor from each combination of two contiguous wards.
>   *Etobicoke:* two aldermen from each of the six wards and one metropolitan councillor from each combination of two contiguous wards.

x. Each city council should have an Executive Committee composed of the mayor, who should also be the chairman, and four members elected by the council from among its members. The Executive Committee should exercise the powers conferred by The Municipal Act on a Board of Control.

xi. The municipal franchise in the four cities should be uniform.

xii. The term of office of members of the four city councils and of the Metropolitan Council should be increased to three years.

3. METRO'S BOUNDARIES AND THE FRINGE AREAS

i. Before considering extension of Metro's boundaries, the Province should give consideration to the position and function of the counties and to municipal reorganization in the fringe areas, including the possible creation of a smaller "Metro" on the western fringe.

ii. Failing satisfactory arrangements by Metro and the Ontario Water Resources Commission to provide the required water and sewage facilities on the northern fringe, the appropriate built-up area north of Steeles Avenue in Vaughan and Markham Townships should be annexed to North York without undue delay, with compensation for loss of assessment to the townships and the County of York.

iii. The Provincial Government should formally recognize the special situation of dormitory municipalities adjacent to Metro by appropriate adjustments in grants for municipal and school purposes.

4. METROPOLITAN PLANNING

i. A Metropolitan Official Plan should be adopted without undue delay. Adoption of the plan should be followed by the preparation, jointly with the local municipalities, of more detailed district plans and the enactment of the necessary changes in zoning by-laws. The plans should be subject to periodic review.

ii. The Municipality of Metropolitan Toronto Act should be amended to declare more explicitly the responsibility of the Metropolitan Corporation, as the designated municipality, for the general direction of the physical development of the Metropolitan Planning Area, with powers:

(a) to establish basic zoning standards and categories;

(b) to participate with an area municipality in redevelopment and urban renewal;

(c) to enact a uniform building by-law and to establish uniform engineering design standards;

(d) to review development applications and proposals and to make recommendations thereon to the provincial agency;

(e) to secure the conformity of local official plans and zoning by-laws in the Metropolitan Planning Area with the Metro Official Plan, reserving to the municipalities a right of appeal to the Ontario Municipal Board. The procedures to ensure conformity of plans should be prescribed by regulations under the legislation.

iii. The Planning Act should be amended to permit municipalities to transfer the functions now vested in local planning boards to a Planning Committee of Council with power to co-opt. The planning staff in area municipalities should be constituted a civic planning department.

iv. The law should provide for a representative of a municipality, which is not otherwise directly represented on the Metropolitan Planning Board, to attend and to be heard when matters originating from, applying to or of particular concern to such municipality are under consideration.

v. In the absence of other regional planning machinery, the area covered by Brampton and its vicinity should be included in the Metropolitan Planning Area and should constitute a fringe district entitled to representation on the Planning Board.

5. METROPOLITAN AND LOCAL SERVICES

i. *Transit*

The chairman of the Metropolitan Council should ex officio be a full member of the Toronto Transit Commission.

There should be a more formal coordination in overall transportation planning between the staffs of the Transit Commission, the Metropolitan Planning Board and other agencies, in order to ensure that proper consideration is given to all forms of transportation required to meet the present and prospective needs of Metro and the surrounding area.

ii. *Roads*

The design of access to metropolitan roads should require the approval of Metro authorities, and Metro should assume appropriate major local arterial roads.

The Metropolitan Corporation should be authorized to assume roads on Metro's boundaries as metropolitan roads.

The Province and Metro should coordinate expressway construction to meet the overall requirements of both transportation and local development.

iii. *Traffic Management*

The traffic engineering services of the Metropolitan Area should be unified under Metro.

Metro should establish an area-wide parking authority with power to operate parking facilities directly or to enter into a contractual arrangement for their operation by the Toronto Parking Authority.

iv. *Public Housing*

The Ontario Housing Corporation should act as a single agency on behalf of the federal and provincial governments in dealing with the Metropolitan Corporation in respect of all further low rental housing developments in the Metropolitan Area, with Metro assuming the remaining municipal financial responsibility therefor.

v. *Health and Welfare*

The Metropolitan Corporation should take steps to provide a metropolitan public emergency ambulance service and should consider a contractual arrangement with the City of Toronto under which the City would operate the service.

A Metropolitan Board of Health Officers, composed of the health officers of the four cities, should be formed to coordinate the public health policies of the municipalities and to advise on health and santitary inspection matters.

It should be the aim of the four cities to make health and welfare services equally available to individuals and families with the same needs, no matter where they live in Metropolitan Toronto.

vi. *Waste Disposal*

The Metropolitan Corporation should assume responsibility for all waste disposal in the Metropolitan Area.

vii. *Sewer Renewals*

The Metropolitan Area as a whole should share in financing the municipal costs of the necessary trunk sewer renewal programmes in the core area.

viii. *Parks and Recreation*

The Metropolitan Corporation should exercise responsibility for the development of the waterfront for park and recreational purposes.

ix. *Police*

The police function should not be divided between Metro and the area municipalities, but more effort should be made to improve relationships between the police force and the area municipalities.

x. *Administration of Justice*

The need for a properly staffed and serviced Metropolitan Juvenile and Family Court, with court facilities in each of the four cities, is sufficiently immediate to warrant the necessary increase in Metro's budget for this purpose, pending a review of the sharing of costs of the administration of justice between the Province and the Metropolitan Corporation.

xi. *Licensing*

The four cities should assume responsibility for the licensing of local businesses which are tied to a specific location, as distinct from metropolitan-wide businesses and activities which should continue to be licensed by the Metropolitan Licensing Commission. The Commission should set minimum standards for local licensing where required.

Consideration should be given to an arrangement between the four cities and the Licensing Commission under which, the municipality having made the decision, the license would be issued on its behalf and at its request by the Commission, with the fee paid to the city concerned.

The law should require approval by the Metropolitan Council of license fees adopted by the Licensing Commission.

xii. *Fire Protection*

Under a four-city system, fire protection should remain the responsibility of the area municipalities, with an effective mutual aid agreement under which each could request assistance from one or all of the others when necessary.

Where centralization is necessary, as in the case of a central communications system, the system should be operated by the City of Toronto under a contractual arrangement.

The fire chiefs of the four cities should constitute an area committee to advise on matters of mutual concern affecting the fire fighting services of the area.

xiii. *Libraries*

The operation of libraries should remain a local responsibility in each of the four cities, with coordination by a Metropolitan Library Board. The recommendations of Report No. 1 (1962) of the Special Committee on Library Services appointed by the Metropolitan Council to study and report upon the Shaw Report should, as far as possible, be implemented.

6. EDUCATION

For public schools, the educational structure in Metropolitan Toronto should be reorganized as follows:

    i. The Metropolitan Area should be divided into eleven school districts, with boundaries fixed on the basis of criteria for determining the viability of school districts. The proposed boundaries are set out in Chapter XII.

    ii. An elected central board, to be called the Metropolitan Toronto Board of Education, should have overall responsibility for school finance and for the development of an acceptable and uniformly high metropolitan standard of education. The administrative responsibilities of the central board should be limited to matters relating to area-wide policies, including teachers' salary scales, to coordination of mutual services, and to the provision of services which can best be provided on a metropolitan basis.

    iii. Local elected boards, to be called District Education Councils, should operate the schools and administer the school programme.

    iv. The central board should be composed of two trustees elected at large in each school district at elections held on the same day as the regular municipal elections, and two representatives of the Metropolitan Separate School Board. The chairman should be elected from among the members. The term of office should be three years.

v. The remuneration for members of the central board should be raised to a figure more commensurate with their responsibilities and the additional responsibilities of the chairman should be recognized by a higher remuneration.

vi. Each District Education Council should be composed of the two trustees elected to represent the district on the central board, one trustee appointed by the Separate School Board, and eight district trustees elected at large in the district. The chairman should be elected from among the members. The term of office should be three years.

vii. A Director of Education should be the chief executive officer of the Metropolitan Toronto Board of Education and a District Superintendent should be the principal officer in each school district, reporting directly to the former.

viii. Educational finance should be coordinated by the central board and a uniform tax for education established throughout Metro. The central board should secure all tax revenue for educational purposes from the Metropolitan Council through the uniform levy.

ix. District education councils should be allocated a fixed percentage of their total budgets to enable them to add to their programme if they desire to provide special equipment or a special service or to undertake educational experiments which are not included in the area-wide budget.

x. The Metropolitan Corporation should assume the local school debt of the area municipalities outstanding on December 31, 1963.

The whole respectfully submitted,

H. CARL GOLDENBERG,
Commissioner.

Toronto, Ont.,
June 10, 1965.

APPENDICES

A. List of Submissions Received at Public Hearings

B. List of Tables

C. List of Maps and Charts

APPENDIX A

LIST OF SUBMISSIONS RECEIVED AT PUBLIC HEARINGS

April 21, 1964—Mr. W. R. Allen, Q.C., Chairman, Metropolitan Council
—Township of York
—Township of North York
—Town of Weston

April 22, 1964—Township of Scarborough
—Town of New Toronto
—Town of Mimico
—Village of Long Branch

April 23, 1964—Township of Etobicoke
—Township of East York
—Town of Leaside
—Village of Forest Hill

April 28, 1964—Village of Swansea
—City of Toronto

April 29, 1964—Metropolitan School Board
—Board of Education, City of Toronto
—Group of Five Trustees of Board of Education, City of Toronto

April 30, 1964—Board of Education, Township of East York
—Board of Education, Township of Etobicoke
—Board of Education, Village of Forest Hill

May 5, 1964 —Board of Education, Town of Leaside
—Board of Education, Township of North York
—Board of Education, Village of Swansea
—Board of Education, Township of Scarborough
—Board of Education, Township of York

May 6, 1964 —Board of Education, Town of Weston
—Lakeshore Board of Education
—Ontario Teachers' Federation
—Leaside Property Owners Association

May 7, 1964 —County of York
—The Southern Six Municipalities of the County of York
—Town of Richmond Hill

May 12, 1964—Township of Pickering and Board of Trustees, School Area No. 2
    —Town of Ajax
    —Township of Toronto
    —Metropolitan Toronto and Region Conservation Authority

May 13, 1964—Town Planning Institute of Canada
    —Urban Development Institute
    —Mr. Eli Comay, Metropolitan Planning Commissioner

May 19, 1964—Toronto Public Library Board
    —York Public Library Board
    —Swansea Memorial Public Library Board
    —North York Public Library Board
    —East York Public Library Board
    —Etobicoke Public Library Board

May 20, 1964—Social Planning Council of Metropolitan Toronto
    —Dr. Albert Rose, University of Toronto

June 2, 1964 —Professor H. Kaplan, York University
    —Toronto and District Labour Council
    —Metro Toronto Council of Public Employees Unions
    —Independent Cab Owners Guild
    —Automotive Transport Association of Ontario

June 3, 1964 —Association of Women Electors of Toronto
    —Metropolitan Toronto Board of Trade
    —Greater Toronto Business Men's Association
    —Mimico Ratepayers Association
    —East York Federation of Ratepayers Associations
    —Reeve Lucien Kurata, Swansea
    —Mr. Karl Mallette, Scarborough
    —Mr. W. A. Edwards, Mimico

June 4, 1964 —Etobicoke Hydro Electric Commission
    —Metropolitan Educational Research Council
    —Communist Party of Canada

June 9, 1964 —Controller Allan Lamport, Toronto
    —Controller W. L. Archer, Toronto
    —Reeve True Davidson, East York
    —Mrs. F. Gell, York
    —Mr. E. H. Farrow, Etobicoke

June 10, 1964—Mrs. Kathleen James and Mrs. Mary L. Axelson, Markham Township
    —Mr. J. C. Van Esterik
    —Mr. J. D. Parker, Etobicoke
    —Mr. Dalton J. Little
    —Mr. L. H. Saunders, East York
    —Mr. N. Maughan

June 11, 1964—Bureau of Municipal Research

APPENDIX B

LIST OF TABLES

		PAGE
Table 1.	Metropolitan Toronto: Area and Population	1
Table 2.	Fringe Municipalities: Area and Population	5
Table 3.	Metropolitan Toronto: Population, 1953 and 1963	11
Table 4.	Metropolitan Toronto: Population: Densities per Acre, 1953 and 1963	12
Table 5.	Metropolitan Toronto: Population: Origins	13
Table 6.	Metropolitan Toronto: Population: Age Distribution	14
Table 7.	Metropolitan Toronto: Population: Occupations	15
Table 8.	Metropolitan Toronto: Population: Per Cent of Labour Force Employed by Occupational Classification	16
Table 9.	Fringe Municipalities: Population, 1953 and 1963	19
Table 10.	City and Suburbs: Population Growth, 1930-1953	22
Table 11.	Taxable Assessment, 1954 and 1964	79
Table 12.	Taxable Assessment Per Capita, 1954 and 1964	81
Table 13.	Non-Residential Taxable Assessment, 1954 and 1964	81
Table 14.	Dwelling Units Completed, 1954 to 1963	83
Table 15.	Tax-Exempt Property, 1954 and 1964	85
Table 16.	General and School Gross Current Expenditure, 1954 and 1963	87
Table 17.	Municipal Gross Current Expenditure, 1954 and 1963: General Government	89
Table 18.	Municipal Gross Current Expenditure, 1954 and 1963: Public Works	91
Table 19.	Municipal Gross Current Expenditure, 1954 and 1963: Protection to Persons and Property	91
Table 20.	Municipal Gross Current Expenditure, 1954 and 1963: Recreation and Community Services	92
Table 21.	Municipal Gross Current Expenditure, 1954 and 1963: Public Welfare	93
Table 22.	Municipal Gross Current Expenditure, 1954 and 1963: Conservation of Health	94
Table 23.	Municipal Gross Current Expenditure, 1954 and 1963: Sanitation and Waste Removal	95
Table 24.	Metropolitan Toronto and Area Municipalities General and School Gross Current Revenue, 1954 and 1963	98
Table 25.	Distribution of Metropolitan General Levy, 1963	101
Table 26.	Distribution of Metropolitan Educational Levy, 1963	103

		PAGE
Table 27.	Area Municipalities General and School Tax Levies for Local Purposes, 1963	104
Table 28.	General and School Mill Rates, 1954 and 1964	106
Table 29.	Debentures Issued by the Municipality of Metropolitan Toronto During the Period 1954-1963, Inclusive, for Own Purposes and for the Purposes of the Area Municipalities	109
Table 30.	Net Debenture Debt for General and School Purposes, 1954 and 1963	112
Table 31.	Net Debt Per Capita for General and School Purposes, 1954 and 1963	113
Table 32.	Net Debt for General and School Purposes Per $1000 of Taxable Assessment, 1954 and 1963	114
Table 33.	Net Debt Charges, 1963	115
Table 34.	Net Debt Charges Per Capita and Per $1000 of Taxable Assessment, 1963	116
Table 35.	Types of Schools in Metropolitan Toronto, September, 1964	120
Table 36.	Public School Enrolment, 1954 and 1964	121
Table 37.	Number of Public Schools, 1954 and 1964	123
Table 38.	Teachers in Public School System, 1954 and 1964	124
Table 39.	Assessment Per Resident Public School Pupil, 1954 and 1964	128
Table 40.	School Maintenance Assistance Payments, 1954 to 1964	130
Table 41.	Public Elementary and Secondary School Costs Per Pupil, 1957 and 1963	133
Table 42.	Area School Board Operating Costs Per Pupil Day, 1963	136
Table 43.	School Mill Rates, 1954 and 1964	138
Table 44.	Distribution of School Population and School Assessment, 1963	139
Table 45.	Proposed School Districts: Population, Enrolment and Schools	148
Table 46.	Fringe Municipalities: Existing Land Use, 1963	159
Table 47.	Fringe Municipalities: Population Projections 1971 and 1980	161
Table 48.	Fringe Municipalities: Assessment Equalized to the Level of Metropolitan Toronto Assessment	162
Table 49.	Fringe Municipalities: Per Capita Assessment Equalized to the Level of Metropolitan Toronto Assessment	164
Table 50.	County Levies: Fringe Municipalities' Share	165
Table 51.	Metropolitan Toronto: Population Forecast, 1971 and 1980	181
Table 52.	Comparison of Net Expenditures: Present System and Proposed 4-City System	185
Table 53.	Comparison of Net Direct Debt: Present System and Proposed 4-City System	187
Table 54.	Composition of Municipal Councils in Metropolitan Toronto, 1965	195

APPENDIX C
LIST OF MAPS AND CHARTS

		PAGE
Plate 1.	The Municipality of Metropolitan Toronto	xvi
Plate 2.	Metropolitan Toronto: Area in Square Miles	3
Plate 3.	Metropolitan Toronto Planning Area	6
Plate 4.	Metropolitan Toronto and Region Conservation Authority	9
Plate 5.	Metropolitan Toronto: Proposed School Districts	147
Plate 6.	Limit of Urban Development under Proposed Metropolitan Toronto Official Plan	160
Plate 7.	Metropolitan Toronto: Proposed Four Cities	183